SOCIAL ECOLOGY

SOCIAL ECOLOGY

A CRITICAL ANALYSIS

BY MILLA AÏSSA ALIHAN

New York

COOPER SQUARE PUBLISHERS, INC.

1964

Published, 1964, by Cooper Square Publishers, Inc.
59 Fourth Avenue, New York, N. Y. 10003
Library of Congress Catalog Card No. 64-24804
Printed in the United States of America

To

R. M. M., E. G. S.

and

M. M. A.

All observation must be for or against some view, if it is to be of any service.—CHARLES DARWIN

ACKNOWLEDGMENTS

THE MOST grateful task that falls to the writer of a critical study is to pay tribute to those who have aided in its preparation.

In particular I most sincerely acknowledge the generous help and interest of Maud and Eustace Seligman without whose unfaltering encouragement the publication of this work would not have been possible.

To Professor MacIver whose wisdom and kindly criticism have guided me in this work I extend my deep gratitude. His patience and understanding did not fail even when he disagreed with the point of view proffered here.

I am indebted to my father for helpful counsel and constant encouragement.

Among my other obligations the following are outstanding: to Steven Cartwright, who gave me invaluable assistance, not only in the task of research, but also in the editorial preparation of this work; to Professor Park and to Professor Burgess, who have freely responded to my requests for clarification of various aspects of their theories and who are in no way responsible, if, after all, I have been guilty of misinterpreting them; to my teachers, Theodore Abel, Alexander von Schelting, Frank Ross, Willard W. Waller, Robert E. Chaddock, and Robert S. Lynd; to Professors Faris, Wirth, and Blumer, of the University of Chicago, who have helped me to elucidate various points in ecological theory; and to Ruth Schwartz, who gave me valuable aid and advice in the revision and final preparation of the manuscript.

M. A. A.

New York, N. Y.
May 16, 1938

CONTENTS

MAPS

TABLE

INTRODUCTION

THE ECOLOGICAL school is one of the most definite and influential schools in American sociology at the present time. It has to its credit not only an important series of factual studies but also a firmly established doctrine. While certain changes and modifications in the ecological theory and methods may well be expected, it has been surmised from the analysis of the development of the school since its inception that it has persisted in its fundamentals and that whatever changes may occur will not markedly affect the essence or the direction of the school. There is apparent, moreover, continued adherence to these fundamental principles in the great majority of the individual factual studies.

It is the object of this study to present and examine the position of the school, its fundamental concepts, and the methodology upon which these studies hinge and which serves as their guiding principle. For it is only as we discern the co-ordinating and organizing factor of the individual researches that we can fully appreciate their significance and their contribution to sociology. With the ever-increasing numbers of ecological researches, there is always danger of losing sight of the wider perspective within which their scientific utility and fruitfulness can be fully recognized. Furthermore, the bearing of the factual studies upon the principles which give the school its name and its claim must serve to indicate the rôle of human ecology in the field of sociology. For in a truly scientific system every research is related to a problem and every problem to a generalization or hypothesis.

For these reasons it was found advisable, indeed essential, to deal with the school as a whole rather than with the individual contributions. The very difficulties encountered by the writer in interpreting the views of the school, in reconciling the statements of the different members of it, and in seeking a coherence between the different concepts go to show that there has been more scholarship expended on the individual studies than on the elucidation of their common significance. Yet it is only through the validation of methods by results and of principles by application that science advances.

There have been some commentaries upon the individual studies by the ecologists themselves and some descriptions of their theory, such as is found in *The Range of Social Theory,* by Floyd House, or references to their methods that are given in various articles in *The Fields and Methods of Sociology*[1] and *Trends in American Sociology.*[2] Probably the outstanding critical evaluation of the methods of human ecology is F. A. Ross's penetrating article "Ecology and the Statistical Method."[3] A monograph such as W. Wallace Weaver's *West Philadelphia: a Study of Natural Social Areas,* which challenges the validity of the concept "natural area" and the methods of delimiting it, may also be mentioned.

However, there has not as yet been any comprehensive critique of the school's point of view, either in the form of theoretical stock-taking by the members of the ecological school, or of an inclusive analysis by other sociologists. This absence of a general critique of the theory of human ecology is but part of a larger picture—the paucity of works dealing with schools of American sociological thought. This

[1] Edited by L. L. Bernard (New York, 1934).

[2] Edited by George A. Lundberg, Read Bain, and Nels Anderson (New York and London, 1929).

[3] *The American Journal of Sociology,* XXXVIII, 507–22.

task has been undertaken in the hope of redressing the former deficiency and of contributing toward the development of analytical studies in sociology in this country.

CHAPTER ONE

THE DOCTRINE AND ITS SETTING

PERHAPS no other period has been so crucial for sociology as the past quarter century. The universe of sociology became pluralistic, if not chaotic. With the search for new methods and techniques, with redefinitions of the scope of sociology, came an unprecedented surge of theories and trends, some still lacking systematized expression, others commanding a definite following. The formal school in Germany; the historical and psychological schools supervening on the biological and geographical ones in England and the United States; the many interpretations which have been labeled sociologistic; in this country the behaviorist groups with their variant leanings; the numerous deterministic theories; all these overlapping systems marked a period of prolific thought, though not always of harmonious agreement. The emulation of the natural sciences fostered manifold techniques. To many, the exclusively empirical approach became the standard, statistical method—the sole criterion of truth.

Among these systems human ecology is one of the youngest. It fulfills the quest for simple and direct explanation of seemingly complex social phenomena. It attempts to interpret the elusive qualitative and intangible social facts in terms of their physical and measurable manifestations. It is a response to the call for the purely empirical research so popularized by behaviorists—action in place of reflection; facts in preference to theory.

The Middle West provided the setting for human ecology,

the post-war years were the period of its articulation. When Europe was changing its philosophic frontiers as an aftermath of its territorial upheavals, when the first echoes of the Russian Revolution were still troubling intellectual America, and when academic thought had not yet completely freed itself from the pressure of propaganda and chauvinism, the Middle West—somewhat removed from the sharp edges of world events—was preoccupied with its own development and fast becoming intellectually self-conscious. At the University of Chicago, while Albion Small was still expounding to his students a sociology which found its roots in Germany, W. I. Thomas was applying the new techniques of realistic research to the study of the Polish peasant. The department of social science was becoming a center of academic influence through the *American Journal of Sociology*.

As early as 1915 there had appeared in the *Journal* an article, "The City,"[1] by Robert E. Park, then a lecturer in sociology at the University of Chicago. This monograph held the first of the threads which were later woven into the distinctive design of human ecology. As Albion Small's influence declined, the new ideas began to take shape, to crystallize into a system, their steadily growing influence in the department being reflected in the pages of the *Journal*.

Today human ecology is a recognized discipline, its influence permeating many universities in the United States and Canada. The plethora of monographs and articles, each elaborating some specific application of the ecological approach, gains in volume each year. Not yet developed into a consistent whole, the theory of human ecology is interpreted by its many disciples with nuances reflecting a variety of backgrounds and experiences. But the soil from which this new theory took its growth is common to both the

[1] *The American Journal of Sociology,* Vol. XX, No. 1.

leaders and the disciples—human ecology is essentially American.

Although twenty years ago American sociology was still regarded as an intruder among the social sciences, without the credentials of a tested and accepted science, it had already reached that stage of development which inevitably demands an indigenous character and setting. Among sociologists reaction had set in, not only against the sweeping generalizations of Lester Ward, Giddings, and Small, but also against their dependence upon foreign influence, particularly that of Herbert Spencer. It was not strange that this reaction sounded its strongest note in the leading university of the Middle West. Intellectually the Pacific coast was still in its pioneer stage, while the East, for obvious historic and geographic reasons, looked across the Atlantic for its direction, and its thought had a cosmopolitan, if not a European, quality. These alien influences reached the Middle West only second hand. The Appalachians, which had cut off the earlier settlers from direct contact with the European heritage, had been more than a geographical barrier; they had served as a symbol of a social and intellectual boundary. Before distances had noticeably shrunk, the country west of Ohio had asserted its distinctive character and pace, with the Middle West holding the reins.

THE FOUNDER

Robert Ezra Park, who was to become the founder and the guiding spirit of the discipline of human ecology, grew up in this setting of the nascent Middle West. Born in 1864, in Pennsylvania, he spent his childhood and youth in a Main Street prairie town in Minnesota.[2] Residence in a

[2] The biographical data have been taken from an unpublished article "Robert E. Park," by Ernest W. Burgess and from *Who's Who in America*, 1935.

Scandinavian community gave him his first glimpse of the immigrant settlers—an experience which inspired a life-long interest in immigrant groups and marginal cultures. He spent a year at the University of Minnesota and graduated from the University of Michigan, in 1887. Here his interest in human sciences began to develop under the influence of John Dewey, then an instructor in the department of philosophy. For the next eleven years he was engaged in newspaper work, during which time he was a reporter in Minneapolis, Detroit, and Chicago. He received a master's degree from Harvard, in 1899, and after a period of study and travel in Europe was given a doctorate in philosophy at the University of Heidelberg, in 1904, his thesis on *Masse und Publikum* revealing his continued interest in the newspaper. He returned to Harvard for a year as an assistant in philosophy and then became secretary to Dr. Barber of the Congo Reform Association and, later, a publicity agent for Booker T. Washington. It was not until 1914 that Park resumed his academic career, being appointed a lecturer in sociology at the University of Chicago and becoming a professor in 1923.

At Harvard, Park came in contact with James Royce, Santayana, and Munsterberg. In Berlin, Strasburg, and Heidelberg, he worked with Simmel and Windelband, writing his dissertation under the guidance of the latter. Knapp gave him an economist's interpretation of the life of the peasant in his community, and Hettner, the geographer, impressed upon him the importance of the geographical basis of human society. William James was another influence; Park found congenial his assertion that it was the actual experience of men and women and not the abstract formulation of it that constituted knowledge. It was this conviction that had earlier attracted Park to newspaper work, which afforded him unrivaled opportunities for observing the active world. It was probably responsible for the investigations which he undertook as a newspaperman, for instance, of the modes of life and problems of a rural Michigan county while he was in Detroit. Again, it was this attitude that prompted him, when at Chicago, to send out his students to various blocks of the city to observe whatever might occur of human interest. For he was convinced that reporting—the inductive methods of the newspaper—had a significant contribution to make to sociology. It was certainly his insatiable curiosity as to human actions and motives that, in addition to fashioning the methods of human ecology, made Park a teacher of pervasive influence.

As a boy, Park had belonged to one of the neighborhood gangs; his hero had been the leader "Black Pete," who was two or three years his senior. As he grew up, he witnessed at first hand the conflicts and adjustments between the varied stream of immigrants and the native settlers. He saw the contrasts between the respective customs and modes of life in both groups. Sweeping changes in industry and transportation were affecting vitally communities such as that in which Park lived. The small prairie towns were being slowly sapped by the cities with their bright lights, their hurried pace of expansion, and their new opportunities.

Park also must have been influenced by the nonconformist puritanism of the small town, with its insistence upon industry, its suspicion of *joie-de-vivre,* its consciousness of moral superiority, and its regard of the city as the "sink of all iniquities." This bias is evident in many of Park's writings; it explains his preoccupation with social problems and social reform, and it sheds light upon the moral approach to sociology which the ecologists are sometimes prone to adopt.

THE BACKGROUND OF HUMAN ECOLOGY

This background Park impressed upon the science he was to shape. The very selection of materials, the approach to social facts, the method of treatment, and the way in which the data were worked into the bas-relief of the system are all expressive of an environmental approach and are thus an intimate reflection not only of Park's early training but also of the scene which his collaborators shared with him.

The Middle West was rapidly expanding, and Chicago had assumed the position of a dominating urban center. But, although the frontier had given way to a metropolitan economy, the pioneer spirit and tradition still persisted. It was a tradition of the conquest of the geographical environment. It was a battle fought primarily in physical terms, and the uncompromising Calvinism which inspired it, sternly turned its back upon the more leisurely traditions of Europe. At the same time, the instruments employed to defeat nature—the "great city," the systems of communications, the unrivaled industrial techniques—so rapidly produced such manifold changes in the environment that there was no time to rationalize or explain them in any terms but the most simple and concrete, if at all.

In this world the human ecologists undertook to explain the social complex by fastening attention upon its salient manifestations, such as the growth of the cities, the spread of industry, the extension of railways and highways, the mosaic of nationalities and races, the movements and distribution of people and utilities. The conditions of social change became to them the *facts* of social change. Thus their universe of discourse became limited to externalities, and the interpretation of social life hinged upon its most concrete aspects. Reducing social behavior to a common denominator of the tangible and the measurable, congenial to the pragmatic intellectual temper of the country, human ecologists became the expounders of the socially "given," the realists of the established order. For they used its own spirit and its own tools to explain in its own language that scheme of things of which they were themselves a part.

Following the point of view which had its immediate roots in the realm of social welfare, human ecologists turned their attention to the concrete problems about them. Nor was there any dearth of such problems. Chicago itself proffered a wealth of material for the "social pathologist." Lincoln Steffens had laid bare the political machine and its corruption in "The Shame of the Cities"; Chicago was gaining a notoriety for crime and gangster activities; slums, hitherto regarded as essentially the prerogative of European cities, had become an American problem. The very severity of conditions prompted the demand for reform. Jane Addams's Hull House had started the settlement trend. Nor was moral guidance neglected. If "muckraking" was somewhat on the wane, there were the social worker, the social preacher, the women's clubs, the propagandists of reform. What is particularly relevant is that investigation was fast becoming the prerequisite of reform.

This ushered in the social survey movement. Charles Booth had earlier given an example of local survey in his *Life and Labour of the People of London.* R. A. Woods's *The City Wilderness,* Jacob Riis's *How the Other Half Lives* and *The Battle with the Slum,* Robert Hunter's *Tenement Conditions in Chicago: Report of the Investigating Committee of the City Homes Association,* Rowntree's *Poverty: a Study of Town Life* were all localized studies paving the path for the increasing development of the survey method. Then came *The Pittsburgh Survey,* which aroused a wide interest. Shortly after followed Galpin's penetrating study, "The Social Anatomy of an Agricultural Community," which seemed to revolutionize the methods of the survey. In Chicago under the auspices of The Chicago School of Civics and Philanthropy, Sophonisba P. Breckinridge and Edith Abbott made studies of Chicago's housing conditions, publishing several articles in *The American Journal of Sociology.*

Taking its cue from these surveys, human ecology found increasingly fertile soil for its development. Here Park saw a timely opportunity for taking sociology out of the realm of abstract academic reflection into the realities of the city life, into the world of the newspaper man.

With his point of view already defined by his early studies, Park developed and verbalized his doctrine in *The Introduction to the Science of Sociology,* which he wrote in collaboration with Burgess and first published in 1921. This text, besides serving as a source of various sociological theories for the many followers of Park and Burgess, gives a clear indication of the direction which the ecological school was to take. Although as yet lacking unity, the theory of human ecology is set here in most of its fundamentals. It was in 1925, however, that the school advanced its first formal presentation of the theory of human ecology in *The City.*[3] By this time the school also had to its credit studies by the graduate students of the department, such as McKenzie's *The Neighborhood, a Study of Columbus, Ohio* and Nels Anderson's *The Hobo: the Sociology of the Homeless Man;* within the next few years appeared Frederick Thrasher's *The Gang,* Wirth's *The Ghetto,* and Zorbaugh's *The Gold Coast and the Slum,* to name only a few. From this period on, both the theoretical presentations and the factual researches increased without stint, and the school attracted growing numbers to its fold.

SOURCES OF HUMAN ECOLOGY

Characteristic of the ecological school is its tapping of many sources for its conceptual framework. Because of their quest to develop sociology into a natural, exact, and special

[3] Park, Burgess, McKenzie, with bibliography by Louis Wirth (Chicago, 1925).

science, human ecologists have turned primarily to biological sciences. As the name of their discipline indicates, they have leaned most heavily upon plant and animal ecologies, particularly the former, on the assumption that man is an organic creature and therefore subject to the general laws of the organic world and that the behavior in plant and animal communities is parallel to certain aspects of behavior in the human community. Thus Burgess claims that "the processes of competition, invasion, succession, and segregation described in elaborate detail for plant and animal communities seem to be strikingly similar to the operation of these same processes in the human community."[4]

From this point of view the school seeks to make a contribution to sociology by dealing with the less evolved aspect of human life common to all living matter. Human ecology emphasizes the more physical and concrete factors and particularly the distribution and the movements of various elements: "Human ecology is the modern name for the study which analyzes the processes involved in the spatial and temporal distribution of human beings and their institutions."[5] Human ecology is also defined as "a study of the spatial and temporal relations of human beings as affected by the selective, distributive, and accommodative forces of the environment."[6] By extending the science of ecology to human groupings ecologists have been obliged to make many modifications. As Park says, "it is not man, but the community; not man's relations to the earth which he inhabits, but his relations to other men, that concerns us most."[7] The

[4] E. W. Burgess, "Can Neighborhood Work Have a Scientific Basis?" in Park, Burgess, *et al.*, *The City,* p. 145.

[5] C. A. Dawson, "Sources and Methods of Human Ecology," in *The Fields and Methods of Sociology,* edited by L. L. Bernard, p. 286. Copyright 1934. Reprinted by permission of the publishers, Farrar and Rinehart, Inc.

[6] R. D. McKenzie, "The Ecological Approach to the Study of the Human Community," in Park, Burgess, *et al.*, *The City,* pp. 63–64.

[7] R. E. Park, "The Urban Community as a Spacial Pattern and a Moral Order," in *The Urban Community,* edited by Burgess (Chicago, 1926), p. 3.

difficulties which human ecologists encounter in leaning so heavily upon organic ecology will become apparent in the course of this study.

Human ecologists have called upon other disciplines for the enrichment of their theory. The list is long, but the more important ones are: physiology, as presented in the writings of C. M. Child; economics, more specifically distribution economics and studies of land values, particularly the work of Richard M. Hurd; human geography and the writings of Vidal de la Blache, Ratzel, Gras, and Brunhes; the demographic and geographic schools of sociology, including the works of Le Play, Buckle, Huntington, and Semple, together with the congeries of subjects which are drawn upon for the various types of social survey; and finally rural sociological works such as those of Galpin and Kolb. Then, too, the materials and discoveries of regional and city planning have been incorporated into their theory. Such diverse conceptions as ecological processes in plant and animal communities, physiological "organismic patterns," and city configurations adapted from real estate studies have all been synthesized in the system of human ecology.

CHAPTER TWO

COMMUNITY AND SOCIETY

FUNDAMENTAL DISTINCTION

THE ECOLOGICAL conceptual frame is built upon a distinction between the two concepts, "community" and "society." These represent for the school the two fundamental aspects of human organization. So distinct are they that the ecologists assign each category to a different discipline. "Community" is regarded as the subject matter of human ecology, while "society" is included in the scope of social psychology. Burgess, in an unpublished article on Robert E. Park, to whom he accords the central place in the development of the ecological school, points out that to Park "relationships of symbiosis, or the factors involved in living together, independent of communication, were to be studied under human ecology, in counter-distinction from relationships of consensus subsumed in the research of social psychology."[1] Burgess goes on to say:

> The significance of this distinction between the community as a distribution of individuals over an area and of society as an organization of persons for corporate action grew upon Park in the years after 1921 when it first crystallized in his mind . . . it led him to the conclusion that social organization has these two primary aspects to be studied by quite different techniques. The study of the community as the natural resultant of the competitive process constitutes the field of human ecology. The study of society as the result of the cultural process is represented by the field of social psychology.[2]

[1] Page 28. [2] Pages 27–28.

The demarcation of the two concepts implies that "community" and "society" define two such different aspects of one whole, or that they are so mutually exclusive, that it is possible and essential to deal with them by different methods within two distinct disciplines and from two distinct approaches.

Park gives another classification of the aspects of human organization, somewhat different from that just presented.[3] He retains the distinction between "community," or the "symbiotic" order, and "society"—the cultural or the moral order, but whereas in the above quotation he seems to identify the political with the social order and the economic with the ecological order, he now distinguishes these as four separate categories:

> The fact seems to be, then, that human society, as distinguished from plant and animal society, is organized on two levels, the biotic and the cultural. There is a symbiotic society based on competition and a cultural society based on communication and consensus. . . However, the interrelations of human beings are more diverse and complicated than this dichotomy, symbiotic and cultural, indicates. This fact is attested by the divergent systems of human interrelations which have been the subject of the special social sciences. Thus human society, certainly in its mature and more rational expression, exhibits not merely an ecological, but an economic, a political, and a moral order. The social sciences include not merely human geography and ecology, but economics, political science, and cultural anthropology.[4]

In essence, the formal distinction remains valid, since Park still regards "community" as the province of human ecology, although the cultural or the moral order now becomes the domain of cultural anthropology rather than of social psychology.

[3] See "Human Ecology," *American Journal of Sociology,* Vol. XLII, No. 1 (July, 1936).

[4] *Ibid.,* pp. 13–14. See also Park, "William Graham Sumner's Conception of Society," *Chinese Social and Political Science Review,* XVII (1933), 438.

Although the latter fourfold classification would seem to divest each of the two concepts of some of its attributes, the human ecologists do not consistently take account of the narrower range thus given to the concepts. In fact, it will later become apparent that the political and the economic organizations comprise the ecological "no man's land" between "community" and "society," so that they are at once part of the "community,"[5] constituent parts of "society,"[6] and, as is evident from quotation given above, entities apart from both "community" and "society."

While formally the distinction is fundamental for the school, the two central concepts not infrequently merge, overlap, are used interchangeably, and in the specific ecological researches they often cease to be significant.

When a technical meaning is given to everyday terms such as "community" and "society," it is not easy to divorce them from their usual significance. For instance, we find that sometimes the ecologists slip into the generally accepted sociological usage; in this case either of the terms covers the whole area of social phenomena. At other times they use them in a specific sense, but interchangeably. An example of the use of "community" in a generic sense is Park's statement to the effect that "the community . . . is the name that we give to this larger and most inclusive social milieu, outside of ourselves, our family, and our immediate neighborhood, in which the individual maintains not merely his existence as an individual, but his life as a person."[7] Park also uses the term "society" to include both concepts when he says "it is an indubitable fact that societies do have this double aspect,"[8] and "ecology conceives society as funda-

[5] Park, "Community Organization and the Romantic Temper," in Park, Burgess *et al.*, *The City*, p. 117.

[6] *Ibid.*, pp. 1–46.

[7] *Ibid.*, p. 104.

[8] "Sociology," in *Research in the Social Sciences*, edited by Wilson Gee (New York, 1929), p. 6.

mentally territorial as well as a cultural organization."[9] The use of the term "community" in a specific sense, but as applied to "society," is shown when Park refers to "community, with the moral order which it embodies."[10]

The theoretical formulations of the ecological school are as yet so few and so fragmentary that a clear-cut presentation of the conceptual framework is extremely difficult, if not impossible. Moreover, it will appear as we proceed that the school's major concepts are fluid in their application and difficult to unify into one consistent conceptual scheme. This is probably due to the fact that the concepts themselves are borrowed from physical or biological sciences and transferred to another universe of discourse. The framework is thus constructed of diverse elements.

It was found advisable to elucidate the concepts "community" and "society" by reference mainly to the works of Park and Burgess and, more particularly, to the former. Although in some of the monographic studies of individual ecologists the conception of "community" deviates to some extent from that originally given by Park and Burgess,[11] the majority of ecologists quote these two authors most extensively, particularly with respect to the concepts under consideration, and on the whole claim to abide by Park's definitions. A great many references in this chapter are drawn from *Introduction to the Science of Sociology,* by Robert E. Park and Ernest W. Burgess, since in this text we find the most thorough and unified formulations and definitions that serve as a clue and a basis for further formulations in the development of the ecological school.

In this chapter and in the following one an attempt will

[9] "Succession, an Ecological Concept," *American Sociological Review,* I, 178.

[10] "The Urban Community as a Spacial Pattern and a Moral Order," in *The Urban Community,* edited by E. W. Burgess, p. 7.

[11] See, for example, H. W. Zorbaugh, *The Gold Coast and the Slum* (Chicago, 1929).

be made to elucidate the meaning and the implications of the two concepts; to examine the validity of the distinction; and, finally, to determine the extent to which the school has abided by the definitions of them and conformed to the assumed limits of the scope of human ecology.

GROUNDS OF THE DISTINCTION

The division of the two concepts of "community" and "society" and the consequent suggestion of the separation of the disciplines dealing with each is based mainly on the attempt to distinguish between the social aspect on the one hand and the physical and economic aspects of group life which ecologists assume to be common to the whole organic world on the other. In the majority of cases, the economic aspect is treated in a physical context, the ecologists claiming that it is fashioned after the economy of the plant and animal communities as interpreted by biological ecologies. What sociologists commonly designate as social co-operation, socialization, or consensus, dependent upon communication, is regarded by the ecologists as the fact of "society," while the process of competition and the reciprocal benefits resulting from exchange of goods and services, involving a "natural" division of labor and mutual, though not conscious, influence of groups upon each other, are conceived of as the essence of "community."

> Society, from the ecological point of view [says Park] is, like the natural as opposed to the institutional family, a symbiotic rather than a social unit. It is a population settled and limited to its habitat. The ties that unite its individual units are those of a free and natural economy, based on a natural division of labor. Such a society is territorially organized, and the ties which hold it together are physical and vital rather than customary and moral.[12]

[12] "Succession, an Ecological Concept," *American Sociological Review,* I (1936), 178.

The division of the two concepts here is in terms of evolutionary development, "community" representing the more "natural," the less evolved biotic aspect, while "society" is the more evolved, the social and cultural aspect which is thought of as superimposed upon the biotic "community." Hence, "community" is looked upon as the more fundamental "organization" and is interpreted as the more universal aspect because it is common to the whole of plant and animal life.

> The same biotic interdependence of individuals and species [states Park] which has been observed and studied in plant and animal communities, seems to exist likewise on the human level, except for the fact that in human society competition and the struggle for existence are limited by custom, convention, and law. In short, human society is, or appears to be, organized on two levels, the biotic and the cultural.[13]

Emphasizing competition as the fundamental process of "community," ecologists interpret it as the determinant of the territorial distribution either of human groups or of utilities and physical structures. Competition is, in this instance, the struggle for existence as it prevails among plants and animals, and it is conceived of apart from consciousness and communication; although the latter attributes are said to limit competition among human beings, by definition they come under the aspect of human life referred to as "society." Moreover, when competition is conscious, it becomes conflict, and it is in this case considered to be a process of "society."[14]

Two ideas are involved in the causal relation of competition and territorial distribution; first, that competition among human beings involves, as it does in plant and animal communities, struggle for spatial and economic "position"

[13] "Succession," *op. cit.*, p. 175.

[14] See Park, "Human Ecology," *American Journal of Sociology,* XLII (1936), 10.

upon the surface of the earth; and second, that competition, being the primary process, both in its genesis and in its universality, is the expression of natural tendencies of living organisms and is concomitant with unrestricted movement or "freedom"; in fact, to ecologists "competition means mobility, freedom," and "restriction of competition is synonymous with limitation of movement."[15] It will later become evident that such categorical identification of competition, free movement, and freedom with the natural order of "community," as against the assumed restriction of all three in "society," is one of the basic hypotheses distinguishing the approach of the ecological school. This conception of competition as the central and fundamental process derives not only from the biological ecologies but also from the philosophical postulates of human ecologists, which hark back to the earlier exponents of the theory of competition and struggle for existence.

The fundamental ecological thesis in the division of "community" and "society" is that the aspect of life which is universal among all living organisms is the "natural," the basic, and the determining one. The phenomena which are found to be "strictly human" are relegated by ecologists to the concept "society," which is understood to be superimposed upon "community." While one is conceived to be the product of nature, the other is a conscious organization for the purpose of controlling its members. However, the relation of these two aspects of life is never consistently defined. For instance, we are warned that "community" and "society" are not separate entities but only aspects of one whole,[16] despite the division of these two concepts into distinct structures with different processes. Again, Park and Burgess state that "society is the more abstract and inclu-

[15] R. E. Park and E. W. Burgess, *Introduction to the Science of Sociology*, revised edition (Chicago, 1924), p. 512.

[16] *Ibid.*, pp. 161–63.

sive term,"[17] and Park adds that "every community is, in some sense and to some degree, a society," whereas "it is certainly true that not every society is a community."[18] And yet in the same article this author asserts that "the term community is employed in a wider connotation" than the term "society."[19]

"Society," which is assumed to be superimposed upon "community" and to be a later development from the "community," is at the same time said to be a control organization for the purpose of limitation of the natural organization of "community." Nevertheless the "community" is not only asserted to represent the more fundamental aspect of life, but its processes and structure are regarded as the causal determinants of those of "society." Obviously the relationship between the two aspects of human organization appears to be one of interaction, but, as we shall see below, the problem which human ecologists set for themselves is to interpret "society" and its changes in terms of the supposedly more fundamental and more concrete manifestations of "community."

INTERPRETATION OF "SOCIETY"

According to Park and Burgess, society is "the social heritage of *habit and sentiment, folkways and mores, technique and culture,* all of which are incident or necessary to collective behavior."[20] It is "made up of social groups, each possessing its own specific type of organization but having at the same time all the general characteristics of society in the abstract."[21] What distinguishes "society" from a "mere collection of individuals" is corporate action.[22] We are told

[17] Park and Burgess, *op. cit.,* p. 163.

[18] "Sociology," in *Research in the Social Sciences,* edited by Wilson Gee, p. 8.

[19] *Ibid.*

[20] Park and Burgess, *op. cit.,* p. 163.

[21] *Ibid.*

[22] See *ibid.,* p. 42.

that "the existence of society presupposes a certain amount of solidarity, consensus, and common purpose"[23] and that

> societies are formed for action and in action. They grow up in the efforts of individuals to act collectively. The structures which societies exhibit are on the whole the incidental effects of collective action. Living in society, the individual gets his interests defined in reference to the larger aims of the groups of which he is a member. In this sense, and to this extent, society controls the individuals who compose it.[24]

"Society" is thus conceived of as a conscious and a purposeful organization.

The cohesive principle of "society" is understood to be interaction, the medium of which is communication, while its mechanisms are suggestion and imitation, so that the limits of "society" are "coterminous with the limits of interaction, that is, of the participation of persons in the life of society."[25] Society, we are told, exists "not merely where there are people but where there is communication."[26] Park and Burgess distinguish three "natural" levels of interaction: (1) the interaction of the senses; (2) the interaction of the emotions; and (3) the interaction of sentiments and ideas. Interaction on the first two levels is said to be "restricted to the communication of attitudes and feelings," designated as the "*natural* forms of communication since they are common to man and to animals."[27] Apparently the third level of interaction is an uniquely human form and, correspondingly, typical of "society." The fact that these authors first refer to the three levels of interaction as natural and then distinguish the first two from the third as the natural forms of interaction can only mean that, as levels of interaction, they are all natural, but as forms of inter-

[23] Park, "Sociology," in *Research in the Social Sciences,* edited by Wilson Gee, p. 7.

[24] *Ibid.,* p. 8.

[25] Park and Burgess, *op. cit.,* p. 341.

[26] *Ibid.,* p. 164.

[27] *Ibid.,* p. 342; italics mine.

action, only the interaction of senses and the interaction of emotions are *natural!*

While competition is assumed to be the basic process of "community," the processes of "society" are those of conflict, accommodation, and assimilation. These social processes evidently represent different aspects of social reality, as is evident in the following quotation:

> Conflict is . . . to be identified with the political order and with conscious control. Accommodation, on the other hand, is associated with the social order that is fixed and established in custom and the mores.
>
> Assimilation, as distinguished from accommodation, implies a more thoroughgoing transformation of the personality—a transformation which takes place gradually under the influence of social contacts of the most concrete and intimate sort.[28]

The relation of competition—the process of "community" —to the social processes of conflict, accommodation, and assimilation, as well as to "society" as a whole, is threefold: (1) Competition is considered the more fundamental, universal, and prior process, in consequence of which and in relation to which all social processes take place. (2) These social processes, at the same time, work in opposition to competition and function to modify and restrict it. "The function of society," states Park, "was everywhere to restrict competition and by so doing bring about a more effective co-operation of the organic units of which society is composed."[29] (3) Although competition may assume the character of a social force, working as if from without "society," at the same time it is said to be a force acting together with the social process of conflict to solidify the social structure:

> Society, in the more inclusive sense in which ecologists have defined it, may be said to exist wherever competition has estab-

[28] Park and Burgess, *op. cit.*, p. 510.

[29] Park, "Human Ecology," *American Journal of Sociology*, XLII, 14.

lished some sort of order or war has established some sort of peace. It is the area within which an intrinsic and functional social order has succeeded one that was extrinsic and mechanical.[30]

In one sense, then, "society" is assumed to "impose itself" upon "community"[31] and to control and restrict the competitive activities of the free individuals of the "community" in the interest of the group: "Society is everywhere a control organization. Its function is to organize, integrate, and direct the energies resident in the individuals of which it is composed."[32] From this viewpoint, "society may be said to exist only so far as this independent activity of the individual is *controlled* in the interest of the group as a whole,"[33] and the evolution of "society" is assumed to have been "the progressive extension of control over nature and the substitution of a moral for the natural order."[34] In describing this aspect of relationship between society and community Park says: "the cultural superstructure [society] imposes itself as an instrument of direction and control upon the biotic substructure [community]."[35]

In another sense, society develops from community through the social processes of conflict, accommodation, and assimilation: "Through the medium of these [social] processes a community *assumes* the form of society."[36]

And finally, competition, in spite of being restricted and diminished in "society," is still regarded as a basic process, both acting upon and operating within "society." For instance: "competition, segregation, and accommodation serve to maintain the social distances, to fix the status, and pre-

[30] "Succession, an Ecological Concept," *American Sociological Review,* I, 176.

[31] See Park and Burgess, *op. cit.,* pp. 508–9.

[32] Park, *loc. cit.*

[33] Park and Burgess, *op. cit.,* p. 508.

[34] *Ibid.,* p. 511.

[35] Park, *op. cit.,* p. 15.

[36] Park and Burgess, *op. cit.,* p. 785; italics mine.

serve the independence of the individual in the social relation";[37] and again, "accommodation . . . is the process by which the individuals and groups make the necessary internal adjustments to social situations which have been created by competition and conflict."[38] Hence, although competition is formally stated to be a process specifically of "community," and although it is supposed to take the form of conflict in "society" inasmuch as it becomes conscious, it is apparent from the above quotation that, withal, competition is regarded as taking place *within* "society" alongside conflict.

The ecologists regard both "society" and "community" as the outcome of a struggle for existence and as dependent upon it for their organizations. "Competition determines the position of the individual in the community; conflict fixes his place in society."[39] Assumedly, "every society represents an organization of elements more or less antagonistic to each other but united for the moment, at least, by an arrangement which defines the reciprocal relation and respective spheres of action of each."[40] It may be recalled that conflict is "conscious" competition and hence a process functioning within society, so that "social organization, with the exception of the order based on competition and adaptation, is essentially an accommodation of differences through conflicts."[41] It is through the process of accommodation that the conflict basic to "society" subsides: "Accommodation is the natural issue of conflicts. In an accommodation the antagonism of the hostile elements is, for the time being, regulated, and conflict disappears as overt action, although it remains latent as a potential force."[42]

In the eyes of the ecologists "society" came into being as

[37] Park and Burgess, *op. cit.*, p. 165.
[38] *Ibid.*, p. 509.
[39] *Ibid.*, p. 574.
[40] *Ibid.*, p. 665.
[41] *Ibid.*, p. 664.
[42] *Ibid.*, p. 665.

a result of conscious effort,[43] and they generally define the processes of society as conscious and as involving social contact. However, although both in conflict and in accommodation the individuals and groups are assumed to be conscious, in assimilation "the process is typically unconscious"[44] and the conscious conflict is reconciled only in the unconscious process of assimilation: "It is only with assimilation that this antagonism, latent in the organization of individuals or groups, is likely to be wholly dissolved."[45] Assimilation is apparently regarded as the most socializing process, as is seen from the statement made by Park and Burgess that "as social contact initiates interaction, assimilation is its final perfect product."[46]

Another distinction between "society" and "community" is that, while the latter is composed of "individuals," the members of "society" are "persons." "The person," Park and Burgess state, "is an individual who has status. We come into the world as individuals. We acquire status, and become persons. Status means position in society. The individual inevitably has some status in every social group of which he is a member."[47] Pointing out that "society" is characterized by consensus and a moral order, Park goes on to say, "within this moral order individuals *assume* the character of persons conscious of themselves and of their rôle in the community."[48] Again, he tells us that

> sociology is not concerned with individuals as such, but with a special type of relation, not fundamentally physical, existing between individuals, and which constitutes them persons. Societies, in the strict sense of the word, are composed of persons, and persons are individuals who have status in some society.[49]

[43] *Cf. infra*, p. 95. [44] Park and Burgess, *op. cit.*, p. 736.
[45] *Ibid.*, p. 665. [46] *Ibid.*, p. 736. [47] *Ibid.*, p. 55.
[48] "Sociology," in *Research in the Social Sciences,* edited by Wilson Gee, p. 34; italics mine. Obviously the term "community" in this quotation signifies "society" as the ecologists define this concept. [49] *Ibid.*, p. 5.

Here, it seems, Park excludes ecology from the field of sociology, confining the latter to the study of "society" and of relationships which are not physical and which take place between persons.

Groupings in "Society" and "Community."—According to Park and Burgess, society in the most inclusive sense of the term,

> turns out upon analysis to be a constellation of other smaller societies, that is to say races, peoples, parties, factions, cliques, clubs, etc. The community, the world-community, on the other hand, which is merely the Great Society viewed from the standpoint of the territorial distribution of its members, presents a different series of social groupings and the Great Society in this aspect exhibits a totally different pattern. From the point of view of the territorial distribution of the individuals that constitute it, the world-community is composed of nations, colonies, spheres of influence, cities, towns, local communities, neighborhoods, and families.[50]

Even though the distinction given in this case between "society" and "community" is explicitly in terms of one factor only, that is, territorial distribution, we have seen that both the structure and the processes of "society" are different from those of "community." Therefore, the term "territorial distribution" must carry with it much wider implications than are apparent in the above statement. For one thing, competition, which is causally related to distribution, is the central process upon which the "communities" are based in contrast to "societies," the latter being regarded as depending more immediately upon social processes. To say that each of the entities enumerated above equally exhibits the ecological and the social aspects would be to distort the fundamental ecological thesis. The very fact that "society" reveals different groupings from those of "community" bears out the distinction between the two entities both

[50] *Op. cit.*, p. 164.

in form and in content. Hence it must be assumed that a group such as the family is basically competitive and that it manifests primarily the specific phenomena which mark it as belonging to "community." On the other hand, a grouping such as "race" or "people" assumedly reveals the more social aspect of human organization and hence is based upon consensus, social processes, and is constituted of "persons" as opposed to the "individuals" who make up the "family." Likewise, communication and a higher form of interaction must necessarily mark the social groupings, such as race, in contrast with those of the family or of "spheres of influence" which are regarded as fundamentally exhibiting such interaction as is "independent of communication."

A dichotomous division of the social organization which is claimed by ecologists to be similar to the ecological classification is that of Tönnies's[51] distinction between *Gemeinschaft* and *Gesellschaft*. This author also includes the family in the category "community," but here we are presented with a very different notion. Tönnies emphasizes the cooperative, mutual characteristics, the organic sympathy and the like-mindedness in the family.

The peculiar viewpoint of ecologists which fashions the family into a symbiotic grouping might be interpreted to mean that they give their attention only to the less evolved, organic aspect of the family. Park occasionally distinguishes the "natural" from the "institutional" family, claiming that the former is a social group "developed on a purely physiological and instinctive basis."[52] But, even if we take this division into consideration, the fact remains that to ecologists the groupings of "community" are essentially com-

[51] See Louis Wirth, "The Sociology of Ferdinand Tönnies," *American Journal of Sociology,* XXXII, 412–22, and "The Scope and Problems of the Community," *Publications of the Sociological Society of America,* XXVII, 61–73.

[52] "Human Ecology," *American Journal of Sociology,* XLII, 13.

petitive and independent of communication. Besides, in the above classification we are not given grounds for including any single aspect of the family in the category "society," since it is without qualification included in "community."

INTERPRETATION OF "COMMUNITY"

Although in their treatment ecologists run the gamut between an entire fusion and a complete separation of the two concepts, nevertheless, most of their theoretical formulations carry the implicit assumption that "community" is categorically distinct from "society."

The definitions of "community" are so variant and diverse that it is extremely difficult to analyze the concept. To cite only a few examples of divergent definitions: Park and Burgess state that "community is the term which is applied to societies and social groups where they are considered from the point of view of the geographical distribution of the individuals and institutions of which they are composed."[53] Here the only distinctive quality of "community" as opposed to "society" is the territorial distribution. McKenzie's statement that "a community . . . is an ecological distribution of people and services in which the spatial location of each unit is determined by its relation to all other units"[54] would appear to confirm the above definition, except that it does not directly imply the inclusion of social phenomena. However, Park deviates from his preceding definition when he declares that community

> is the name that we give to this larger and most inclusive social milieu, outside of ourselves, our family, and our immediate neighborhood, in which the individual maintains not merely his existence as an individual, but his life as a person. The community, including the family, with its wider interests, its larger purposes,

[53] Park and Burgess, *Introduction to the Science of Sociology,* p. 163.

[54] "The Scope of Human Ecology," in *The Urban Community,* edited by Burgess, p. 169.

and its more deliberate aims, surrounds us, incloses us, and compels us to conform; not by mere pressure from without, not by the fear of censure merely, but by the sense of our interest in, and responsibility to, certain interests not our own.[55]

Here, surely, the author is describing "society" as defined above! But, then again, in the same publication Park tells us that

the simplest possible description of a community is this: a collection of people occupying a more or less clearly defined area. But a community is more than that. A community is not only a collection of people, but it is a collection of institutions. Not people, but institutions, are final and decisive in distinguishing the community from other social constellations.[56]

Park offers a more substantive description of "community" by saying that it characterizes that aspect of social life in which individuals "act independently of one another . . . compete and struggle with one another for mere existence, and treat one another, as far as possible, as utilities."[57] He further differentiates "community" in terms of processes when he states:

Within the limits of this [closed] system the individual units of the population are involved in a process of competitive co-operation, which has given to their interrelations the character of a natural economy. To such a habitat and its inhabitants—whether plant, animal, or human—the ecologists have applied the term "community."[58]

But the same author asserts that "it is in this *community,* with its various organizations and its *rational,* rather than traditional, schemes of control, and not elsewhere, that we have delinquency."[59]

[55] "Community Organizations and Juvenile Delinquency," in Park, Burgess, *et al., The City,* p. 104. [56] *Ibid.,* p. 115.

[57] "Sociology" in *Research in the Social Sciences,* edited by Wilson Gee, p. 6.

[58] "Human Ecology," *American Journal of Sociology,* XLII, 4.

[59] Park, Burgess, *et al., op. cit.,* p. 106; italics mine.

To Burgess "community" signifies "individuals, families, groups, or institutions located upon an area and some or all of the relationships which grow out of this common location."[60] Here we have a definition which approaches that given to community by sociologists generally, but which scarcely clarifies the distinctively ecological concept.

McKenzie's definition, cited earlier, is enlarged upon in the following statement and in fact seems to include the social as well as the ecological phases of human organization: "The unit of ecological study is the communal organism, which is at once an aggregation of individual persons, a geographical and cultural habitat, and an interrelated and interdependent biosocial unity."[61]

In his article "Sociology,"[62] Park defines "community" by stating that while it is "not always identical with society, [it] is, at the very least, the habitat in which alone societies grow up. It provides the economic organization and the necessary conditions in which societies are rooted; upon which as upon a physical base, they can be established." He adds that

> this is one reason why sociological research may very properly begin with the community. A more practical reason is the fact that the community is a visible object. One can point it out, define its territorial limits, and plot its constituent elements, its population, and its institutions on maps. Its characteristics are more susceptible to statistical treatment than society.[63]

This statement emphasizes the more fundamental character of "community" as against "society," its visible and more concrete nature with territorial distribution and the eco-

[60] Park, Burgess, *et al., op. cit.*, p. 144.

[61] "Demography, Human Geography, and Human Ecology," in *The Fields and Methods of Sociology*, edited by L. L. Bernard, p. 59, New York. Copyright 1934. Reprinted by permission of the publishers, Farrar & Rinehart, Inc.

[62] *Research in the Social Sciences*, edited by Wilson Gee, p. 9 *et seq.*

[63] *Ibid.*, p. 9.

nomic organization within a tangible, physical embodiment as its definitive qualities.

The territorial distribution of populations and that of utilities and physical structures (or "institutions" as the two are referred to sometimes) are the central factors with which ecologists are concerned. In fact, ecological organization is identified with "community" and territorial organization: "A society that is organized ecologically, that is on a territorial basis, is not merely a society, it is a community."[64] This territorial organization, as already indicated, is determined by competition. "Competition," say Park and Burgess, "is the process through which the distributive and ecological organization of society is created."[65] More specifically, "competition determines the distribution of population territorially and vocationally. The division of labor and all the vast organized economic interdependence of individuals and groups of individuals characteristic of modern life are a product of competition."[66] Competition thus accounts for both territorial distribution and occupational divisions and, as we shall see later, these two types of distribution are intrinsically related in the ecological theory.

Competition and "Community."—Competition, then, emerges as a key to the understanding of the concept "community"; it is thought of by ecologists as the most fundamental process in human organization, and "community" is regarded as its product. There are various nuances in the respective interpretations of this important process suggested by individual ecologists. Park, for example, stresses the biological significance of competition, whereas McKenzie

[64] Park, "William Graham Sumner's Conception of Society," *Chinese Social and Political Science Review,* XVII (1933), 433. This monograph, as its title suggests, is an evaluation of Sumner's approach. However, Park interprets his subject from such a markedly ecological point of view, that it seems justifiable to quote from the article in elucidating Park's own theory.

[65] Park and Burgess, *Introduction to the Science of Sociology,* p. 508.

[66] *Ibid.*

leans toward an essentially economic interpretation, as may be gathered from his *Metropolitan Community* and other writings in which he presents his ecological formulations.

More often than not Park uses competition in a sense more inclusive than that of economic competition and with a different emphasis. He employs the term "competition of life" and identifies it with Darwin's "struggle for existence." He says that "man is everywhere involved in a struggle with other men—and with the living organisms by which he is surrounded—for a place and a position within the limits of the habitable world."[67] Together with Burgess, Park asserts that "competition, unqualified and uncontrolled as with plants, and in the great impersonal life-struggle of man with his kind and with all animate nature, is unconscious."[68] This unconscious process Park calls "biotic competition,"[69] and he looks upon it as essentially biological:

> The active principle in the ordering and regulating of life within the realm of animate nature is, as Darwin described it, "the struggle for existence." By this means the numbers of living organisms are regulated, their distribution controlled, and the balance of nature maintained. Finally, it is by means of this elementary form of competition that the existing species, the survivors in the struggle, find their niches in the physical environment and in the existing correlation or division of labor between the different species. . . These manifestations of a living, changing, but persistent order among competing organisms—organisms embodying "conflicting yet correlated interests"—seem to be the basis for the conception of a social order transcending the individual species, and of a society based on a biotic rather than a cultural basis, a conception later developed by the plant and animal ecologists.[70]

While economic competition in its rudimentary form is probably implied in the above quotation, it is not clear

[67] Park, *op. cit.*, p. 433. [68] Park and Burgess, *op. cit.*, p. 574.

[69] "Human Ecology," *American Journal of Sociology*, XLII, 13.

[70] *Ibid.*, p. 3.

whether Park also intends to include here the concept as it is generally used in the science of economics. He says, for instance, that "status has been described as an effect of conflict. But it is clear that economic competition frequently becomes conscious and so passes over into some of the milder forms of conflict."[71] The inference is that economic competition, like biotic competition, is regarded as essentially unconscious. Park also stipulates that "economic competition, as one meets it in human society, is the struggle for existence, as Darwin conceived it, modified and limited by custom and convention. In other respects, however, it is not different from competition as it exists in plant and animal communities."[72] Therefore, in its elements economic competition is biotic competition—an unconscious struggle for existence—except that it is modified and limited by custom and convention. Or, to put it in another way, when biotic competition is modified and limited by custom and convention it becomes economic competition. Park and Burgess hold that "competition on the economic level, i.e., of struggle for livelihood, had its origins in the market place."[73] Apparently the limitation and modification of competition transform the very quality of biotic competition in that the struggle for existence becomes struggle for livelihood and for status, the former being economic competition and the latter conflict:

Competition among men . . . has been very largely converted into rivalry and conflict. The effect of conflict has been to extend progressively the area of control and to modify and limit the struggle for existence within these areas. The effect of war has been, on the whole, to extend the area over which there is peace. Competition has been restricted by custom, tradition, and law, and the

[71] Park and Burgess, *op. cit.*, p. 670.

[72] "Succession, an Ecological Concept," *American Sociological Review,* I, 176.

[73] Park and Burgess, *op. cit.*, p. 555.

struggle for existence has assumed the form of struggle for a livelihood and for status.[74]

Thus, in spite of the inference that economic competition is intrinsically unconscious, the fact that it is modified, limited, and restricted by custom, convention, and other social factors changes this process, gives it a social quality which distinguishes it from the natural process of biotic competition. The individual may not know his competitors personally, but he is aware of competition about him, he is aware of competing with others, and he directs his competitive actions and employs various methods of competition in relation to this awareness. It is perhaps with this in view that Park states that "competition persists in human society and continues to manifest itself, as does the sexual instinct, in manifold indirect and insidious ways."[75] It is within the control imposed by "society" and in the manner acceptable to the social mores that economic competition takes place; "restriction of competition," we are told, "is synonymous with limitation of movement, acquiescence in control, and telesis, Ward's term for changes ordained by society in distinction from natural process of change."[76]

It is not that the biotic competition has no restrictions, but these are said to be of a different kind from the ones imposed upon economic competition. Although "competition, on the biotic level, as we observe it in the plant and animal communities, seems to be relatively unrestricted,"[77] Park claims that "the restraint in the case of symbiotic society (as, for example, in the plant community) is physical and external. In the case of cultural, i.e., human, society the restraints upon the individual are, so to speak, internal and moral, i.e., based on some sort of consensus."[78]

[74] Park and Burgess, *op. cit.*, p. 512.

[75] Park, "Succession, an Ecological Concept," *American Sociological Review*, I, 177.

[76] Park and Burgess, *op. cit.*, p. 512.

[77] Park, "Human Ecology," *American Journal of Sociology*, XLII, 14.

[78] Park, *op. cit.*, p. 176.

Park emphasizes this distinction between the biotic and economic competition in terms of the disciplines which deal with each process. He refers to human ecology as biologic economics and points out:

Ecology (biologic economics), even when it involves some sort of unconscious co-operation and a natural, spontaneous, and non-rational division of labor, is something *different* from the economics of commerce; something quite apart from the bargaining of the market place. Commerce . . . is one of the latest and most complicated of all the social relationships into which human beings have entered. Man is the only animal that trades and traffics.

Ecology, and human ecology, if it is not identical with economics on the distinctively human and cultural level is, nevertheless, something more than and different from the static order which the human geographer discovers when he surveys the cultural landscape.[79]

Here Park adheres scrupulously to his claim that the subject matter of human ecology is the organization and behavior of human beings on the organic level as opposed to the manifestations of phenomena which are uniquely human and, therefore, more evolved.

The relationship of the two aspects of human organizations, "community" and "society," in terms of competition is well expressed in the statement below:

It is when, and to the extent that, competition declines that the kind of order which we call society may be said to exist. In short, society, from the ecological point of view, and in so far as it is a territorial unit, is just the area within which biotic competition has declined and the struggle for existence has assumed higher and more sublimated forms.[80]

Thus "society" is the organization in which biotic competition has been transformed into other processes, whether they be economic competition, conflict, or rivalry. Social control eliminates biotic competition, and hence the more there is of conscious economic or social competition, the less

[79] Park, *op. cit.*, p. 12; italics mine. [80] *Ibid.*, p. 7.

of biotic struggle for existence; the more there is of "society," the less of "community." From this point of view, competition on the biotic level or in "community," is free in that it is neither limited nor modified by factors of "society": "In human as contrasted with animal societies, competition and the freedom of the individual is limited on every level above the biotic by custom and consensus."[81] Consequently, "community" exists only in so far as the biotic competition has not been limited or transformed by social control. Ecologists hold that "the evolution of society has been the progressive extension of control over nature and the substitution of a moral for the natural order."[82] Interpreted in terms of the ecological thesis, this statement would mean that "society" is progressively encroaching upon the sphere of "community" and, hence, that biotic competition or "competition of life" has an ever-diminishing function. Moreover, because "restriction of competition is synonymous with limitation of movement,"[83] it follows that the increasing limitation of competition would denote increasing limitation of movement. This conclusion, though, ecologists would hardly accept, since they hold that one of the main characteristics of the highly evolved modern city is the intense physical mobility of its population.[84]

If ecologists had consistently maintained this point of view, "community" would clearly define the ecological scope. The distinction of "community" from "society" would then be easily apparent. However, ecologists do not only qualify the above assumptions but often repudiate them. Although biotic competition becomes economic competition once it is limited and modified by social control, and although the bi-

[81] Park, *op. cit.*, p. 13.

[82] Park and Burgess, *op. cit.*, p. 511.

[83] *Ibid.*, p. 512.

[84] See, for example, Park, "Sociology," in *Research in the Social Sciences*, edited by Gee; and Nels Anderson, "The Trend of Urban Sociology," in *Trends in American Sociology*, edited by Lundberg, Anderson, and Bain.

otic level is free from such social curbs, Park advances other statements which contradict this position:

> A social organization on either the biotic or social level, so far as it involves the incorporation of individuals into a more intimate association, imposes limits, control, and direction upon these individual units. One may regard the plant and animal community as an association that is wholly anarchic and free. In that case, however, every form of association on the cultural level will involve a limitation of freedom of the individual.[85]

That biotic competition does not exist in its pure, unmodified form becomes apparent: "With man the free play of competition is restrained by sentiment, custom, and moral standards, not to speak of the more conscious control through law."[86] More specifically, "human ecology has . . . to reckon with the fact that in human society competition is limited by custom and culture. The cultural superstructure imposes itself as an instrument of direction and control upon the biotic substructure."[87] And, in fact, this restriction and modification by social factors evidently effects a complete metamorphosis of "community":

> In human communities . . . unlike plant and animal communities, we are not dealing merely with space and sustenance relationships, but invariably find these elementary relationships complicated by economic, political, and cultural factors. Space and time are translated into cost; the struggle for life becomes a struggle for living, and competitive co-operation becomes conflict and conscious collaboration toward a common goal.[88]

The biotic level either is or is not limited, restricted and modified by social control. If we overlook the contradictory statements given with such finality, then the only assumption left is that in "community" there is a different degree

[85] Park, "Succession . . .," *American Sociological Review,* I, 176.
[86] Park and Burgess, *op. cit.,* p. 512.
[87] Park, "Human Ecology," *American Journal of Sociology,* XLII, 15.
[88] Wirth, Louis, "The Scope and Problems of the Community," *Publications of the Sociological Society of America,* XXVII, 69.

or kind of social control from that which functions in "society"; this, however, is not revealed to us. We are told in one context that the biotic level, *qua* biotic, is not limited by custom and consensus; when it is so limited it changes its character and becomes economic competition. In another, we are told that the biotic level is controlled and limited by custom and consensus; in this case the distinction between biotic and economic competition is lost.

Since human ecologists regard and treat competition as the central process in the ecological "organization," its comprehension is of utmost importance. The very validity of the distinction between "community" and "society" and the delimitation of the scope of human ecology depend upon the definition of this process.

It is evident, however, that the ecologists have not formed a full understanding of the concept of competition. They have not uniformly differentiated between biotic and economic competition, and they have not satisfactorily indicated the relation of the two processes either to "community" or to "society." What puts a particular difficulty in the path of the reader is the loose use of the term competition. Unless the process is qualified as being biotic or economic, it is impossible to surmise the meaning the ecologists intend to give to it in any particular context. Yet they use the term competition in one case as including all forms of it, in another as a particular kind of competition often neglecting to state whether it is biotic, economic, or social. To cite only one example, Park and Burgess state in the same text that: (*a*) "competition among men . . . has been *very largely converted into rivalry and conflict,*" or "competition has been restricted by custom, tradition, and law";[89] and (*b*) "the freedom which commerce sought and gained upon the principle of laissez faire has *enormously*

[89] Park and Burgess, *op. cit.*, p. 512; italics mine.

extended the area of competition and in doing so has created a world-economy where previously there were only local markets."[90] These two statements can only be reconciled if we assume that the term competition has a different meaning in each of the two contexts.

Biotic versus Economic Competition.—If, as Park states, ecological competition is specifically biotic and distinct from economic competition, then the statement that "the economic organization of society, so far as it is an effect of free competition, is an ecological organization,"[91] would necessarily limit ecological organization to that aspect of economic organization which is essentially organic or less evolved. Likewise, we might reasonably assume that the terms "competition," "economic competition," "economic organization," and "economic forces," when used in relation to "community" or "the ecological organization," have a very specific connotation and always signify the biotic, "natural" type of phenomena.

However, in their treatment of "community" and of the synonymous concept of "ecological organization," the ecologists do not restrict themselves to the organic aspect of economic life. For example, Park and Burgess state:

> Competition is a struggle for position in an economic order. The distribution of populations in the world-economy, the industrial organization in the national economy, and the vocation of the individual in the division of labor—all these are determined, in the long run, by competition. The status of the individual, or a group of individuals, in the social order, on the other hand, is determined by rivalry, by war, or by subtler forms of conflict.[92]

The very essence of the ecological set-up involves the highly complex modern structure of cities and regions. McKenzie defines ecological distribution as "the spatial distribution of human beings and human activities resulting from

[90] *Ibid.*, p. 505; italics mine. [91] *Ibid.*, p. 508. [92] *Ibid.*, p. 574.

the interplay of forces which effect a more or less conscious, or at any rate dynamic and vital, relationship among the units comprising the aggregation."[93] Ecological unit is defined by the same author as "any ecological distribution—whether of residences, shops, offices, or industrial plants—which has a unitary character sufficient to differentiate it from surrounding distributions"[94] and ecological distance as a "time-cost concept rather than a unit of space . . . [which] is measured by minutes and cents rather than by yards and miles."[95] The ecological pattern depends upon modern systems of communication, modern methods of commerce and industry, and the culture of today. We are told that "an ecological organization is in process of constant change, the rate depending upon the dynamics of cultural, and particularly technical, advance"[96] and that "the spatial and sustenance relations in which human beings are organized are ever in process of change in response to the operation of a complex of environmental and cultural forces."[97] Of the four classes of ecological factors the geographical, which includes "climatic, topographic and resource conditions,"[98] represents the only kind of phenomena which may be regarded as natural; the other three are economic factors, "which comprise a wide range and variety of phenomena such as the nature and organization of local industries, occupational distribution, and standard of living of the population"; cultural and technical factors including "in addition to the prevailing condition of the arts, the moral attitudes and taboos that are effective in the distribution of population and services"; and political and administrative measures, "such as tariff, taxation, immigration laws, and rules governing public utilities."[99]

[93] "The Scope of Human Ecology," in *The Urban Community*, edited by E. W. Burgess, p. 168.

[94] *Ibid.*, p. 169.

[95] *Ibid.*, p. 170.

[96] *Ibid.*, p. 169.

[97] *Ibid.*, p. 167.

[98] *Ibid.*, p. 171.

[99] *Ibid.*, p. 172.

Hence, in spite of the professed limits of human ecology it cannot be said that either the strictly ecological subject matter or the forces that determine ecological phenomena are confined to the organic, or natural, aspects of human organization. The thought underlying the inclusion of aspects other than organic in such concepts as economic competition or organization is presumably that if the modern economic system with its highly rational and complex organization has developed from "biotic competition" it must perforce come under the category "community." This identification of cause and effect hardly bears logical analysis. Upon this principle society, as interpreted by ecologists, would likewise have to be identified with "community," since the assumption of the school is that the phenomena of community are the determining factors of social reality, as is seen from Park's statement that ecology "assumes that most if not all cultural changes in society will be *correlated* with changes in its territorial organization, and every change in the territorial and occupational distribution of the population will *effect* changes in the existing cultures."[100] By this token the division of the two concepts would be futile, if not impossible. Yet surely the causes may be inherent in one aspect of life, while the effects may reveal themselves in another.

Competitive Co-operation.—Even though the ecologists speak of competition as the basic process of "community," they often employ the term "competitive co-operation" in its stead. While in many cases ecologists use the term "co-operation" to signify social co-operation as it is generally understood by sociologists, the addition of the term "co-operation" to competition is evidently intended to signify the impersonal co-ordination and mutuality of economic

[100] "Succession, an Ecological Concept," *American Sociological Review,* I, 179; italics mine.

services. Co-operation, in this case, is not deliberate and is independent of communication. Thus, in discussing plant communities Park and Burgess state:

Co-operation and community, so far as it exists, consists merely in the fact that within a given geographical area, certain species come together merely because each happens to provide by its presence an environment in which the life of the other is easier, more secure, than if they lived in isolation.[101]

The same authors find that "the plant community is the best illustration of the type of social organization that is created by competitive co-operation because in the plant community competition is unrestricted."[102] Burgess gives the following specific illustration of competitive co-operation:

Certain of these basic necessities [technical services] of urban life are possible only through a tremendous development of communal existence. Three millions of people in Chicago are dependent upon one unified water system, one giant gas company, and one huge electric light plant. Yet, like most of the other aspects of our communal urban life, this economic co-operation is an example of co-operation without a shred of what the "spirit of co-operation" is commonly thought to signify. The great public utilities are a part of the mechanization of life in great cities, and have little or no other meaning for social organization.[103]

In this way, then, the competing individual, while pursuing his own ends, "inevitably contributes through the mutual exchange of services . . . to the common welfare."[104] This "competitive co-operation," distinct from conscious co-operation and social effort, is referred to as "symbiosis" when the relationship aspect is stressed. It denotes the fact of mutual interdependence arising out of complementary demands of the organisms upon the habitat and upon each other.

[101] "Succession," *op. cit.*, p. 201.

[102] *Ibid.*, p. 507. See also p. 165.

[103] "The Growth of the City," in Park, Burgess, *et al.*, *The City*, p. 53.

[104] Park and Burgess, *op. cit.*, p. 507.

Symbiosis.—The term "symbiosis" is borrowed from biology and stands for "the habitual living together of organisms of different species" where the relationships between them are usually "beneficial to at least one of the participants and harmful to none."[105] Among plants:

Species that form a community must either practice the same economy, making approximately the same demands on its environment (as regards nourishment, light, moisture, and so forth), or one species present must be dependent for its existence upon another species, sometimes to such an extent that the latter provides it with what is necessary or even best suited to it; a kind of symbiosis seems to prevail between such species.[106]

Symbiosis in human organization apparently involves division of labor and the impersonal mutual service resulting from exchange of goods and services. "People come together," says Park, "much as do different plant species that constitute a plant community, because they are useful to one another."[107] Burgess refers to relationships of symbiosis as "the factors involved in living together independent of communication."[108] In its broadest sense, Park conceives of it as extending over the world community where, he says,

we are in relations that are rather more symbiotic than social with vast numbers of people who, without knowledge of us or we of them, are toiling silently, in remote places, to maintain this vast structure of international exchange and division of labor in which we live. But even in the small local communities, where we are in some sort of personal contact with one another, the competition of life goes on, below the level of economic competition, in ways of which we are not wholly conscious and over which we have little control.[109]

[105] "Symbiosis," *Columbia Encyclopaedia,* 1935.

[106] Park and Burgess, *op. cit.,* adapted from Eugenius Warming, *Oecology of Plants,* p. 176.

[107] Park, "William Graham Sumner's Conception of Society," *Chinese Social and Political Science Review,* XVII, 434.

[108] Burgess, unpublished article on Robert E. Park, p. 28.

[109] Park, *op. cit.,* p. 440.

Symbiosis is regarded by ecologists as the basis of cohesion in the biotic community, and Park emphasizes the point that "the ties which hold it [the community] together are physical and vital rather than customary and moral.[110] It is with this point in view that he regards the "natural area" as "an area of competitive co-operation."[111] We are told that "each area . . . has its internal pattern of divisions of labor which operate as a basic mechanism in the selection of appropriate population elements."[112] The areas thus differentiated are also assumed to be in symbiotic relations with one another. Dawson, for instance, states that "the expanding city is gradually differentiated into natural areas which have marked specialization of function. . . These are interdependent, and their close proximity in an area, is a matter of very great advantage to each unit."[113] He goes on to say that beside the financial center and areas concerned with administration of industry and commerce, "there are still other areas of industry and residence in the metropolitan region which, taken together, form a major regional symbiotic pattern."[114]

Symbiosis thus serves as the basis of cohesion of each "natural area" and hence assumedly delimits it from other areas; symbiosis also links the different areas into a larger unit. We are not told, however, the difference in the degree or in the kind of symbiosis in the two instances. If it is the particular function which delimits each area, as is partly suggested in the above quotation of Dawson, then symbiosis cannot be said to serve as the cohesive principle any more or less for any particular area than it does for the larger

[110] Park, "Human Ecology," *American Journal of Sociology,* XLII, 15.

[111] *The Urban Community,* edited by Burgess, p. 12.

[112] C. A. Dawson, "Human Ecology," in *The Fields and Methods of Sociology,* edited by L. L. Bernard, p. 294, New York. Copyright 1934. Reprinted by permission of the publishers, Farrar & Rinehart, Inc.

[113] *Ibid.,* pp. 293–94. [114] *Ibid.,* p. 294.

area of which it is a part. Consequently, the general statement that a natural area is "an area of competitive co-operation" does not in any way define it. A natural area to which a part of another area is added arbitrarily can still be described as "an area of competitive co-operation."

A somewhat different slant is given to symbiosis by Wirth. In his book *The Ghetto* he assumes that the "natural area" populated by Jews is an entity by virtue of its social cohesion but that the relationships of the Ghetto with the other areas are distinctly symbiotic. He says:

> The relations between the two groups in such instances are usually relations of externality. Problems are settled by rules and laws, not by personal contact and intimate discussion. It is because the contacts between the larger and the smaller, between the dominant and the subordinate groups, are confined to mere externals that they are able to live so close to each other at all. In such cases human groups manage to live side by side, much like plants and animals, in what is known as *symbiosis*. The economy that arises persists without consciousness being at all involved. But among human beings consciousness and feelings will arise, and two groups can occupy a given area without losing their separate identity because each side is permitted to live its own inner life, and each somehow fears the other or idealizes the other. This relationship has been properly described as accommodation, to distinguish it from the assimilation that takes place when two people succeed in getting under each other's skins, so to speak, and come to share each other's inner life and thus become one.[115]

In describing the relationships of symbiosis in terms of rules and laws Wirth assumes that symbiosis involves consciousness and feelings, fear and idealization, and finally he regards it as coincident with the process of "society"—accommodation.

Dominance.—One of the most important concepts in human ecology is that of "dominance" and although the ecologists do not always clearly specify its relation to sym-

[115] Louis Wirth, *The Ghetto* (Chicago, 1928), pp. 282–83; italics mine.

biosis, their statements carry an implication that symbiosis results in various stages of ecological forms of organization, the crystallized form being that of dominance and subordination between either individuals or groups or between types of utilities or, again, between territorial units. "Dominance" in the ecological writings refers to the ascendancy to a more controlling position of one or more units among competing elements. It obviously involves the idea of "survival of the fittest" and, in addition, the control exerted by the "fittest" over the less able competitors. When this form of organization emerges, ecologists assume a temporary cessation of extreme competition and a consequent state of equilibrium. It is this "principle of dominance" that is understood to "determine the general ecological pattern of the city and the functional relation of each of the different areas of the city [community] to all others."[116] In other words, competition results in a relationship of dominance and subordination of the units, the dominance of one or more, in turn, determining the "position" of each unit. Park states, for instance, that "the so-called natural or functional areas of a metropolitan community—for example, the slum, the rooming-house area, the central shopping section and the banking center—each and all owe their existence directly to the factor of dominance and indirectly to competition."[117] The ecological processes, that is, the movements and the allocation of the population and of the utilities in the community, are also determined by the principle of dominance.[118] Finally, the stabilization, not only of the "community" but also of the cultural organization of "society," is determined by "dominance."[119]

Social or Nonsocial?—It is clear from the foregoing state-

[116] Park, "Human Ecology," *American Journal of Sociology,* XLII, 9.

[117] *Ibid.,* p. 8.

[118] See chap. vi on Ecological Processes.

[119] See Park, *op. cit.,* p. 9.

ments that ecologists conceive of community as representing that aspect of human life which is in its main features asocial. The very division of community and society in terms of the two levels, the biotic and the cultural, assumes the nonsocial character of "community." Furthermore, the relationships of symbiosis as opposed to those of consensus are independent of communication and are "biological rather than social."[120] Park and Burgess say that

the plant community offers the simplest and least qualified example of the community. Plant life, in fact, offers an illustration of a *community* which is *not a society*. It is not a society because it is an organization of individuals whose relations, if not wholly external, are, at any rate, "unsocial" in so far as there is no consensus.[121]

In other words, in the absence of consensus the relationships in a "community" are unsocial. This is what Park means when he states that "such a society [community?] is territorially organized and the ties which hold it together are physical and vital rather than customary and moral."[122] Both the above statements apply to the human as well as to the plant or animal "community" since this concept is based upon the assumption that there exists in one aspect of human organization behavior parallel to that of plants and animals. What distinguishes the human from plant and animal behavior is that, besides the biotic relationships, human beings exhibit social behavior which is not found among plants and animals. To embrace this social behavior the ecologists employ the concept "society."

Having pointed out that relations in a plant community are "unsocial," Park and Burgess then completely reverse their position and call these relations social. They say:

120 Park, "William Graham Sumner's Conception of Society," *Chinese Social and Political Science Review,* XVII, 439.

121 Park and Burgess, *op. cit.,* p. 165.

122 Park, "Human Ecology," *American Journal of Sociology,* XLII, 15.

"The members of a plant community live together in a relation of mutual interdependence which we call *social* probably because, while it is close and vital, it is not biological. It is not biological because the relation is a merely external one and the plants that compose it are not even of the same species."[123] This is indeed an extraordinary statement. Because a relation is "merely external," it is not biological—so it is called social. The distinction between "society" and "community" depends on the fact that the former involves mutual awareness—and now a relation is called social primarily because it lacks this factor. The only justification is contained in such a statement as the following, which seems only to make confusion worse confounded.

> If we are to assume that the economic order is fundamentally ecological, that is, created by the struggle for existence, an organization like that of the plant community in which relations between individuals are conceivably at least wholly external, the question may be very properly raised why the competition and the organization it has created should be regarded as social at all. As a matter of fact sociologists have generally identified the social with the moral order. . . The fact is, however, that this character of *externality* in human relations is a fundamental aspect of society and social life.[124]

Here Park and Burgess suggest the use of the term "social" in a sense inclusive of competitive factors, but the suggestion is never consistently carried out, as is shown in those statements given above where social is counterposed to competitive and to organic. It is Park who asserts that "symbiotic" relations are "biological rather than social,"[125] or "symbiotic rather than social,"[126] and that, "in the larger

[123] Park and Burgess, *op. cit.*, p. 506; italics mine.

[124] *Ibid.*, p. 508.

[125] Park, "William Graham Sumner's Conception of Society," *Chinese Social and Political Science Review*, XVII, 439.

[126] Park, "Succession, an Ecological Concept," *American Sociological Review*, I, 178.

world community, we are in relations that are rather more symbiotic than social."[127] Obversely, having made the distinction between the natural order of "community" and the social or moral order of "society," Park in his later writings speaks of "community" as a social order, as in the following quotation: "Human ecology, in so far as it is concerned with a *social order* that is based on competition rather than consensus, is identical, in principle at least, with plant and animal ecology."[128] Thus it would seem that both of the words "social" and "unsocial" have not merely variant meanings in the ecological terminology but actually contradictory ones.

The ambiguous use of the term "social" is succinctly illustrated by a passage of Park's in which he speaks of "a social organization on either the biotic or social level."[129] The author nowhere differentiates between "level" and "organization"; therefore, if both levels or organizations are social, why call one social and the other biotic? Evidently Park attaches a different meaning to each of the words "social"; the first generic, including both the social and the biotic levels, and the second specific, distinguishing the social from the biotic level.

Not the least of the difficulties in the analysis of "community" and "society" is the vague use of the term "society." It changes its hues and content in such fashion that it is often a matter of speculation to find the meaning intended by the authors. For example, in one and the same article we encounter passages such as the following:

Society, from the ecological point of view, and in so far as it is a territorial unit, is just the area within which biotic competition

[127] Park, *op. cit.*, p. 440.

[128] Park, "Human Ecology," *American Journal of Sociology*, XLII, 14; italics mine.

[129] "Succession, an Ecological Concept," *American Sociological Review*, I, 176.

has declined and the struggle for existence has assumed higher and more sublimated forms.[130]

Society, as ecologists have conceived it, is a population settled and limited to its habitat. The ties that unite its individual units are those of a free and natural economy, based on a natural division of labor. Such a society is territorially organized and the ties which hold it together are physical and vital rather than customary and moral.[131]

It will be seen that both statements are definitions of "society," both conceived from the ecological point of view, and both referring to territorial organization. Yet the first describes an organization in which biotic competition has declined, while the second stipulates a free and natural economy.

Abstraction versus Reality.—From the many contradictions found in the ecological formulations of "community" and "society," it will have become evident that ecologists themselves have no clear-cut conception of the two categories. One of their main difficulties lies in the confusion between abstraction and reality. Some of this confusion might have been avoided if the school had been familiar with the "ideal type" method of investigation. The concept "community" is approached in a way that denies its social attributes. In its very definition it is an abstraction of the asocial aspect of human behavior. Yet the ecologists find themselves compelled in many ways to take account of the social factors which in reality are intrinsically related to and bound up with the asocial community. Had ecologists persisted in dealing with the concept of the "natural order" as an abstraction, or as an "ideal type," for the purposes of study these social factors could be treated apart from "community," as conditioning, concomitant, and intrusive phenomena of the "natural order." We would then have only the problem of

[130] Park, *op. cit.*, p. 7.

[131] *Ibid.*, p. 15.

the validity and scientific utility of a particular classification and of the particularistic philosophical ideology underlying the delimitation of the category "community."

But ecologists do not pursue this course consistently; what is to them an abstraction at one time becomes a reality at another. So, on the one hand, we have the statement that there is a biotic level which represents an expression of natural behavior and which involves free competition, unrestricted mobility, unconscious relationships of symbiosis —all these in their pure form. As an abstraction, this conception permits the ecologists to denude "community" of its social aspects by relegating them to "society." The biotic level remains an asocial entity, apart from "society." But then, on the other hand, we have the statements that all these phenomena of "community" are modified and limited in every phase of human organization, that competition is never entirely free, that symbiosis is inextricably bound up with conscious, social relationships, that among human beings as opposed to the rest of the organic world social control penetrates and to a degree absorbs the biotic level. Although the category "community" still persists, it is now envisaged as a reality and defended in terms of that reality. Not only are social phenomena seen as conditioning factors, but the very fact that they condition or intrude upon "community" changes the quality of "community" from biotic to social. Social factors become so essentially a part of the natural community that the latter acquires a social character.

CHAPTER THREE

SOCIETY AND THE NATURAL ORDER

"COMMUNITY" AND "NATURE"

ECOLOGISTS speak of the "natural order" of community and of the "moral order" in society. The conception is of essential importance, since it involves the specific philosophical basis of the ecological theory. What do ecologists mean by the term "natural"?

Since competition, the struggle for existence, is construed as the central and all-pervading process in the natural order of community, self-preservation is the fundamental fact, and it implies, as Park suggests, the existence of "the self-assertiveness and insurgence of the creature."[1] Competition here is the expression of the organic needs of the individual, and it is in this sense that ecologists use the term "natural" as manifesting tendencies inherent in the object or in the situation.[2]

Moreover, since competition is for sustenance or self-preservation, it is a biological, natural process, that is, natural as opposed to rational or planned. Involving no conscious organization or planning, the system of relations in the "community" is that which spontaneously arises in the aggregation of men and animals alike. Thus, whatever organization or structure results, it is the product of the orderly working of natural laws, and in this sense it is in-

[1] Park, "Succession . . .," *American Sociological Review,* I, 177, quoting Arthur J. Thompson.

[2] See, for example, Park, "Sociology," in *Research in the Social Sciences,* edited by Gee, pp. 27–38.

evitable and hence predictable.[3] Human will and purpose do not interfere here to deflect the course of nature. Each element has its function to perform in relation to all the other elements about it. Park says, for example: "A region is called a 'natural area' because it comes into existence without design, and performs a function, though the function, as in the case of the slum, may be contrary to anybody's desire. It is a natural area because it has a natural history."[4]

Consequently, the expression of the basic, inherent tendencies of all living beings in a state of nature and the products of these tendencies are assumed to be natural. For instance, the division of labor, regarded as the product of competition[5] and the subsequent interdependence designated as symbiosis are natural processes analogous to the biological mutual dependence of plant and animal communities.

"Position" in the Natural Order.—The natural order is the distributive organization in which men, utilities, physical structures, and districts, compete for "position." Ecologists generally include under the term position both spatial and "sustenance" positions: "Competition among human beings involves struggle for position—that is, for a sustenance niche and a spatial location in which the individual or institution may survive and function."[6] Spatial and "sustenance" positions are closely related in the minds of ecologists, and ecological distribution is intended to include both types of position.

Under the influence of an intensified competition, and in the increased activity which competition involves, every individual and

[3] See Park, "The City," in Park, Burgess, *et al., The City,* p. 9.

[4] Park, "The City as a Social Laboratory," in *Chicago: an Experiment in Social Science Research,* edited by T. V. Smith and Leonard White, p. 9.

[5] Park and Burgess, *op. cit.,* p. 506.

[6] McKenzie, "The Field and Problems of Demography, Human Geography, and Human Ecology," in *Fields and Methods of Sociology,* edited by L. L. Bernard, p. 59, New York. Copyright 1934. Reprinted by permission of the publishers, Farrar & Rinehart, Inc.

every species, each for itself, tends to discover the particular niche in the physical and living environment where it can survive and flourish with the greatest possible expansiveness consistent with its necessary dependence upon its neighbors.[7]

The sustenance relationship of the individual with the physical environment, which is direct in a state of nature, becomes indirect in a civilized environment. Park points out that man is not so immediately dependent upon his physical environment as are other animals because: (1) "as a result of the existing world-wide division of labor, man's relation to his physical environment has been mediated through the intervention of other men. The exchange of goods and services have co-operated to emancipate him from dependence upon his local habitat";[8] (2) "man has, by means of inventions and technical devices of the most diverse sorts, enormously increased his capacity for reacting upon and remaking, not only his habitat but his world"; and (3) "man has erected upon the basis of the biotic community an institutional structure rooted in custom and tradition."[9]

Although the spatial is thus physically separated from the sustenance position, the latter becoming an economic position, and although the place of work is not any more directly related to the place of shelter, the ecologists claim that the relationship between territorial and economic positions still holds. They make a twofold classification: from the point of view of population they speak of spatial position and economic position; and from the point of view of the use of land they speak of residential and functional location. Thus sustenance position acquires two aspects—the physical place in which individuals work and the economic occupation, which, it would seem, is divorced from the territorial location. However, a further assumption is

[7] Park, "Human Ecology," *American Journal of Sociology,* XLII, 10.

[8] *Ibid.,* p. 12.

[9] *Ibid.*

that the economic position is generally related to the place of work since there is a territorial specialization of functional areas; at the same time, the economic position is related to the place of residence, for the territorial segregation in the latter case is in terms of people's income. Upon these arguments ecologists base their treatment of both types of position as closely related categories belonging to the same universe of discourse.

As opposed to a state of nature, what defines man's spatial position within a community, such as the city, is no longer the geographical locus, the surface of the earth, from which he may derive both his food and shelter, but the value of the land upon which he settles. In this way land values decide the pattern of the distribution of populations. Land values are seen as the primary selective factors in the allocation of populations, as well as of utilities, and they are regarded as "the chief determining influence in the segregation of local areas and in the determination of the uses to which an area is to be put."[10] The spatial position acquires an economic significance, and economic position becomes the determinant of the spatial position rather than the obverse as it is in the organic world.

Ecologists maintain that populations, utilities, and physical structures all compete for a spatial position, so that territorial situation as such is regarded as an object of competition.[11] Park tells us that "business and industry seek advantageous locations and draw around them certain portions of the population."[12] People also compete for position in the community, so that "in this competition for position the population is segregated over the natural areas of the

[10] Wirth, "A Bibliography of the Urban Community," in Park, Burgess, *et al., The City,* p. 203.

[11] McKenzie, *loc. cit.,* p. 59.

[12] Park, "The City," in Park, Burgess, *et al., The City,* p. 6.

city."[13] Furthermore, spatial position is seen as the determinant of the success or failure of an "institution."[14] In this way spatial position both determines and signifies the degree of success in competition and therefore, by implication, the economic and social position.

The Rôle of Physical Factors in the Natural Order.—Although territorial position is translated by ecologists into an economic value, geographic and other physical factors are regarded by them as directly related to man's existence. Not only do individuals in the "natural order" compete for spatial position, but they are also attracted and conditioned by physical factors. For instance, although populations may settle in places where their incomes correspond to the land values, the geographic factors, be they natural resources of the earth, or topographical phenomena, such as hills, ravines, rivers, and lakes, are of a determining influence in their distribution. The natural resources are assumed to play an important rôle in the settlement of groups in larger regions. Here ecologists follow the geographers in assuming that populations settle at or near the natural resources, with the qualification that the development of modern technology has complicated this relation of populations to natural resources.[15]

The physical factors are of two kinds, the topographical and the artificial, the first being natural elevation and depression in the land, rivers, and so forth, the second, factors such as artificial changes in elevation, parks, boulevards, artificial lakes, and various systems of communication and transportation. Ecologists designate all these as

[13] Zorbaugh, "The Natural Areas of the City," in *The Urban Community*, edited by Burgess, p. 222.

[14] See, for example, Paul G. Cressey, *The Taxi Dance-Hall* (Chicago, 1932).

[15] See McKenzie, "Ecological Succession in the Puget Sound Region," *Publications of the American Sociological Society*, XXIII (1928), 60–80.

physical factors and treat both the natural and the artificial as *natural* in so far as they determine the pattern of the natural order of the "community." Park says for example: "Physical geography, natural advantages and disadvantages, including means of transportation, determine in advance the general outlines of the urban plan."[16]

Within a "community," such as the city, physical factors serve to attract or to repel populations and utilities, to condition and partly to determine land values, and to impede or to facilitate movements of the various elements, thus influencing their disposition and their relationship to each other. In this way they make up the framework, the pattern, of the city:

> The structure of the individual city . . . is built about this framework of transportation, business organization and industry, park and boulevard systems, and topographical features. All of these break the city up into numerous smaller areas, which we may call natural areas, in that they are the unplanned, natural product of the city's growth. Railroad and industrial belts, park and boulevard systems, rivers and rises of land acting as barriers to movements of population tend to fix the boundaries of these natural areas, while their centers are usually intersections of two or more business streets. By virtue of proximity to industry, business, transportation, or natural advantages each area acquires a physical individuality accurately reflected in land values and rents.[17]

It is to barriers which delimit "natural areas" that ecologists give a particular emphasis: "Streets, rivers, railroad properties, street-car lines, and other distinctive marks or barriers tend to serve as dividing lines between the natural areas within the city."[18] In accordance with the ecological principle, these physical factors divide the community into social and economic units, because "geography, occupation and all the other factors which determine the distribu-

[16] Park, *op. cit.*, p. 5.

[17] Zorbaugh, *op. cit.*, p. 222.

[18] Wirth, *op. cit.*, p. 188.

tion of population determine so irresistibly and fatally the place, the group, and the associates with whom each one of us is bound to live."[19] Burgess finds that in Chicago "the lines of physical separation, with some few exceptions, were also the dividing lines between local communities."[20]

The Natural Order as a Physical Entity.—Physical factors are more than limiting conditions of the social organization. Ecologists conceive of them as determining not only physical movements and physical distribution, but also social changes and social structure. Burgess reveals this point of view in his definition of the ecological community, of "this apparently 'natural' organization of the human community, so similar in the formation of plant and animal communities," when he poses the following questions:

How far has the area itself, by its very topography and by all its other external and physical characteristics, as railroads, parks, types of housing, conditioned community formation and exerted a determining influence upon the distribution of its inhabitants and upon their movements and life? To what extent has it had a selective effect in sifting and sorting families over the area by occupation, nationality, and economic or social class? To what extent is the work of neighborhood or community institutions promoted or impeded by favorable or unfavorable location? How far do *geographical distances* within or without the community *symbolize social distances?*[21]

The two principles, (1) the identification of the physical with economic facts, and (2) the broader restatement of the first, that the physical phenomena are fundamental determinants of social behavior, depend upon particular philosophic postulates. We saw that not only is the natural order a competitive and distributive organization but it is

[19] Park, *op. cit.*, 17–18.

[20] Burgess, "Basic Social Data," in *Chicago: an Experiment in Social Science Research,* edited by T. V. Smith and Leonard White, p. 59.

[21] Burgess, "Can Neighborhood Work Have a Scientific Basis?" in Park, Burgess, *et al., The City,* p. 144; italics mine.

also free in the sense that it is the aspect of life which, although progressively diminishing, is not yet within the currents of social control. Three characteristics, competition, freedom, and mobility (the condition of distribution), constitute the core of this natural order and the assumption of their intrinsic relation in essence defines the conception.

Mobility, a term used by ecologists as equivalent to physical movement of all kinds,[22] is apparently regarded as one of the primary means of survival and hence becomes not only a condition but a concomitant of the process of competition. It is assumed that through change of location organisms are better able to seek more favorable conditions for survival, so that mobility in this case determines success in competition and implies freedom of selection within the limits of the environment. In fact, the degree of freedom of movement is related to the degree of freedom of competition. Park and Burgess declare that "from the standpoint of the individual *competition means mobility, freedom,* and, from the point of view of society, pragmatic or experimental change."[23] They also assert that "restriction of competition is synonymous with limitation of movement."[24] Thus freedom of competition means freedom of movement and vice versa. But more than that, mobility as such is the essence of freedom because "freedom is fundamentally freedom to move,"[25] and "capacity of independent locomotion is the basis and the symbol of every other form of independence."[26] Hence, mobility defines freedom as well as competition.

Moreover, if mobility is a concomitant of competition, then immobility is assumed to correspond to quiescence; if physical movement reflects the competitive process, then

[22] Park, "Sociology," in *Research in the Social Sciences,* edited by Gee, p. 17.

[23] Park and Burgess, *op. cit.,* p. 512; italics mine.

[24] *Ibid.*

[25] *Ibid.,* p. 508.

[26] *Ibid.*

physical position tallies with the sustenance position. It is this assumption of an intrinsic nexus between competition and mobility which is the key to the ecologists' interpretation of economic and social phenomena in terms of physical factors. Since the competitive "community" is the fundamental order from which "society" emerges and upon which "society" rests, ecologists think of the phenomena of "community" both as determining factors and as indices of the phenomena of "society." Because physical mobility is found to be a concomitant of competition and physical position is seen as related to sustenance position, physical mobility and spatial position measure not only competition and economic position but also the social factors of which competition is either an index or a determinant. In this way physical movement in all its aspects becomes directly correlated with social movements. "Movement and migration are not merely an *incident* but a *cause* of almost every form of social change."[27] These considerations lead Park to assert:

> It is because social relations are so frequently and so inevitably correlated with spacial relations; because physical distances, so frequently are, or seem to be, the indexes of social distances, that statistics have any significance whatever for sociology. And this is true, finally, because it is only as social and psychical facts can be reduced to, or correlated with, spacial facts that they can be measured at all.[28]

Nels Anderson adheres to the same point of view when he claims that social mobility is the subjective aspect of physical mobility and that the former is generally the result of the latter:

> The two forms of mobility are essentially two aspects of a single phenomenon, social mobility being more subjective and generally a resultant of mobility. Once people shift through space, they

[27] Park, *op. cit.*, p. 15; italics mine.

[28] Park, "The Urban Community as a Spacial Pattern and a Moral Order," in *The Urban Community*, edited by Burgess, p. 18.

have no choice but to form new habits and set up new social relationships.[29]

Thus ecologists try to establish a correspondence between "the physical formation of the city with its areas separated by river, elevated railroad walls, industrial belts, and parks and boulevards" and "the currents of the economic and social life." According to Burgess, in Chicago it was found that "while these local communities were in a state of change, more or less rapid as the case might be, the changes taking place were more or less localized by the effects of these permanent physical barriers."[30]

The Individual and the Person.—The assumption that the natural order is characterized by freedom leads ecologists to designate the "natural" beings within it as individuals, in contrast to persons, in the moral order.[31]

> The term *individual* [says Burgess] is reserved for "that atomic viewpoint" of a self-sufficient unit, namely the biological organism with physical, temperamental, and mental traits reacting to environmental stimuli. The term *person* is introduced for "the organic viewpoint" of the individual as "an integral part of his social setting."[32]

Individuals are here assumed to be independent and free, concerned entirely with their individual needs. They struggle with each other for the satisfaction of these needs, and in their midst "such order as exists is the order of nature."[33] Again, "they are spatially separated, territorially

[29] Anderson, "The Trend of Urban Sociology," in *Trends in American Sociology*, edited by G. Lundberg, *et al.*, p. 286.

[30] Burgess, "Basic Social Data," in *Chicago: an Experiment in Social Science Research*, edited by Smith and White, p. 58.

[31] Park, "The Urban Community," in *The Urban Community*, edited by Burgess, p. 17.

[32] Burgess, "What Social Case Records Should Contain to be Useful for Sociological Interpretation," *Social Forces*, VI (Sept., 1927–28), 526.

[33] Park, "Sociology," in *Research in the Social Sciences*, edited by Gee. p. 8.

distributed, and capable of independent locomotion."[34] To Park and Burgess, freedom is "fundamentally freedom to move and individuality is inconceivable without the capacity and the opportunity to gain an individual experience as a result of independent action,"[35] the implication being that independent action is in turn dependent upon independent movement or locomotion. Park states that communities "are composed of individuals who act independently of one another, who compete and struggle with one another for mere existence, and treat one another, as far as possible, as utilities."[36] Since "the moral and political order . . . imposes itself upon this competitive organization,"[37] it is in "society" that "individuals" are formed into "persons" that is, they acquire status and membership in a social organization. "Within this moral order individuals assume the character of persons conscious of themselves and of their rôle in the community,"[38] and "it is the social environment to which the person, as distinguished from the individual, responds."[39] The freedom of the individual within the "natural order" is not only freedom to express the inherent self-assertive tendencies, but it is freedom from control, because "society may be said to exist only so far as this independent activity of the individual is *controlled* in the interest of the group as a whole."[40]

The antithesis between the individual and the person is clearly revealed when Park states that in society,

men and women are bound together by affection and common purposes; they do cherish traditions, ambitions, and ideals that are not all their own, and they maintain, *in spite of natural impulses to the contrary,* a discipline and a moral order that *enables*

[34] Park and Burgess, *op. cit.,* p. 508. [35] *Ibid.*

[36] Park, *op. cit.,* p. 6. [37] Park and Burgess, *op. cit.,* p. 508.

[38] Park, *op. cit.,* p. 34. Community in this quotation is used to signify what we have so far designated as "society."

[39] Park, "Community Organization and Juvenile Delinquency," in Park, Burgess, *et al., The City,* p. 100. [40] Park and Burgess, *op. cit.,* p. 508.

them to transcend what we ordinarily call nature and through their collective action, recreate the world in the image of their collective aspirations and their common will.[41]

The Essence of the Natural Order.—It is apparent that the ecologists' conception of the "natural order" reflects their implicit adherence to biological Darwinism. The peculiarly individualistic bias underlying the treatment of "community" and its description as an automatic organization without awareness, resting upon division of labor and economic interdependence, is also reminiscent of Adam Smith, who envisaged a freely automatic system working out a form of order through the self-centered economic drives of individuals. Adam Smith, too, regarded this order as "natural," though occasionally he attributed its equilibrium to the "invisible hand."

In its essence then, the "natural order" signifies the organization which is the direct embodiment and the result of the fundamental and inherent characteristics of living organisms. It is the aspect which reveals the laws of nature that are unplanned and inevitable. When ecologists speak of the "natural history" of an area[42] or of a newspaper, they mean a history that describes the development inherent within that entity—not only the unplanned sequence of change, but also the course of development which it is assumed must and will take place in spite of planning.[43] When ecologists speak of a "natural area" they follow the suit of plant ecology, where the plant formation is a "natural unit in which all of its associes . . . fall into their proper developmental relation."[44] The "community" is conceived of

[41] Park, "Sociology," in *Research in the Social Sciences,* edited by Gee, pp. 6–7; italics mine.

[42] See Park, "The City," in Park, Burgess, *et al., The City,* p. 32.

[43] See Park, "The Natural History of the Newspaper," in Park, Burgess, *et al., The City.*

[44] F. E. Clements, *Plant Succession: an Analysis of the Development of Vegetation* (Washington, 1916), p. 143.

as a natural organism, whose pattern and whose processes are rigidly defined by natural laws.

The attributes which define the "natural order" in themselves are natural entities, so that competition and symbiosis, locomotion and freedom, distribution and spatial relations, natural and artificial physical phenomena, no matter how different from similar manifestations in the state of nature, are all natural phenomena, subject to natural laws of their own, apart from the rational and purposeful design of men.

MORAL REGIONS

Because the term "natural" acquires a specific meaning in the ecological terminology and because the "natural order" describes one of the two aspects of human organization, we may take it for granted that whatever is a characteristic of the other aspect, that is, the social or the moral order, is not to be treated as specifically natural. It is also clear that a thing or a quality is designated natural not only by virtue of its particular definitive attributes but also because it is derived from or has its roots in the natural order. That is to say, because competition is assumed to be a natural process, whatever organization or phenomenon is based upon it, or is the direct outcome of it is also treated as natural. This is evident in the inclusion of economic and industrial factors in the ecological organization; and, although Park has given us a few statements which would imply that only the biotic aspect of the economic organization is treated by ecology, his other statements do not show such a distinction. In fact, none of the ecologists limit their scope to the biotic.[45] On the contrary, ecological factors and ecological processes, upon further investigation, turn out to be highly evolved and rationalized, whether they are descriptive of social or economic organizations.

[45] See, for example, McKenzie's treatment of economic factors in *The Metropolitan Community* (New York, 1933).

It is in the light of the distinctive definition of the natural that the "moral region" will be discussed, because this concept is an illustration of a deviation from the definition in question. Moral regions are forms of segregation in the ecological community and are described by Park as "regions in which a divergent moral code prevails, because it is a region in which the people who inhabit it are dominated, as people are ordinarily not dominated, by a taste or by a passion or by some interest which has its roots directly in the original nature of the individual."[46] The implication in this statement is obviously that there are also other forms of behavior which are not directly rooted in the original nature of the individual. Park and Burgess define ceremonial, public opinion, and law as

> characteristic forms in which social life finds expression as well as a means by which the actions of the individual are co-ordinated and collective impulses are organized so that they issue in behavior, that is, either (a) primarily expressive—play, for example—or (b) positive action.[47]

These authors find that

> art, play, religious exercises, and political activity are either wholly or almost wholly forms of expression, and have, therefore, that symbolic and ceremonial character which belongs especially to ritual and to art, but is characteristic of every activity carried on for its own sake. Only work, action which has some ulterior motive or is performed from a conscious sense of duty, falls wholly and without reservation into the second class.[48]

This division in terms of motives and attitudes between "expressive behavior" and "work" is the basis of the concept "moral region." Park says that "we should seek to distinguish, as far as possible, between those abstract mental qualities upon which technical excellence is based and those more fundamental native characteristics which find expres-

[46] Park, "The City," in Park, Burgess, *et al., The City,* p. 45.

[47] Park and Burgess, *op. cit.,* p. 788.

[48] *Ibid.*

sion in temperament."[49] The segregation of population in a "community," in this case the city, is apparently distinguished in terms of these two types of behavior, which are treated as basic determinants of various groupings. Park makes such a distinction when he says that

> in the organization which city life spontaneously assumes the population tends to segregate itself, not merely in accordance with its interests, but in accordance with its tastes or its temperaments. The resulting distribution of the population is likely to be quite different from that brought about by occupational interests or economic conditions.[50]

Park gives a special meaning to the term "interest" and refers to it as rational, mobile, making for change, and as implying the existence of a consciousness between means and ends.[51] He tells us that "money is the cardinal device by which values have become rationalized and sentiments have been replaced by interests"[52] and that "the effect, under conditions of personal competition, of this increasing interdependence of the parts is to create in the industrial organization as a whole a certain sort of social solidarity, but a solidarity based, not on sentiment and habit but on community of interests."[53] Thus, economic or occupational distribution assumes a character distinct from that of the distribution which is the result of fundamental native characteristics. Furthermore, in so far as the basis of economic or occupational distribution is described in terms of interests, it acquires a rational character and is thus distinguished from or opposed to "natural" forms of segregation.

"Moral regions" include places of resort as well as of abode.

> Such a region would differ from other social groups by the fact that its *interests are more immediate and more fundamental.* For

[49] Park, *op. cit.,* p. 42. [50] *Ibid.,* p. 43. [51] *Ibid.,* p. 16.
[52] *Ibid.* [53] *Ibid.,* pp. 15–16.

this reason its differences [from other regions] are likely to be due to moral, rather than intellectual, isolation.[54]

They are regions in which

"vagrant and suppressed impulses, passions, and ideals emancipate themselves from the dominant moral order."[55]

Expressive behavior, its roots directly in the original nature of the individual, serves as a function of escape from social control and is a vicarious expression of natural tendencies. In Park's words:

> The fact seems to be that men are brought into the world with all the passions, instincts, and appetites, uncontrolled and undisciplined. Civilization, in the interests of the common welfare, demands the suppression sometimes, and the control always, of these wild, natural dispositions. In the process of imposing its discipline upon the individual, in making over the individual in accordance with the accepted community model, much is suppressed altogether, and much more finds a vicarious expression in forms that are socially valuable, or at least innocuous. It is at this point that sport, play, and art function. They permit the individual to purge himself by means of symbolic expression of these wild and suppressed impulses.[56]

Apparently vice of various sorts and crime also belong to this type of "expressive" behavior.[57] Park, moreover, includes under "expressive" behavior other social phenomena such as "strikes, wars, popular elections, and religious revivals [which] perform a similar function in releasing the subconscious tensions."[58]

"Moral regions," then, are areas in which particular types of "expressive" behavior are dominant, in contrast to other regions (we are not told what kind) in which apparently people work or act from a sense of duty. Because moral regions are a product of the "original nature of the individ-

[54] Park, *op. cit.*, p. 45; italics mine. [55] *Ibid.*, p. 43. [56] *Ibid.*, p. 43.
[57] See Park, "Human Ecology," *American Journal of Sociology*, XLII, 1–15.
[58] Park, *op. cit.*, p. 44.

uals," Park regards them as "part of the natural, if not the normal, life of a city."[59]

Expressive behavior, as enumerated by Park and in part by Burgess, consists of activities such as art, play, sport, religious exercises, political activity (including strikes, wars, and popular elections), vice, crime, and eccentric and exceptional behavior which deviates from the social norm. Park refers to areas inhabited by the poor also as "moral regions," but in this case he does not state the exact activities which make this type of segregation natural, or rooted "directly in the original nature of the individual."

The distinction between the natural and the moral, the cultural, or the social which was given in connection with the division of "community" and "society," now acquires a new meaning, inconsistent with that given earlier. Whereas before we were told that those relationships are natural which are independent of communication, which are not conscious, and which are based on competition, we now find that phenomena such as play, "religious exercises," and political, criminal, or delinquent activities are also natural. Thus, in view of the categorical designation of "community" as the natural order, these activities would logically come under the concept "community." This is corroborated by Park's statement that

> it is in this community with its various organizations and its rational, rather than traditional, schemes of control, and not elsewhere, that we have delinquency. Delinquency is, in fact, in some sense the measure of the failure of our community organizations to function.[60]

In other words, delinquency is the expression of natural impulses in the face of the failure of rational control organiza-

[59] Park, *op. cit.*, p. 45.

[60] Park, "Community Organization and Juvenile Delinquency," in Park, Burgess, *et al.*, *The City*, p. 106. The use of the term "community" in this particular passage is challenged, *cf. infra*, pp. 75–77.

tions to limit or suppress them. Here we still have rational activities as an aspect of "society," although such traditional or customary modes of behavior as "religious exercises" and political activities, which were earlier considered to belong to "society," would have to be included in "community." The inclusion of these functions in the natural order would result either in the assumption that all the above mentioned activities are independent of communication, are the outcome of competition, and primarily involve symbiotic relationships, or that "community" is not a competitive organization and depends upon communication as much as does "society," or, again, that "society," too, is partly a natural order.

The very distinction between "expressive" behavior as natural and work as strictly human may be questioned. When the motives underlying the particular form of behavior are made the basis of distinction, as is done by Park and Burgess, expressive behavior being "activity carried on for its own sake," while work is "action which has some ulterior motive or is performed from a conscious sense of duty,"[61] then one might still question the assumption that one class of motives is necessarily less evolved or less conscious than the other.

An objection may be raised that "expressive" behavior is not meant by ecologists to be included in the scope of "community" and that there is a difference between the biotic or the economic activities, which are a direct expression of man's natural tendencies and which develop apart from social control, and religious exercises, play, and political activities, which are a vicarious expression of man's native impulses and which serve as an escape from social control. However, we have already been told that the biotic organization is limited and controlled by "society" so that

[61] Park and Burgess, *op. cit.*, p. 788.

the factor of repression is present in both cases. Moreover, ecologists themselves label expressive activities as "natural" and state that they have roots directly in the original nature of the individual, so that the distinction in essence is lost between these two types of behavior.

The inclusion of expressive behavior in the natural order narrows down the scope of "society" to activities and relationships which depend upon a rational basis. This, in fact, completely reverses the position Park takes when he tells us that "community of interests"—that is, the rational organization—represents the kind of solidarity which is not based on sentiment and habit and that this type of solidarity is exemplified in the economic and industrial organization. It is the economic and industrial organization, based upon rational interests, which now becomes the definitive substance of "society." This, of course, is in direct contradiction with the ecologists' assumption that "the economic organization of society, so far as it is an effect of free competition, is an ecological organization."[62]

The designation of "expressive" behavior as natural would also imply that these activities are more directly affected by their distribution in space[63] and perhaps it is with this idea in mind that the problems of delinquency, vice, political groups, and areas inhabited by "the poor" are made the subject of ecological studies. All these studies approach the problems of the "expressive" forms of behavior with the assumption that they are modes of escape from the repression and control of "society" and are therefore studied in terms of the degrees of disorganization and organization of "society."

It is the nonconformity of these groups to the social standards and social control that is the basis of their problem behavior. But, at the same time, nonconformity enters

[62] Park and Burgess, *op. cit.*, p. 508. [63] See *infra*, pp. 81–82.

into "society" in other ways, as Park reveals when he states that "it is by non-conformity, nevertheless, that the individual develops his personality and society ceases to be a mere mass of inert tradition."[64] He goes on to say that the individual "may distinguish himself and become ambitious. He may fail; he may cheat; he may do the unpardonable thing and suffer the pangs of remorse. In any case, as a result and to the extent of his collision with the existing social order he is likely to become acutely conscious of himself" and, by implication, in this way develop his personality.[65] Earlier, we saw that society is an instrument of social control and the individuals of community assume the character of persons in that they

> are bound together by affections and common purposes; they do cherish traditions, ambitions, and ideals that are not all their own, and they maintain, in spite of natural impulses to the contrary, a discipline and a moral order that enables them to transcend what we ordinarily call nature and, through their collective action, recreate the world in the image of their collective aspirations and their common will.[66]

Hence the individual is a person in so far as he conforms, and yet this individual develops his personality in so far as he does not conform.

CRITICAL CONSIDERATIONS

When two concepts are marked by different processes and structures, by different levels and types of behavior, and when they are said to be governed by distinct laws—"community" by natural laws and "society" by social principles —there is no escaping the conclusion that they are separate categories. And yet the ecologists find several ways of obviating the difficulties inherent in the strict observance of this principle. They waver between the complete scission of the

[64] Park, "Sociology," in *Research in the Social Sciences,* edited by Gee, p. 40. [65] *Ibid.* [66] *Ibid.,* pp. 6–7.

two concepts, on the one hand, and their fusion, on the other. They discard the specific meaning given to each, so that either "community" or "society" is used in a sense inclusive of both or with the meanings generally attached to these terms by the majority of sociologists. As the ecological formulations become more definite, the ecologists increasingly obliterate the demarcation between the concepts and extend the scope of the ecological discipline at the expense of the non-ecological concept "society." This is particularly evident in the school's research work, where the ecologists apparently find it impossible to maintain the distinction either as a working principle or even as an heuristic hypothesis. Concomitantly with the extension of the scope of human ecology, the ecologists, paradoxically enough, subdivide "community"—the avowed subject matter of human ecology—into three or four types of organization, only one of which is named the "ecological community" or the "ecological organization."

Even in those cases in which the theoretical distinction is adhered to, ecologists find it desirable to enlarge the scope of their theory, as is seen in Park's definition of the specifically ecological process "succession."

> In view . . . of the complexity of social change and of the peculiar manner in which change in the social superstructure is involved in change in the biotic or symbiotic substructure, it seems desirable to include within the perspective and purview of the concept, and of the studies of succession, every possible form of orderly change so far as it affects the interrelations of individuals in a community or the structure of the society of which these individual units are a part.[67]

This statement, if taken at its face value, is tantamount to a denial of the possibility of distinction between the two concepts "community" and "society."

[67] Park, "Succession, an Ecological Concept," *American Sociological Review,* I, 177.

The contradictions pointed out in the following discussion might be attributed to the changes and adjustments occasioned by the progressive development of the theory over a period of time. Yet the inconsistencies in the formulations do not occur only between the earlier and the more recent works, but also between contemporaneous writings and even within a single text. With the exception of a few admitted disagreements within the school, nowhere do we find any explicit statements of retraction of earlier hypotheses. Presumably, then, the ecologists envisage new classifications or concurrent formulations which do not appear to the reader to be coherent, as being logically integrated into their scientific context. It is in the light of these considerations that the following criticisms are broached.

Specific Inconsistencies.—The confusion between "community" and "society" is illustrated in the shifting of the various aspects of human association from one to the other. Many grounds may be offered to show the vacillating inclusion of the political, the economic, and the moral, in either the ecological community or in "society."

It was seen that the formulations of the ecologists assume a dichotomous division of the human organization, "community" defining the "biotic level" and "society" describing the "cultural level." The four basic processes are divided accordingly, competition being the process upon which "community" is based, and conflict, accommodation, and assimilation representing the three basic processes of "society." Conflict is identified with the political order, which is included in "society." Park and Burgess point out that "competition determines the position of the individual in the community; conflict fixes his place in society,"[68] and that "it is in what has been described as the *political process* that society consciously deals with its crises."[69] However,

[68] Park and Burgess, *op. cit.*, p. 574. [69] *Ibid.*, p. 509.

political activity is designated by Park as expressive behavior and as belonging to the natural order of "community." Hence, at one time conflict, the process of political order, is specifically attributed to "society" and, at another, it is relegated to "community" without reason being given for the interchange.

The same authors assume that "the economic organization of society, so far as it is an effect of free competition, is an ecological organization."[70] However, in another context Park states:

> The interrelations of human beings are more diverse and complicated than this dichotomy, symbiotic and cultural, indicates. This fact is attested by the divergent systems of human interrelations which have been the subject of the special social sciences. Thus human *society, certainly in its mature and more rational expression,* exhibits *not merely an ecological, but an economic, a political, and a moral order.*[71]

Elaborating this he goes on to say:

> It is interesting also that these divergent social orders seem to arrange themselves in a kind of hierarchy. In fact they may be said to form a pyramid of which the ecological order constitutes the base and the moral order the apex. Upon each succeeding one of these levels, the ecological, economic, political, and moral, the individual finds himself more completely incorporated into and subordinated to the social order of which he is a part than upon the preceding.[72]

Here, then, in spite of statements to the contrary[73] the economic order is considered an organization apart from the ecological. The same applies to the political organization, which is also classified apart from the moral or social order.[74]

[70] Park and Burgess, *op. cit.*, p. 508.

[71] Park, "Human Ecology," *American Journal of Sociology,* XLII, 14; italics mine.

[72] *Ibid.*, p. 14.

[73] Cf. ch. ii, sec. 4.

[74] If the hierarchal arrangement of the four orders is related to the ecological theory, where the ecological order is the least evolved and the most free from social control, while the moral order is the most evolved, the

It may be assumed that in the fourfold classification of human society, the term "society" is used in a generic sense and that therefore the "ecological order" is synonymous with "community" as we have been given to understand before. However, Park finds that "community," too, contains its own three organizations: (*a*) the ecological organization, (*b*) the economic organization, and (*c*) the cultural and political organization.[75] Either Park uses "community" here, as he does "society" above, in a generic sense, or he gives it the meaning usually assigned to it by sociologists, overlooking the specifically ecological definition. Burgess also finds that "community life, as conditioned by the distribution of individuals and institutions over an area, has at least three quite different aspects."[76] These he designates as the ecological, cultural, and political communities.[77] As all three are approached from the point of view of territorial distribution, they definitely fall within the purview of "community."

Whether or not Park's use of the term "community" coincides with that of Burgess, it is clear from the statements of both that the ecological community is now stripped of its inclusive connotation cited in the pages above. First, the economic organization is separated from the ecological; then, the ecological community, as such, becomes only one of several aspects of the "community." "Community" thus ceases to define the ecological scope. Although Burgess approaches

---

most controlled and rational, then the implication is that the economic order is less rational and on a lower evolutionary level than the political, which is in turn less rational and less evolved than the moral order. This concurs with Park's statement that "the individual man [has] . . . more freedom on the economic level than upon the political, more upon the political than the custom or moral level." ("Succession, an Ecological Concept," *American Sociological Review,* I, 176–77.)

[75] See "Community Organization and the Romantic Temper," in Park, Burgess, *et al., The City,* pp. 114–18.

[76] *Ibid.*, p. 144.

[77] *Ibid.*, see pp. 144–47.

the three aspects of "community" from the point of view of their territorial significance, nevertheless all but the ecological community are conceived of as something other than ecological categories. While the territorial basis is regarded by Burgess as substantive for the ecological community, it becomes only a limiting or a conditioning factor in the cultural and the political "communities."[78] How are we to reconcile this all-inclusiveness of "community" and the contraction of the concept "ecological community" with the unqualified statement that "a community, then, is an ecological distribution,"[79] where, we are told, distribution is used synonymously with organization?

As formulated by Park and Burgess, "moral order" pertains to "society," but Park sometimes includes it in "community."

> Every *society* [he states] imposes some sort of discipline upon its members. Individuals grow up, are incorporated into the life of the community, and eventually drop out and disappear. But the *community, with the moral order which it embodies,* lives on.[80]

Although Park speaks of "society" as imposing discipline upon its members, in accordance with his own conception of "society," at the same time, he relates the moral order to "community." Either he intends to obliterate the division made between community and society, or he gives a new and a different meaning to each of them in the above quotation. In the same passage Park speaks of the process of assimilation as taking place in the "community," although this process, as was cited earlier, is stated to be one of the basic processes of "society." According to this author

[78] See Burgess, "The Growth of the City," in Park, Burgess, *et al., The City.*

[79] McKenzie, "The Scope of Human Ecology," in *The Urban Community,* edited by E. W. Burgess, p. 169 and note.

[80] "The Urban Community as a Spacial Pattern and a Moral Order," in *The Urban Community,* edited by Burgess, p. 7; italics mine.

the life of the community . . . involves a kind of metabolism. It is constantly assimilating new individuals, and just as steadily, by death or otherwise, eliminating older ones. But assimilation is not a simple process, and, above all else, takes time.[81]

In fact, the process of assimilation turns out to be one of the basic processes upon which the metabolism of the "community" depends.[82]

In one and the same article Park defines "community" as an economic and a physical entity, as a visible object and also as an organization of discipline, of standards, and of common purposes. He says that community "provides the economic organization and the necessary conditions in which societies are rooted; upon which, as upon a physical base they can be established," and adds that "the community is a visible object."[83] As against this, however, he states:

Status . . . is a matter of consensus. It is determined in any single case largely by the extent to which the individual man is able to participate in the common purposes of the community, conform to its standards, submit to its discipline or, through the force of personal prestige and influence, impose his own purposes upon his fellows.[84]

The confusion of the two concepts "community" and "society" and the loss of the specific meaning given to them heretofore is particularly pronounced in the following passage from Park:

In the family and in the neighborhood such organization as exists is based upon custom and tradition, and is fixed in what Sumner calls the folk-ways and the mores. At this stage, society is a purely natural product; a product of the spontaneous and unreflective responses of individuals living together in intimate, personal, and face-to-face relations. Under such circumstances conscious efforts to discipline the individual and enforce the social code are directed merely by intuition and common sense.

[81] *Ibid.*, p. 7.

[82] See Park, "Sociology," in *Research in the Social Sciences,* edited by Gee, pp. 3–49. [83] *Ibid.*, p. 9. [84] *Ibid.*, p. 34.

In the larger social unit, the community, where social relations are more formal and less intimate, the situation is different. It is in the community, rather than in the family or the neighborhood, that formal organizations like the church, the school, and the courts come into existence and get their separate functions defined. With the advent of these institutions, and through their mediation, the community is able to supplement, and to some extent supplant, the family and the neighborhood as a means for the discipline and control of the individual. . . It is in this community with its various organizations and its rational, rather than traditional, schemes of control, and not elsewhere, that we have delinquency.[85]

Here Park refers to "society" as a natural product, because it is a result of "unreflective responses" and because its organization is based upon custom and tradition and fixed in folk-ways and mores. So far, we have been given the factors of tradition, custom, and mores as the distinctive attributes of "society" and as contrasted to the natural order of "community." We do not find any formal statement indicating a division of customs and mores into those which are a product of unreflective responses, and which are therefore natural, and those which are a product of conscious and rational interests and hence, are social. Again, it is "society" that has been earlier defined as an organ of "discipline and control of the individual" as contrasted with the free, competitive "community." In both cases the meaning of the concepts "community" and "society" is reversed. And, finally, we are told that "community" has rational schemes of control, as opposed to traditional ones in "society." Gone is the fundamental distinction of "community" as a "biotic" organization, independent of communication, and based upon unconscious relationships. The very inclusion of institutions such as the church, the school, and the courts and of their function as a means of control in the

[85] "Community Organization and Juvenile Delinquency," in Park, Burgess, *et al.*, *The City*, pp. 105–6.

aspect representing "community" breaks down the formulation of this concept as "symbiotic rather than societal."[86] Park himself, in describing the biotic community, states that "the ties which unite its individual units are those of a free and natural economy, based on a natural division of labor," and that this order is "territorially organized and the ties which hold it together are physical and vital rather than customary and moral."[87] But in the quotation under consideration the natural organization for some reason becomes rational, although it is still contrasted with the customary. We saw earlier that the biotic order corresponds to the organic, the less evolved, level of all living creatures; and now, because an organization has a scheme of control that is not traditional, but rational, it is included in the concept "community."

A definition of "community" which deviates from those of the rest of the ecologists is that of Louis Wirth. In his article "The Scope and Problems of the Community,"[88] he states that community has come to refer

> to group life when viewed from the standpoint of symbiosis. . . A territorial base, distribution in space of men, institutions, and activities, *close living together on the basis of kinship* and organic interdependence, and *a common life based upon the mutual correspondence of interests* tends to characterize a community.[89]

While the attributes of organic interdependence and symbiotic relationships concur with those in other formulations of "community," the factor of "common life based upon the mutual correspondence of interests" would surely come un-

[86] Park, "Human Ecology," *American Journal of Sociology,* XLII, 4.

[87] *Ibid.,* p. 15.

[88] Louis Wirth, "The Scope and Problems of the Community," *Publications of the Sociological Society of America,* Vol. XXVII, No. 2 (May, 1933).

[89] *Ibid.,* p. 62; italics mine. Wirth's definition here seems to reflect Tönnies's conception of "Gemeinschaft" except that Wirth also includes interests.

der the concept "society," since it implies a relationship based primarily upon communication and social contact. In his article "The Ghetto," Wirth states that:

What makes the Jewish community—composed as it is of heterogeneous cultural elements and distributed in separate areas of our cities—*a community* is its capacity *to act corporately*. It is a cultural community and constitutes as near an approach to *communal life* as the modern city has to offer. The ghetto, be it Chinese, Negro, Sicilian, or Jewish, can be completely understood only if it is viewed as a socio-psychological, as well as an ecological, phenomenon; for it is not merely a physical fact, but also a state of mind.[90]

Here Wirth speaks, first, of "community," then of "cultural community," and finally of an "ecological phenomenon" as equivalent to a "physical fact." To him, apparently, community, together with the corporate action which he assumes to characterize it, is an entity separate from the ecological phenomenon. Community here corresponds to the concept "society" as defined earlier, and the ecological organization is apparently assumed to be merely a physical fact.

A definition of community given by Harvey W. Zorbaugh in his ecological monograph *The Gold Coast and the Slum* cuts across both concepts "society" and "community" in their specific meanings. Neither the distinctive processes nor the particular aspect of human life which the concept "community" defines for ecologists are stressed and differentiated. A community, according to this writer, "is a local area over which people are using the same language, conforming to the same mores, feeling more or less the same sentiments, and acting upon the same attitudes."[91] The cohesive principle of the community, as seen by Zorbaugh, is similarity of psychological, social, and cultural phenom-

[90] Wirth, "The Ghetto," *American Journal of Sociology*, XXXIII (July, 1927), 71; italics mine.

[91] *Ibid.*, p. 223.

ena, while the definitive condition is a common and contiguous territory.

The same confusion is seen in the definitions of "society." Wirth, for example, states that "society . . . has come to refer more to the willed and contractual relationships between men, which, it has been assumed, are less directly affected than their organic relationships by their distribution in space."[92] But we have just seen that Park subsumes rational schemes of control and institutions such as the school, the church, and the courts, under the concept "community"; hence either Park or Wirth deviates from the ecological theory. Furthermore, Park and Burgess tell us that "the economic order is fundamentally ecological, that is, created by the struggle for existence, an organization like that of the plant community in which the relations between individuals are conceivably at least wholly external,"[93] and likewise Park speaks of the economic community.[94] Consequently either the "economic community" is included in the ecological organization, in which case "willed and contractual relationships between men" would also have to come under this category, or the economic organization is a distinct entity, in which case Park's inclusion of it in the ecological community and even his designation of the economic organization as a "community" are inconsistent with the ecological theory. It is possible that the economic community is conceived of by ecologists apart from the "willed and contractual relationships between men" as is suggested elsewhere by Park, but in this case the preceding statement of Park and Burgess is too sweeping and needs qualification. Other considerations interfere with the assumption that ecologists intend only to include the biotic phase of the

[92] Wirth, "The Scope and Problems of the Community," *Publications of the Sociological Society of America,* XXVII, 62.

[93] Park and Burgess, *op. cit.,* p. 508. [94] See *supra,* ch. ii, sec. 4.

economic organization within the ecological scope. Park tells us that

> industrial competition and the division of labor, which have probably done most to develop the latent powers of mankind, are possible only upon condition of the existence of markets, of money, and other devices for the facilitation of trade and commerce. . . The old adage which describes the city as the natural environment of the free man still holds so far as the individual man finds in the chances, the diversity of interests and tasks, and in the vast unconscious co-operation of city life the opportunity to choose his own vocation and develop his peculiar individual talents.[95]

In his article "Human Ecology," Park uses the term "society" for both community and society. He tells us that "human society, as distinguished from plant and animal society, is organized on two levels, the biotic and the cultural. There is a symbiotic society based on competition and a cultural society based on communication and consensus."[96] The substitution of either term for the other often results in vagueness of the meaning which ecologists attempt to convey. The following statement of Park's is an example:

> In human as contrasted with animal societies, competition and the freedom of the individual is limited on every level above the biotic by custom and consensus. The incidence of this more or less arbitrary control which custom and consensus imposes upon the natural social order complicates the social process but does not fundamentally alter it—or, if it does, the effects of biotic competition will still be manifest in the succeeding social order and the subsequent course of events.[97]

Here a question arises as to what Park means by the term "social" and whether this term has a consistent meaning

[95] Park, "Suggestions for the Investigation of Human Behavior in the Urban Environment," in Park, Burgess *et al.*, *The City*, p. 12.

[96] Park, "Human Ecology," *American Journal of Sociology*, XLII, 4.

[97] *Ibid.*, p. 13.

throughout the quotation. He first states that custom and consensus limit competition and freedom of the individual on every level except the biotic, that is, competition and freedom are not limited in "community." Then he tells us that custom and consensus impose a control upon the natural social order which complicates the social process! If "social" is used in a generic sense here, then the natural order is that of "community." But we have just been told that consensus does not impose a control upon the biotic or the natural order. If, however, by the term "social" Park means the quality or attribute of society as ecologists have specifically defined it, then why the "natural social" order? Nor can he mean the combination of both the natural and the social orders, since he has just said that the natural, or the biotic, order is free from control. Furthermore, in saying that the control imposed by custom and consensus complicates the social process, does he mean social in a specific or generic sense?

"Community" and Ecological Studies.—The fundamental assumption of ecologists is that every action or phenomenon or move of living beings is territorially based. The essential attributes of the concept "community" are the territorial basis and organic, spontaneous reactions on the animal level. However, in the distinction between the concepts "community" and "society" there is an inference that some human actions have a more specific relation to territory than others. In fact, in the correlation of ecological distribution and animal or organic behavior it is more or less generally assumed that the more rational or conscious activities are less dependent on territorial factors. This assumption is apparent in most of the theoretical formulations of the school and is explicitly given in Wirth's statement that the willed and contractual relationships between men in "society" are "less directly affected than their organic relationships by their

distribution in space."[98] It would seem to follow, therefore, that a study made on ecological premises would be directed more to the asocial or purely organic activities of man. It is this logical conclusion that the ecologists themselves reach when they occasionally point out the "unsocial" character of the concept "community."[99] However, the actual "ecological" studies cannot follow out this distinction, because if we take a territorially demarcated unit as a basis for study we do not discriminate between certain activities carried on within the area as those of "society" and others which are those of "community." When ecologists themselves subdivide "community" into various communities, economic, political, cultural, and ecological, we seem to be tracking the territorially determinant factor down to narrower bounds. But this conclusion becomes untenable, since these other "communities" are indifferently included in the scope of ecological studies. Nor do the researches conform to the initial distinction, upon which they are supposed to depend any more than does the theoretical application of the ecological principle. To make the matter even more obscure, "community" is taken in its broadest scope and mingled with what was first defined as "society." The only help we have in this regard is that we are sometimes warned that certain studies are not "purely" ecological.

To cite only a few examples: Nels Anderson's study, *The Hobo,* while admittedly approaching the type from the point of view of locomotion, deals to a great extent with the cultural background and the social activities of the hobo. In fact, no distinction is attempted on the lines suggested above. The same may be said of *The Gold Coast and the Slum,* by Harvey W. Zorbaugh. The areas are taken as the frame within which the social phenomena occur, but the phenomena themselves are neither those of community as ecologists

[98] Wirth, *op. cit.,* p. 62.

[99] See *supra,* p. 45.

conceive it, nor those of society in their specific sense. Rather are these monographs general sociological studies in which territorial distribution is taken account of in reference to sociological data.

It might be said that Clifford Shaw's delinquency study[100] more nearly bears upon ecological distribution, but he neither investigates symbiotic and competitive relations, nor does he probe into the organic, natural reactions of the delinquents. In fact, there is little in Shaw's study to suggest Park's and other ecologists' interpretation of the biotic substructure. Instead, Shaw confines himself to the finding of correlations between the frequency of a social phenomenon, delinquency, in various areas and the relative distance of these areas from the center of the city, following the ideal zonal pattern into which every city supposedly tends to fall. This done, he interprets delinquency primarily in terms of social, cultural, and economic factors. He does not submit any evidence to show that the different frequencies of delinquency in different areas are ecological adaptations to the particular areas.

Such studies as *The Gang,* by Frederick Thrasher, and *The Taxi Dance-Hall,* by Paul G. Cressey, are subject to the same observation. The gang, for example, is assumed to be a natural group and is then studied in its sociological setting. We have no glimpse of what the biotic aspect of this group represents, unless we assume that it is natural in the sense that it constitutes a "moral region." But we do not find this group described in terms of the natural behavior independent of communication and expressing, in particular, tendencies common to all living organisms rather than strictly human characteristics. In fact, the gang as treated by Thrasher is not specifically and essentially an ecological group, but rather a social grouping exhibiting a certain type of social

[100] Clifford R. Shaw, *Delinquency Areas* (1929).

behavior. The only "ecological" fact considered by the author is the delimitation of the territorial area in which the gang concentrates. Excellent though this study may be from the sociological point of view, it does not confine itself to community as formulated by the ecologists.

When we consider studies such as R. D. McKenzie's *Metropolitan Community* and "Ecological Succession in the Puget Sound Region,"[101] they are seen to fall more within the ecological scope, save that McKenzie includes in the ecological community the economic organization in its broadest and "most evolved" sense. He makes no attempt to abstract the natural economy from the highly complex economic relationships any more than he tries to isolate biotic competition from conscious competition. In fact, he strongly emphasizes communication as a determining factor as well as a process inherent in the organization with which he deals. It is true that he studies the movements and distribution of populations and goods and on the whole approaches the subject of economic relations from an external point of view, but in essence his works cover the field of distribution economics rather than the less evolved aspect of human processes and structure. Nor is McKenzie concerned with the product of free, as opposed to controlled, competition or with the natural division of labor as distinguished from any other type.

Conclusions.—So intertwined are the two aspects which ecologists would sever into two distinct entities that the treatment of them invariably results in their fusion, while the theoretical statements come to the contradictions just dealt with. Taking their clue from the processes in plant and animal colonies, the ecologists discover common elements between these and the human community and try to delimit this simpler aspect of behavior. At the same time,

[101] *Publications of the American Sociological Society*, Vol. XXIII, 1928.

however, they find that the presence of "group economy," which defines a plant or an animal colony, is in human community so highly evolved and so intrinsically a part of other social phenomena that the analogy becomes worthless, and the ecologists are forced to define the very concepts intended to describe this organic aspect of life in terms of the assumed social psychological concept "society." Consequently, what is said to be unsocial in one instance is asserted to be social in another.

Assuming that symbiotic relationships correspond to an existing phase of group life, it is still difficult to perceive how in the study of the "biologic economic" organization of the "community" one can abstract the "organic interdependence" and the "common life based upon the mutual correspondence of interests" characteristic of "community" from the "willed and contractual relationships between men" which define "society." Nor is it clear where the line is drawn between free and controlled or limited competition nor, for that matter, between biotic and social interdependence. Although the economic organization is claimed to be the product of competition, it is also said to be the effect of accommodation: "The equilibrium based on accommodation . . . is not biological; it is economic and social and is transmitted, if at all, by tradition."[102] Accommodation is in turn the outcome of conflict.[103] Thus the three processes are closely related and serve as determinants of the economic organization, while, at the same time, conflict and accommodation are determined by competition. However, conflict and accommodation are non-ecological processes and, in fact, they restrict the ecological process of competition. We are not told how these processes of "society" are separated from the ecological process of competition, nor is there any definite means of severing them except by the arbitrary as-

[102] Park and Burgess, *op. cit.*, p. 664. [103] *Ibid.*

sumption that a particular aspect of the economic organization is natural and another is not natural.

When we come to the factual ecological studies, there seems to be no distinction between the "natural" aspects of the economic organization, which result from competition, and the cultural, or those which are the product of accommodation and conflict—nor, for that matter, between any unconsciously effected phenomena and those brought about consciously.[104] Even when ecologists do distinguish between the natural and the planned, it seems that the planned phenomena eventually take their natural course of development. For example, Park states:

> The newspaper has a history; but it has, likewise, a natural history. The press, as it exists, is not, as our moralists sometimes seem to assume, the wilful product of any little group of living men. On the contrary, it is the outcome of a historic process in which many individuals participated without foreseeing what the ultimate product of their labors was to be. . . *In spite of all the efforts of individual men and generations of men to control it* and to make it something after their own heart, it has continued to grow and change *in its own incalculable ways.*[105]

The two levels of human behavior, "that which is common to all organic life" and "that which is strictly human," have never yet been successfully separated by science, perhaps, for the very reason that one is found to be a continuation of and a development from the other; not only is the more evolved aspect rooted in the less evolved, but one imperceptibly shades into the other, the two interact continuously and in fact are one. C. O. Whitman's remark illustrates the realization of this merging of the two aspects of life:

[104] See McKenzie, *The Metropolitan Community,* Wirth, *The Ghetto,* Ruth S. Cavan, *Suicide.*

[105] Park, "The Natural History of the Newspaper," in Park, Burgess, *et al., The City,* p. 80; italics mine. This point is further elaborated in Chapter VII, section on "Historical versus Logical Sequence."

We are apt to contrast the extreme of instinct and intelligence to emphasize the blindness and inflexibility of the one and the consciousness and freedom of the other. It is like contrasting the extremes of light and dark and forgetting all the transitional degrees of twilight. . . Instinct is blind; so is the highest human wisdom blind. The distinction is one of degree. There is no absolute blindness on the one side, and no absolute wisdom on the other.[106]

Division such as the ecologists make of human behavior is born of the absolutist assumption of a constant, unchanging nature, where evolution is approached as a simple additive process. But does not the cumulative process of natural and social evolution mean transformation as well as addition? Can reality, social reality in particular, be reasonably interpreted in terms of "more or less," especially if we seek to interpret the "more" by the "less" and not vice versa? The very distinction which ecologists make between the struggle for existence on the animal level and the struggle for livelihood on the human level would necessarily imply change in the quality of the so-called struggle. There may be a difference of degree, but there is also a difference in kind, not only in the struggle itself, but also in the total situation of which the struggle is an expression. Human beings differ from plants and animals, not only in that they control their environment,[107] but also in that they *desire* to control it and that with this desire they consciously seek and find the means to create a new environment. The processes which are unconscious on the plant or animal level become infused with consciousness of various degrees on the human level. The competition of plants for soil and water has no corresponding factual process in the competition of human beings within any physical area. Since any

[106] Quoted in C. C. Adams, "The Relation of General Ecology to Human Ecology," *Ecology*, XVI (July, 1935), 322.

[107] See McKenzie, "The Ecological Approach to the Study of Human Community," in Park, Burgess, *et al.*, *The City*, pp. 64–65.

crowding is translated into conscious struggle in human groupings, where the very expression and the methods of competition are not only conditioned and complicated by this consciousness but also are actually determined by it, is it possible to speak of biotic competition among men?

Although the division of community and society carries the implication of the abstraction of the biotic from the civilized form of competition, and although the ecologists themselves admit this implication, they have nowhere succeeded in effecting it. What they often do, is to concentrate their attention upon the external factors of human behavior, such as distribution and movements of populations, utilities, and physical structures—these usually being interpreted with a particular stress upon the economic and technological factors as the determining ones. There is not a vestige of the "natural" order in the movements and allocation of these elements, in the highly developed forms and methods of communication and transportation, and in the elaborated design and framework of organization within which these mobile forces function. Likewise, nothing specifically natural is revealed either in the scheme of motivations or in the technical economic and other external conditions determining the distribution of the elements in human organization.

There is no objection to the abstraction of these external phenomena to serve the ends of scientific investigation, but the relevant point is that these are not the intrinsic factors of the community as we have found it defined by ecologists.

If ecologists intend to abstract certain external manifestations in human groupings, even if based upon an analogy with organic life, they might develop a discipline which would treat of the civilizational aspect of society as against its cultural facets; or, with a difference in emphasis, they might found a discipline dealing specifically with spatial phenomena; in any case, human ecology would mark either a specific approach or a selected subject matter.

But the ecologists' theory, particularly their distinction between "community" and "society," is based upon a priori assumptions, and it is upon the relevance, validity, and application of these assumptions that the scientific claims of human ecology rest. It is also these same a priori assumptions that, although not always consistently, direct the development and the scope of human ecology. Some of them have already been suggested in the course of the preceding discussions. Others will appear later. Here we may point to the assumption of an intrinsic association between the less evolved organic structure and the external physical phenomena. There is also the assumption of an inherent nexus between spatial and economic phenomena, between locomotion and competition, and, again, between locomotion and freedom. If we take the last of these, the supposed intrinsic relation of locomotion and freedom, thinking of these two concepts in their naked and simplest sense, as probably the ecologists have done, then the one factor can properly be regarded as the obverse of the other. Yet freedom, as ecologists deal with it in their theory, ceases to be freedom on an animal level but becomes freedom to live in a society as we know it today—the freedom which has been the subject of innumerable queries by philosophers and political theorists and of endless strife between soldiers and between priests.

For such a widening and enriching of the concept "freedom," we have another a priori assumption by Park that "mind is an incident of locomotion" and that "the first and most convincing indication of mind is not motion merely but . . . locomotion."[108] It seems superfluous to inquire into

[108] "Community Organization and Juvenile Delinquency," in Park, Burgess, *et al.*, *The City*, p. 156.

this relation of locomotion and mind in the case of animals or, even more to the point, in the case of birds. If the intrinsic association of freedom and locomotion is assumed to remain constant in spite of the change of the meaning of the concepts and of the reality which each represents, then surely by the same principle locomotion would be expected to have an identical relation to mind whether among plants, animals, or human beings. Any concept which may qualify locomotion on the human level, such as purpose, may, for example, be equally applied to animals and birds. There is no wider difference between the freedom among plants or animals and the freedom among human beings than there is between purpose among the former and purpose among the latter.

Another a priori assumption inherent in the ecological theory is that in a civilized society the division of labor has a more organic basis than customs or mores which have grown from the intimate relationships of human beings. If as Park and Burgess state "custom is group habit,"[109] there is as much basis for speaking of custom among animals, such as the songs belonging to any species of birds, as there is for regarding the division of labor in the animal world as being the equivalent of the division of labor in the human organization. Moreover, to take only one aspect, it is still a matter of speculation as to whether it is the survival of the individual or the survival of the species which is the "concern of nature." We have no single theory which has finally proved and pigeon-holed the derivation of customs as against the derivation of division of labor, of social as against economic phenomena. If the intricate pattern of the modern division of labor is a product of organic needs of human beings, so are the manifold modern customs and mores, whatever the worth of either, whatever the consistencies or inconsist-

[109] Park and Burgess, *op. cit.*, p. 799.

encies of both. If consciousness characterizes the social aspect, it also characterizes the economic; if division of labor has its roots in nature, so have customs and traditions. Yet the differences and similarities existing between these categories are differences and similarities which must perforce be discerned and interpreted on the level on which they are found—the human organization. Finally, the designation of competition as the primary, the universal, and the fundamental process, as against assimilation, accommodation, cooperation, or, for that matter, any other process, is also a matter of a particularistic ideology. The approach to human organization from the angle of competition is one thing, but a claim that competition is the process basic to all other processes is another. Cooley's discussion of Tarde's treatment of the process of imitation brings out this point:

I think, that other phases [than imitation] of social activity, such for instance, as communication, competition, differentiation, adaptation, idealization, have as good claims as imitation to be regarded as the social process, and that a book similar in character to M. Tarde's might, perhaps, be written upon any one of them. The truth is that the real process is a multiform thing of which these are glimpses. They are good so long as we recognize that they are glimpses and use them to help out our perception of that many-sided whole which life is; but if they become doctrines they are objectionable.

The Struggle for Existence is another of these glimpses of life which just now seems to many the dominating fact of the universe, chiefly because attention has been fixed upon it by copious and interesting exposition. As it has had many predecessors in this place of importance, so doubtless it will have many successors.[110]

[110] Charles Horton Cooley, *Human Nature and the Social Order* (New York, 1922), p. 272.

CHAPTER FOUR

THEORETICAL BACKGROUND

THE SCHISM between human nature and human reason or will, which has served as a root principle in many philosophies and most religions, is the hypothesis upon which the ecologists build the distinction between their two primary concepts and their putative division of the two disciplines within sociology. Park and Burgess, in *The Introduction to the Science of Sociology,* criticize the one-sided views of both the individualistic and organic schools. They attempt to reconcile the two principles, but this they do by implying that each corresponds to a separate order of human organization; moreover, they assume that the individualistic is the natural and the fundamental order.

Thinkers in all ages have been prone to glorify reason as distinct from and even antagonistic to nature and to think of society in a restrictive aspect. The ethical schemes of Christianity, of Buddhism, and of Mohammedanism are built upon this schism. Thinkers of many different types, St. Paul, the Sophists, Hobbes, Rousseau in his early writings, Nietzsche, Spencer, Benjamin Kidd, and all those who regard law as antagonistic to nature have suggested this duality.

This dualism contains the seeds of another point of view which is becoming more and more prevalent in modern science. The division between society and the individual still exists in this philosophy, but it is not based upon the conception of an inherent antagonism between the two. The underlying assumption is that man's nature is so many-sided, that it has so many potentialities, social and unsocial, competitive and co-operative, that at any one point all these facets of his nature cannot find expression. As society becomes more complex, however, it provides more and more outlets for the individual's self-expression. Locke's idea of the mind as a *tabula raza,* on which nature and society write what they will, implies this point of view.

In its extreme version this principle becomes environmental determinism, where nature is almost negated and nurture becomes the prime mover of behavior. A certain degree of conflict is still seen between the two, but it is overcome by the process of molding and habituation, which brings out some of the human potentialities while it represses others. Thus Graham Wallas and William James give importance to habit, while John B. Watson thinks of nature as entirely plastic and molded by nurture.

The third school regards society as the fulfillment of man's nature. The conflict between the individual and the social fades, and the individual is looked upon as an intrinsic part and an outcome of society, while society is thought of as a complex and multiple expression of the nature of the individual. In one form, it is assumed that the fundamental instincts, drives, and potentialities are realized in society and can be realized to any degree of completeness in the interaction of nature and environment. The variance between the social and the individual is taken account of more in terms of the situation than in terms of the original antagonism between the less evolved, or the natural, tendencies of man and the more evolved social aspect of life.

The co-operative organization and activities of men in society are thought of as the expression and the fulfillment of their intrinsic nature, revealed through the manifold interactions of individuals and groups and through the adjustments they make both to one another and to the outer environment. Neither heredity nor environment is stressed, but both are regarded as intertwined and interacting, and it is the very interaction of these two that defines society. Here, of course, is a great range of variation in the interpretation of the interaction, from the mechanistic and deterministic causal conception to that of emphasis upon human volition and human evaluation. Sociologists such as Cooley, Fouillée, and Lévy-Bruhl indicate this point of view. The Hegelian school may also be mentioned in this connection, as well as Durkheim, to whom the individuality of man is the specific embodiment of greater forces animating societies as wholes.

The philosophical background of the ecological group is essentially that of the first type. As we have attempted to show, the division between nature and reason is strongly emphasized. Here lies the source of the distinction between the natural and the designed, between community and society, between the individual and the person, and between symbiosis and consensus. The social is construed as equivalent to the moral order, which imposes on man a discipline alien to his primary nature. Society is thus, as it were, the product of reason which subordinates the impulses of "natural" human beings to their common well-being, and in this way enables them "to recreate the world in the image of their collective aspirations and their common will."[1] Hence the social organization is conceived of as comprising "limitations of the natural wishes of the individual."[2]

THE HOBBESIAN ELEMENT

There is more than a superficial similarity in this outlook with the social contract theories of the seventeenth and eighteenth-century philosophers, specifically with Hobbes's

[1] Park, "Sociology," in *Research in the Social Sciences,* edited by Wilson Gee, p. 7.

[2] Park and Burgess, *op. cit.,* p. 509.

individualistic philosophy. Some sort of covenant is implied by ecologists in their conception of the individual's surrender to forces which are not in harmony with his innate nature. In the formation of society, according to Park and Burgess, there came a stage in which "men first consciously united their common efforts to improve and conserve their common life."[3] Like the "natural man" of Hobbes, the ecological "natural individual" is a detached, unsocial creature, who, were he able to live according to the dictates of his nature and apart from social control, would abandon himself to his predatory drives and meet his like primarily in a competitive struggle. It must be remembered that competition, of whatever form, is the foundation of the ecological natural order:

> The natural condition of the individual in society is one of conflict; conflict with other individuals, to be sure, but particularly conflict with the conventions and regulations of the social group of which he is a member.[4]

Park explains the antithesis of the individual and society as follows:

> The fact seems to be that men are brought into the world with all the passions, instincts, and appetites, uncontrolled and undisciplined. Civilization, in the interests of the common welfare, demands a suppression sometimes, and the control always, of these wild, natural dispositions.[5]

There is an implicit assumption that the "natural individual" gives up his natural independence, which is equivalent to the "natural rights" of the social contract theory, in this case, not to the state, but to "society," which performs for the individual the "function of a mind," because "like mind in the individual man, society is a control organization."[6]

[3] *Ibid.*, p. 953.

[4] Park, "Community Organization and Juvenile Delinquency," in Park, Burgess, *et al.*, *The City*, p. 105.

[5] *Ibid.*, p. 43.

[6] Park and Burgess, *op. cit.*, p. 848.

Ecologists agree with Hobbes in their implicit assumption that law and freedom are opposites. To Hobbes law is "public conscience," to ecologists law is a means of control of the individual, and consequently the more law there is in "society," the less freedom. Freedom, as in Hobbes's theory, exists "in the interstices of law."

In some ways ecologists go further than Hobbes in the emphasis on the antithesis of the "natural order" and "society." Hobbes sees the almost complete surrender of the individual to the state, while ecologists assume that the nature of man is never completely molded by the rational and moral control of "society." Park expresses this notion as follows:

> So ill-adapted is the natural, undomesticated man to the social order into which he is born, so out of harmony are all the native impulses of the ordinary healthy human with the demands which society imposes, that it is hardly an exaggeration to say that if his childhood is spent mainly in learning what he must not do, his youth will be devoted mainly to rebellion. As to the remainder of his life, his recreations will very likely turn out to be some sort of vacation and escape from this same social order to which he has finally learned to accommodate, but not wholly reconcile, himself.[7]

Here social control is conceived of as almost an external force, acting upon the individual in such opposition to his natural tendencies that rebellion and a search for escape are his natural reaction to repression by "society." However, another statement of Park's implies a surrender of the individual to the social order:

> Men and women are bound together by affection and common purposes; they do cherish traditions, ambitions, and ideals that are not all their own, and they maintain, in spite of natural impulses to the contrary, a discipline and a moral order that enables them to transcend what we ordinarily call nature and,

[7] Park, *op. cit.*, pp. 99–100.

through their collective action, recreate the world in the image of their collective aspirations and their common will.[8]

It is obvious that the first statement carries an implication of deep antagonism between the individuals' nature and the demands of society, whereas the second passage assumes a willing surrender to "society." While at first sight, these statements appear to be contradictory, the ecological point of view holds that it is the individual who is out of harmony with "society," while the person not only is in complete harmony with it, but also is the conscious instigator of control of himself as well as of society. It is reason and conscious effort against the nonsocial, natural behavior of man.

The factor of repression is strongly emphasized by Park in all his writings. He assumes that social heritage is cumulative and seems to imply that, as the scope of "society" becomes ever wider and its impress deeper, so the nature of the individual is more repressed:

> One reason why human beings, in contrast with the lower animals, seem to be so ill-adapted to the world in which they are born is that the environment in which human beings live is so largely made up of the experience and memories and the acquired habits of the people who have preceded them.
>
> This experience and these memories—crystallized and embodied in tradition, in custom, and in folk-ways—constitute the social, as distinguished from the biological, environment; for man is not merely an individual with certain native and inherited biological traits, but he is at the same time a person with manners, sentiments, attitudes, and ambitions.[9]

In other words, the individual is in conflict not only with "society" but also with that part of himself which ecologists designate as "person." Moreover, the cumulation and changes which take place in the acquired heritage—"society"—do not seem to change effectually and substantially the real

[8] "Sociology," in *Research in the Social Sciences,* edited by Wilson Gee, pp. 6–7.

[9] Park, *op. cit.,* p. 100.

nature of the individual; whereas, implicit in the above statements is the idea that the person changes in concomitance with "society," of which he is maker as well as part and product. Thus the individual's nature is relatively constant, not only in that it represents the more general biotic aspect exhibited by all living beings, but also in that the social forces do not so much modify his nature as they limit or repress its expression. This postulate, implicit in the reasoning of the ecologists, partly explains why, with all the emphasis upon nature and the natural organization, they nevertheless interpret the phenomena of human behavior in terms of environmental determinism. Furthermore, this assumption of the relatively constant and unchanging nature, or state of nature, concurs with the rigidity of the natural pattern and its assumed susceptibility to prediction in exact mathematical terms.[10]

MATERIALISTIC IMPLICATIONS

An interesting modification colors the ecological point of view. The expression of the natural tendencies of the individual is related to the physical, economic, and technological aspects of group living. Most of the civilizational factors are regarded as natural factors; hence the emphasis upon the physical, concrete, visible phenomena. Essentially, this derives from the assumption that the "natural" process of life is competition. The cultural factors are those brought about by social design, by the efforts of the competing individuals to live in a group as social creatures. The division is not clear-cut, and the two aspects of behavior are intermixed and overlapping. For instance, when Park defines "expressive" behavior as rooted in human behavior and sets it

[10] See Robert M. MacIver, *Society, Its Structure and Changes,* New York, 1931, chap. xxiv, for a discussion of deterministic approach which conceives of nature as constant.

against "work," which he calls purposive behavior, he deviates from his fundamental distinction.

The symphysis of the "natural" order and of the concrete and physical civilizational phenomena is important to the understanding of the ecologists' theory and to their causal interpretation of social phenomena. For, in spite of the delimitation of the scope of human ecology in terms of the asocial, the "natural" order of human life, the ecologists' quest is to interpret social phenomena; and it is with this purpose in view that they regard all the physical and technological factors as central. These factors acquire causative efficacy in the school's interpretation of social organization, but some are emphasized more than others. Although competition is regarded as the fundamental process, and the division of labor, or occupational distribution, is thought of as a primary ecological force, and although technological developments are said to be the basis of social change, essentially ecologists seek to interpret social organization in terms of physical movement and location.

The place which ecologists accord to movement and location is seen in Park's statement that "it is in locomotion . . . that the peculiar type of organization that we call 'social' develops."[11] Here is the simple, long sought for answer to the problem of the history of mankind, as ecologists see it. Park tells us that "it is in the processes of locomotion—involving, as they do, change of scene and change of location—that mankind is enabled to develop just those mental aptitudes most characteristic of man, namely, the aptitude and habit of abstract thought."[12] To Park, "it is this fact of locomotion . . . that defines the very nature of society."[13]

If locomotion is the basis and the cause of the develop-

[11] Park, "The Mind of the Hobo: Reflections upon the Relation between Mentality and Locomotion," in Park, Burgess, *et al.*, *The City*, p. 157.

[12] *Ibid.*

[13] *Ibid.*, p. 159.

ment of society, location is the basis of its preservation:

In order that there may be permanence and progress in society the individuals who compose it must be located; they must be located, for one thing, in order to maintain communication, for it is only through communication that the moving equilibrium which we call society can be maintained.[14]

Here Park raises the problem of a complex process, such as communication, but he does not give it much thought. The primary factor in "permanence and progress in society" is the fact of location: "All forms of association among human beings rest finally upon locality and local association."[15] Park adds social factors to his interpretation of society, as when he says:

The extraordinary means of communication that characterize modern society—the newspaper, the radio, and the telephone—are merely devices for preserving this permanence of location and of function in the social group, in connection with the greatest possible mobility and freedom of its members.[16]

However, these references do not seem on the whole to deflect him from the main course of his theory. Like the rest of the ecological school, he finds the explanation of social phenomena primarily and essentially in their physical manifestations.

Park advances the fundamental thesis of ecological interpretation of social change in the following statement:

Human ecology, in approaching the study of society from the aspect presented by its biotic substructure, assumes that the origin of social change, if one could trace it to its source, would be found in the struggle for existence and in the growth, the migration, the mobility, and the territorial and occupational distribution of peoples which this struggle has brought about.[17]

[14] Park, "The Mind of the Hobo," *op. cit.*, p. 159.

[15] *Ibid.*

[16] *Ibid.*

[17] Park, "Succession, an Ecological Concept," *American Sociological Review*, I, 178.

Here we have competition as the basic process, mobility and location as its basic means and expression, and finally, occupational distribution as the product of competition.

An even more extreme point of view is revealed in another statement of Park's: "The organization of the city, the character of the urban environment and of the discipline which it imposes is finally determined by the size of the population, its concentration and distribution within the city area."[18] Thus, to Park, numbers, density, and allocation—all things that are susceptible to measurement—are not only indices of social phenomena but also their determinants.

Although Park enumerates several causal factors of social change, he finally reduces all these to one—namely, mobility. According to him, "movement and migration are not merely an incident but a cause of almost every form of social change."[19] The inclusion of other factors besides mobility among the determinants of social change is apparently due to Park's idea that these bring about mobility. Of such factors, he mentions physical growth, increase in population, the principle of dominance, economic changes, and inventions.

> The amount of change that inevitably takes place in a growing community is, moreover, multiplied and intensified by the invention of new mechanical devices for the production of goods, by new facilities for transportation and communication, and by the incidental extension of the division of labor.[20]

Or, again:

> The present economic, political and cultural order in Europe has come into existence with the growth in population and the migration and the territorial expansion of Europe. This expansion has been made possible by a series of inventions which have, at dif-

[18] Park, "The City: Suggestions for the Investigation of Human Behavior in the Urban Environment," in Park, Burgess, *et al., The City*, p. 6.

[19] Park, "Sociology," in *Research in the Social Sciences*, edited by Gee, p. 15.

[20] *Ibid.*

ferent epochs in its history, revolutionized and transformed the prevailing methods of transportation and communication.[21]

Park also tells us that "every change in the conditions of social life manifests itself first and most obviously in an intensified mobility and in movements which terminate in segregation."[22] Thus mobility is initiated by changes in social conditions. However, according to Park, these in turn are caused by mobility since movement and migration are "a *cause* of almost every form of social change."[23]

Once the causes of social phenomena are traced, the ecologists make these causes the indices of the phenomena themselves:

In society we not only live together, but at the same time we live apart, and human relations can always be reckoned, with more or less accuracy, in terms of distance. In so far as social structure can be defined in terms of position, social changes may be described in terms of movement; and society exhibits, in one of its aspects, characters that can be measured and described in mathematical formulas.[24]

These principles and these methods are accepted and reiterated by the great majority of the ecological school, although with some variations. Burgess follows them, as does McKenzie. The latter says, for example:

"Society is made up of individuals spatially separated, territorially distributed, and capable of independent locomotion." These spatial relationships of human beings are the products of competition and selection, and are continuously in process of change as new factors enter to disturb the competitive relations or to facilitate mobility. Human institutions and human nature itself become accommodated to certain spatial relationships of human beings. As

[21] Park, "Succession . . .," *American Sociological Review,* I, 179.

[22] Park, *op. cit.,* p. 33.

[23] *Ibid.,* p. 15; italics mine.

[24] Park, "The Urban Community," in *The Urban Community,* edited by Burgess, p. 4.

these spatial relationships change, the physical basis of social relations is altered, thereby producing social and political problems.[25]

So inclined are human ecologists to interpret social manifestations in terms of physical factors that Park and Burgess suggest that the four fundamental wishes as formulated by W. I. Thomas can be envisaged in spatial terms:

As wishes find expression in characteristic forms of behavior they may also be thought of in spatial terms as tendencies to move toward or away from their specific objects. The wish for security may be represented by position, mere immobility; the wish for new experience by the greatest possible freedom of movement and constant change of position; the wish for response, by the number and closeness of points of contact; the wish for recognition, by the level desired or reached in the vertical plane of superordination and subordination.[26]

This simplification of social phenomena, this identification of the processes and structures of society or societies with their physical concomitants or with what Aristotle called the "necessary accidents" associated with them, is the core of the ecological approach. Park tells us that

It is because social relations are so frequently and so inevitably correlated with spacial relations; because physical distances, so frequently are, or seem to be, the indexes of social distances, that statistics have any significance whatever for sociology. And this is true, finally, because it is only as social and psychical facts can be reduced to, or correlated with, spacial facts that they can be measured at all.[27]

Faced with the intricate and elusive social phenomena which sociology regards as its subject matter, human ecologists have sought to resolve into physical terms the complexities involved in social manifestations, thus meeting the

[25] McKenzie, "The Ecological Approach to the Study of the Human Community," in Park, Burgess, *et al.*, *The City*, p. 64.

[26] Park and Burgess, *Introduction to the Science of Sociology*, p. 442.

[27] Park, *op. cit.*, p. 18.

difficulties inherent in social interpretation by evading them. Through this emphasis upon physical factors, moreover, the ecologists have endowed the social with a physical character and have attributed to it physical and mechanistic principles and properties.

It is thus that they interpret "society" in terms of "community." Upon the premise that the external factors of "community," such as mobility, position, and distance in space, are both causes and indices of social changes, social structure, and social relations, ecologists propose, by this short cut, to submit to exact quantitative measurement the complex and qualitative phenomena of society. It seems that measurement and description in mathematical formulae are essential to raise sociology to the level of science, and this is the method which the ecologists propound. How great the ecologists' propensity is for measurement may be seen in Park's statement:

> We are very much concerned in the social as in all other sciences about indices. It is only through indices that we can establish units and apply quantitative methods to our descriptions of things. To be sure, it sometimes happens that sociologists, like the psychologists with their intelligence tests, do not know just what they are measuring. Nevertheless, it is possible in this way to give precision to our comparisons of one object with another, even if we do not quite know what the things we are measuring measure.[28]

THE ORGANISMIC HYPOTHESIS

Underlying the ecological approach is the conception of "community" as an organism. In his definition of community McKenzie states that "the unit of ecological study is the communal organism, which is at once an aggregation

[28] Park, "Sociology," in *Research in the Social Sciences,* edited by Gee, p. 11.

of individual persons, a geographical and cultural habitat, and an interrelated and interdependent biosocial unity."[29] Park advances the same point of view:

Every community has something of the character of an organic unit. It has a more or less definite structure and it has "a life history in which juvenile, adult and senile phases can be observed." If it is an organism, it is one of the organs which are other organisms. It is, to use Spencer's phrase, a superorganism.[30]

The organismic analogy is applied by the ecologists to both "community" and "society," but, while the cyclical theory is involved throughout, the particular application of the organismic concept takes variant forms, depending upon the category under consideration. The processes of "society" are viewed broadly and *in abstracto* as corresponding to organic processes,[31] whereas those of "community" are seen as the manifestations of a territorial and concrete entity, where patterns and configurations are interpreted in biological terms. The basic processes of "society," conscious interaction and consensus, are included under social metabolism. Organization and disorganization, which are considered to be the resultants of assimilation and elimination of individuals and groups in the social organism, are assumed to correspond to the anabolic and katabolic processes of a biological organism.[32] By contrast, symbiosis or eco-

[29] "Demography, Human Geography and Human Ecology," in *The Fields and Methods of Sociology*, edited by L. L. Bernard, p. 59. New York. Copyright 1934. Reprinted by permission of the publishers, Farrar and Rinehart, Inc.

[30] Park, "Human Ecology," *The American Journal of Sociology*, XLII (July, 1936), 4.

[31] See Park, *op. cit.*, pp. 11–16; and Burgess, "The Growth of the City," in Park, Burgess, *et al.*, *The City*, pp. 53–62.

[32] *Ibid.* Ecologists place social metabolism in both "community" and "society." Although it would seem more logical to consider it under "society" in accordance with their presuppositions, it is difficult to ascertain to what extent the process is transferred from one to the other through the loose use of terms and to what extent by actual intention.

logical interdependence, division of labor, and ecological dominance and subordination are the cohesive processes of the "community" organism. In McKenzie's words:

All the spatially fixed aspects of our communal structure, such as roads, homes, shops, factories, institutions, become integrated into rather definite pattern forms with the relation of dominance and subordination as the dynamic organizing principle.[33]

The organismic analogy with the emphasis upon spatial relationship is further explained by Burgess:

A human community, like a biological organism, grows by the process of subdivision. As a city grows, its structure becomes more complex and its areas more specialized. Increasing differentiation, however, involves more rather than less co-operation and interdependence. The specialized areas of the city, as the central retail business district, the industrial community, the residential neighborhood, and suburban towns and villages are all organic parts of the city because of rather than in spite of their differentiated functions.[34]

Finally, while in "society" it is the agencies of social control which are referred to as the "mind" of the social organism,[35] in "community" it is the trade center, regarded as the point of ecological dominance, which is compared with the cerebral cortex of a biological organism.

The differentiation of areas, the distribution of institutional units, and their complex integration take place with reference to the center of dominance somewhat after the manner in which a higher organism has its parts coördinated and controlled by means of the specialized and central cerebral cortex.[36]

[33] McKenzie, "The Concept of Dominance and World Organization," *The American Journal of Sociology,* XXXIII, 29.

[34] Burgess, "Urban Areas," in *Chicago: an Experiment in Social Science Research,* edited by Smith and White, p. 113.

[35] *Cf. supra,* p. 95.

[36] Dawson, "Sources and Methods of Human Ecology," in *The Fields and Methods of Sociology,* edited by L. L. Bernard, p. 295, New York. Copyright 1934. Reprinted by permission of the publishers, Farrar and Rinehart, Inc.

Beyond the fact that human ecologists adhere to the organic school of sociology, as is borne out in the foregoing discussion of "community" and "society," there are two points of departure for their organismic treatment of "community." First, they have taken their clue from the physiological writings of Professor Child. Second, in borrowing concepts from plant ecology, they have also adopted analogically the organismic approach employed by that school.[37] In drawing upon these two different sources for their organismic analogy, human ecologists have also adopted from them various terms, several of which are common to both systems.

[37] It may be noted that Richard Hurd, from whom the ecologists have drawn part of their theoretical formulations, also regards the city as an organism. See *Principles of City Land Values* (New York, 1911).

CHAPTER FIVE

SPECIFIC BORROWINGS

THE PHYSIOLOGICAL THEORY OF CHILD

PROFESSOR Child's thesis, upon which the human ecologists have called extensively, is advanced by him in *The Physiological Foundations of Behavior*[1] and in "Biological Foundations of Social Integration," a paper given before the American Sociological Society in 1928.

According to this author, every organism is integrated into what he designates an "organismic pattern," which is developed in the process of relation and reaction to the environment. In this pattern the parts of the organism are related in terms of dominance and subordination. He distinguishes several types of "organismic pattern" in the evolution from the simple to the multicellular organisms, ranging from the "interior-surface" pattern of the simplest organisms to the "axiate" pattern of the more complex multicellular ones. In the former the point of dominance is asserted to be on the surface, because that region is most active and most exposed to the environment: "Since the surface is the medium of relation and exchange with the external world, it exercises a certain control over what happens in the interior."[2] In the more evolved organisms, however, besides the "interior-surface" pattern, Child finds an "axiate pattern," which involves a more centralized point of dominance, this dominance depending upon the

[1] Henry Holt & Co., New York, 1924.

[2] Child, "Biological Foundations of Social Integration," *Proceedings and Papers of the American Sociological Society*, XXII (June 21, 1928), 28.

higher rate of physiological activity of a part of the organism in relation to other parts. The "axiate pattern" here refers to physiological polarity and symmetry which are the expressions in the organism of "orderly arrangements and relations which are referable to certain so-called axes passing in certain directions in the body."[3] The author states that "the processes of living, or certain of them, are going on most rapidly at one end of such an axis, and from this end their rate decreases along the axis."[4] It is, presumably, these differences in the rate of living that determine the formation of different organs.

For example, the head, and primarily the brain, develops from the most active region of the polar axis and the regions of the central nervous system posterior to the head from the most active regions of the axis of symmetry. Other organs arise in definite order along the axes.[5]

The differentials in physiological activity determine not only the formation of organs but also the integration of the organism. "Apparently all that is necessary for the beginning of orderly integration in protoplasm is a quantitative difference in rate of living and the possibility of communication."[6]

This quantitative difference in the "rate of living," or the rate of physiological activity, is expressed in "gradients" of activity. The region of dominance which, as we have seen, is assumed to be the region of the highest rate of living is the determinant of the gradient or the ratio of activity. Child says:

The activity locally induced does not remain sharply localized, but spreads to adjoining regions, the effect decreasing with increasing distance from the point of origin. The active region then becomes the dominant factor in determining a gradient in activity. It exercises a control over regions within a certain distance

[3] *Ibid.*, p. 29. [4] *Ibid.* [5] *Ibid.* [6] *Ibid.*, p. 42.

from it because it is the chief factor in determining the degree of their activity. This influence of an active region on adjoining regions is apparently due primarily to the transmission of energy changes from it and it is probable that electric currents resulting from the differences in condition between it and the adjoining regions are factors in such transmission. This relation between a more active and a less active region appears to be the foundation of physiological dominance or control.[7]

Thus the region of the highest rate of activity controls the other regions of the organism; it determines the gradient of activity in the organism, its dominance decreasing with increasing distance. The author also points out that these gradients do not arise autonomously in the protoplasm but are caused by "the reaction of the protoplasm to a differential in its environment."[8] This physiological dominance depends primarily upon communication rather than "commercial exchange" or "transportive relations," although, with increased differentiation in the organism, a basis for transportive relations between parts of the organism is provided.[9]

Application of Child's Hypothesis.—Human ecologists have taken Child's principles, as outlined above, and applied them to the phenomena which they claim fall within the scope of human ecology. They have not followed the sug-

[7] Child, "Biological Foundations of Social Integration," *op. cit.*, p. 31.

[8] *Ibid.*, p. 30.

[9] The conception of gradients or differentials of physiological activity in the living organism concomitant with differentials in its environment is also inherent in the theory of plant ecology with respect of plant communities and their environment (see F. E. Clements, *Plant Succession: an Analysis of the Development of Vegetation,* Carnegie Institution of Washington, 1916). Moreover, Professor Child is in agreement with plant ecologists in that the development of the organism represents a record of the reaction of that organism to its environment. As Professor Child put it: "The establishment of a new persistent axis of polarity or symmetry in a cell or a cell mass represents a record in the protoplasm of reaction to environment. This record of past behavior becomes a fundamental factor in determining the character of all later behavior" (*op. cit.*, p. 30).

gestion of Child to draw an analogy between "organismic pattern" and social organization,[10] but have made the "ecological organization" the analogue of the "organismic pattern." In the development of this latter analogy they have made particular use of two aspects of Child's analysis: (*a*) that of the increasing differentiation of the parts of an organism and the increasing concentration of the point of dominance by virtue of evolutionary growth; and (*b*) that of the "axiate" organismic pattern involving dominance and subordination between parts of the organism, and of the gradients of activity ranging from the central point of dominance. The first of these aspects served the ecologists as a basis for the historical as well as the contemporary classification of communities, and the second gave rise to the concepts of "dominance," "gradient," and "axiate pattern."

The historical development of communities is compared to the evolution of the physiological integration of the organism by McKenzie in his article "The Concept of Dominance and World-Organization."[11] He draws an analogy between the "interior-surface" organismic pattern and the primitive human community—the village and the walled city. Similarly, he finds a parallel between the more evolved "axiate pattern" of the organism and the modern city:

As we ascend the scale of animal life . . . we find an increasing differentiation of parts and concentration of the area of dominance, until we reach the human animal, in which the brain or cerebral cortex has become a highly specialized center of dominance co-ordinating and controlling the complexly integrated parts of the body. In social evolution somewhat similar steps stand out in the spatial pattern characteristics of human aggregations.[12]

[10] Child points out the similarity between a biological organism and a social organism, particularly with respect to function and processes, but he makes the qualification that the continuity of the units in a biological organism is not present in human society. See Child, *ibid.*

[11] *American Journal of Sociology,* XXXIII (July, 1927), 29–34.

[12] *Ibid.,* pp. 29–30.

Evolution and Dominance.—McKenzie finds that in the earliest stages of the evolutionary process primitive human communities, like organisms with the simplest organismic pattern, are

> livest at the periphery or part that is most exposed to the hazards of the environment. The primitive village is usually a mere aggregation of dwellings without any specialized center of activity save that which is associated in some cases with a temple or shrine. The chief region of attention is the outer edge, where at night watchmen are usually stationed to guard against marauders.[13]

This treatment illustrates the point recently made that the wholesale transference of a concept from one science to another is likely to lead to forced interpretations. In order to fit his hypothetical primitive village into the primitive "organismic pattern," McKenzie conceives that its chief center of activity is the periphery where at dead of night a hypothetical watchman strains his eyes at the darkness beyond.

The author goes on to argue that, as communities evolve, they become more differentiated, and the points of dominance become more concentrated. "The trend of social evolution, like that of organismic evolution, is toward the axiate form of spatial pattern with dominant center and subordinate integrated parts,"[14] so that the modern city is found to be like the human organism, with a center of dominance similar to the human brain. In other words, the city's center or area of dominance is "where the intelligence is received and transmitted, where brains and ability concentrate, where the community is most alive."[15] In this way McKenzie classifies communities according to their evolutionary stage in "the transition from the symmetrical to the axiate pattern,"[16] so that an absence of the axiate pattern in cities today is supposed to reveal a less evolved state. By the same

[13] *American Journal of Sociology,* XXXIII, 30.

[14] *Ibid.* [15] *Ibid.,* p. 35. [16] *Ibid.,* p. 31.

token, the evolved type of city is assumed to show the more specialized and differentiated pattern, with the point of dominance in the city's business center, which is usually the spatial center as well.

Not only the center of the city, but also the trade center of any area is regarded by human ecologists as the point of dominance for that particular area. As in the biological organism, dominance is assumed to diminish as the distance from the center increases[17] and in this way is said to suggest "a center and a margin of activity, an inner locus and an outer periphery."[18] Moreover, just as, according to Child, dominance or the difference in the rate of certain physiological activities along the axes accounts for the formation and the order of the organs, so in the case of the ecological areas the dominant center "functions as the integrating unit"[19] and determines the position of areas in relation to it.[20] With the development of new systems of communication and transportation, which make possible free movement in every direction, "trade areas and hinterlands of cities have tended to assume a more compact, symmetrical, and radial form and every urban center has come into more complete possession of the area and the region that it dominates."[21] Again, as in an organism, the areas of a community are functionally dependent on the dominant center and on the city as a whole.

> There are, for example, satellite cities, where the heavier industries are located, residential suburbs, golf settlements, and so-called dormitory towns. There are harbors of refuge, also, in

[17] See McKenzie, *The Metropolitan Community*, pp. 81, 313, and Park, "Urbanization as Measured by Newspaper Circulation," *American Journal of Sociology*, XXXV, 65.

[18] McKenzie, "The Concept of Dominance and World Organization," *American Journal of Sociology*, XXXIII (1927), 36.

[19] McKenzie, *op. cit.*, p. 313.

[20] See McKenzie, *op. cit.*, especially p. 32.

[21] Park, *op. cit.*, p. 79.

which vice and crime seek safety, particularly during periods of reform in cities. Every suburb exists because it performs for the city some function which the city cannot perform for itself so well or so economically.[22]

More specifically, Park asserts that

the so-called natural or functional areas of a metropolitan community—for example, the slum, the rooming house area, the central shopping section and the banking center—each and all owe their existence directly to the factor of dominance, and indirectly to competition.[23]

The center of dominance is understood to be the controlling organ of the city organism, as the cerebral cortex is in the biological organism. In his interpretation of ecological concepts, Dawson, one of the younger ecologists, states that dominance is the outcome of "the process of centralization under modern conditions of rapid communication." He adds:

Centers of dominance emerge at focal points in transportation and communication whether they are world centers of dominance or local centers of dominance, as for instance, the down-town centers of modern cities. A center of dominance implies a wider constituency of subordinate areas and centers. The differentiation of areas, the distribution of institutional units, and their complex integration take place with reference to the center of dominance somewhat after the manner in which a higher organism has its parts coördinated and controlled by means of the specialized and central cerebral cortex.[24]

This spatially conceived ecological "dominance" is generally employed as being equivalent to economic dominance, as is seen, for example, in McKenzie's use of these terms when he states that the shift from political dominance in

[22] Park, *op. cit.*, p. 65.

[23] Park, "Human Ecology," *American Journal of Sociology,* XLII, 8.

[24] Dawson, "Sources and Methods of Human Ecology," *The Fields and Methods of Sociology,* edited by L. L. Bernard, p. 295, New York. Copyright 1934. Reprinted by permission of the publishers, Farrar and Rinehart, Inc.

modern times is to "economic *or* ecological dominance."[25] There is a further assumption, however, that the economic or ecological dominance determines the social (or cultural) and political character of a "community," this relationship being usually implied in the concept of ecological dominance.[26] Park, discussing the findings of Galpin in the monograph, "The Social Anatomy of an Agricultural Community,"[27] states that, "the web of personal relations in which customs and institutions grow up does, on the whole, tend to conform to the area of trade relations and of common interest. Trade comes first, but political and social institutions follow."[28] He explains further that, "As the ultimate source of a common culture is, in a manner of speaking, common talk, the market place, wherever it is, has been, and still remains, a cultural center for the territory tributary to it."[29] In fact, as is evident throughout this work, there is, in the approach of this school, an implicit assumption that the economic factors determine the cultural and social character of a "community."[30]

In turn the economic structure and changes are assumed to be brought about in part by certain technological changes.[31] Hence, ecological dominance is a function of transportation and communication. "Wherever modern means of transportation and communication are introduced,

[25] McKenzie, *op. cit.*, p. 33; italics mine.

[26] The term "political" is here used in a special sense, meaning "the more formal control of public opinion and law." Burgess says, "Neighborhood work is concerned with political forces whenever social action is desired. Our whole scheme of social work may be regarded, from this standpoint at least, as social politics." *The City*, p. 153.

[27] Madison, Wis., 1915.

[28] Park, "Urbanization as Measured by Newspaper Circulation," *The American Journal of Sociology*, XXXV (July, 1927), 61.

[29] *Ibid.*, p. 62.

[30] *Ibid.*, pp. 65–79.

[31] See Park, in *The Urban Community*, and "Succession . . .," *American Sociological Review*, Vol. I, No. 2.

the symmetrical undifferentiated pattern of spatial grouping is replaced by the axiated and differentiated pattern."[32] It is the new modes of communication and the divergence of "speed in the transmission of ideas and objects" which are said to have brought about "concentration of intelligence," such as financial and business control, in the center of dominance of a "community"; at the same time these have tended to effect a decentralization of industrial and commercial activities: "Industries and other business enterprises may now be located at great distances from the source of their management and control."[33] The way the introduction of a new system of communication determines the development of an "axiate pattern" and therefore of a central point of dominance in a city is described by McKenzie:

> The introduction of the railway and modern mechanisms of communication tends everywhere to produce similar results with reference to spatial redistribution. As a rule the railroad penetrates the old city wall and locates its terminus at or near the geographical center of the community. Immediately spatial reorganization begins. The new center of the community gains in relative importance over all other parts. Axiate intramural transportation systems are introduced. Central land values rapidly increase. Hotels, office buildings, banks, and department stores arise in or near the center. Population and utilities become redistributed with reference to the new center of dominance and land-value levels.[34]

Gradients.—As a corollary of the concept of "dominance," human ecologists have adopted the physiological concept of "gradient." Although human ecologists have made numerous studies to establish gradients in various types of areas, they make exceedingly few theoretical statements by way of interpreting this concept. Burgess defines

[32] McKenzie, *op. cit.*, p. 30.

[33] *Ibid.*, p. 34.

[34] *Ibid.*, p. 31. See Hurd, *Principles of City Land Values,* New York, 1911, especially pp. 145–46, where relation of methods of communication and axiate growth are clearly presented.

gradient as "the rate of change of a variable condition like poverty, or home ownership, or births, or divorce, from the standpoint of its distribution over a given area."[35] More specifically Dawson speaks of the gradient as "the notion . . . used to measure the degree of dominance which a center exercises in successive zones out toward its periphery."[36] Apparently human ecologists have closely followed Child in that they, too, assume that the point of dominance determines the gradient of activity from the center to the circumference of the city or of any other area. The rate of activity is interpreted in one sense in terms of the degree of mobility. We are told that "the area of greatest mobility, i.e., of movement and change of population, is naturally the business center itself"[37] and that "within the area bounded on the one hand by the central business district and on the other by the suburbs, the city tends to take the form of a series of concentric circles. These different regions, located at different relative distances from the center, are characterized by different degrees of mobility of the population."[38]

The concept of "dominance" is defined above only in a formal, not in a substantive, sense. In other words, we are shown, not the character of this dominance, but only the pattern which it is supposed to assume in relation to the structure over which it dominates. How it operates, by what instruments it acts, how it maintains itself—we have still to discover.

Human ecologists accept the fundamental assumption of

[35] "The Determination of Gradients in the Growth of the City," *Publications of the American Sociological Society,* XXI (1927), 178.

[36] Dawson, "Sources and Methods of Human Ecology," *The Fields and Methods of Sociology,* edited by L. L. Bernard, p. 295, New York. Copyright 1934. Reprinted by permission of the publishers, Farrar & Rinehart, Inc.

[37] Park, "The Urban Community as a Spacial Pattern and a Moral Order," in *The Urban Community,* edited by E. W. Burgess, p. 10.

[38] *Ibid.*

Child that the basis of dominance is the higher rate of activity in the dominant region of the organism. The central area is marked by higher mobility, where "mobility" means, in Park's words, "all the movements, migrations, and changes of location that take place within the community, or in any way affect the routine of communal life."[39] The dominant region is, therefore, relatively unstable, and the stability and "wholesomeness" of the city areas apparently increases as we move from the center to the periphery.[40]

THE ECOLOGICAL THEORY OF CLEMENTS

The second source of the organismic concept held by human ecologists is plant ecology. In this science, according to F. E. Clements, plant formations or communities are envisaged as analogous to an individual organism:

> The unit of vegetation, the climax formation, is an organic entity. As an organism, the formation arises, grows, matures, and dies. Its response to the habitat is shown in processes or functions and in structures which are the record as well as the result of these functions. Furthermore, each climax formation is able to reproduce itself, repeating with essential fidelity the stages of its development. The life-history of a formation is a complex but definite process, comparable in its chief features with the life-history of an individual plant. The climax formation is the adult organism, the fully developed community, of which all initial and medial stages are but stages of development. Succession is the process of the reproduction of a formation, and this reproductive

[39] Park, "Sociology," in *Research in the Social Sciences,* edited by Gee, p. 17.

[40] This assumed correlation between high mobility and instability is expressed by Park in the following quotation: "Migration, movement, and changes in economic conditions break up existing forms of social order and undermine status. New means of locomotion, like the automobile, for example, have already profoundly changed the conditions and the character of modern life. The automobile has been charged with the responsibility for new forms of crime and new types of criminals." "Sociology," in *loc. cit.,* pp. 34–35.

process can no more fail to terminate in the adult form in vegetation than it can in the case of the individual plant.[41]

Human ecologists, too, conceive of community in terms of life cycles. For instance, Park says:

The community, as distinguished from the individuals who compose it, has an indefinite life-span. We know that communities come into existence, expand and flourish for a time, and then decline. This is as true of human societies as it is of plant communities.[42]

The same author speaks of the organic conception of biotic communities in terms of interdependence:

These symbiotic societies are not merely unorganized assemblages of plants and animals which happen to live together in the same habitat. On the contrary, they are interrelated in the most complex manner. Every community has something of the character of an organic unit.[43]

Park further elaborates the organic conception—this time in terms of competition:

What more than anything else gives the symbiotic community the character of an organism is the fact that it possesses a mechanism (competition) for (1) regulating the numbers, and, (2) preserving the balance between the competing species of which it is composed. It is by maintaining this biotic balance that the community preserves its identity and integrity as an individual unit through the changes and the vicissitudes to which it is subject in the course of its progress from the earlier to the later phases of its existence.[44]

Derived thus from the scheme of organic ecology, the concepts of human ecology are permeated with the implications of the organismic principle. A brief description of the approach of the plant ecologists will show the corre-

[41] F. E. Clements, *Plant Succession: an Analysis of the Development of Vegetation,* Carnegie Institution of Washington, 1916, pp. 124–25.

[42] Park, *op. cit.,* pp. 6–7.

[43] Park, "Human Ecology," *American Journal of Sociology,* XLII, 4.

[44] *Ibid.,* pp. 4–5.

spondence between their treatment and that of the human ecologists. *Mutatis mutandis,* they use the same formulae. Thus plant formations are said to be arranged in a succession of zones, which are stages of growth of the plant-community organism. The zones are generally perceived to be successive stages of evolutionary growth, the higher life-forms usually succeeding the lower ones. The more evolved plant life-form pushes out the existing population of an area, which then settles in a zone on the rim of its original habitat. As more and more evolved types succeed each other, the displaced plants congregate in a sequence of zones.[45]

Zonation is due to the gradient arrangement of the environmental factors, such as water content of the soil, from a central point of excess or deficiency, and to the reaction of different evolutionary life-forms of plants upon these environmental factors. Each plant life-form is said to modify its habitat by reaction, creating more median conditions and thus making the habitat less favorable to itself and more suitable for the invasion of the next higher life-form.

Zonation is the practically universal response of plants to the quantitative distribution of physical factors in nature. In almost all habitats, one or more of the physical factors present decreases gradually in passing away from the point of greatest intensity. The result is that the plants of the habitat arrange themselves in belts about this point, their position being determined by their relation to the factor concerned.[46]

[45] Evolutionary stages as revealed in the ecological life-forms differ somewhat from those accepted in biology, in that in plant ecology trees are regarded as the most evolved: "Forest is in all places the last natural stage of evolution of vegetation, excepting where the development of trees is checked by substratum of rock, lack of nutriment, water, cold or drought." (Warming, *Oecology of Plants,* p. 365.)

The ecological order as given by Clements is as follows: "One primary sere . . . may show rock, gravel, grassland, and woodland. The corresponding life-form stages would be lichen, moss, herb, grass, scrub, forest, and algae, herb, sedge, grass, scrub, forest." (Clements, *Plant Succession,* p. 100.)

[46] Clements, *Research Methods in Ecology,* p. 274.

This modification by reaction continues until the final stage of vegetation (for the climate and soil type of the particular area) becomes the dominant life-form in the area. The reaction to the habitat of this most evolved type is such that it keeps the habitat favorable to itself and in this way prevents further invasion. This marks the "climax" stage which is stable and "permanent," subject to disturbance only from external factors such as changes of climate. Thus, dominance signifies the stabilized, equilibrated relation of plants and habitat. It also indicates the control of the higher life-forms over those of lower evolutionary stages which have preceded it and which have moved out or are in the stage of moving out. The series of invasions in an area are described in terms of the process "succession," which is "a sequence of plant communities marked by the change from lower to higher life-forms."

In human ecology, too, we shall see that zones are construed as successive stages in the growth of the city. The succession of elements in the human community also implies succession of different types of elements through various stages of occupancy or use which tend toward stabilization in a "climax" community. "Dominance" of the higher over the lower ecological types and the recession of this dominance in terms of "gradients" also have their correlates in human ecology. In fact, as will be seen in the following chapters, human ecologists depend for their concepts more upon the biological ecologies than upon any other discipline.

The adoption of coterminous concepts from both physiology and plant ecology involves human ecologists in certain difficulties, if not in actual contradictions. For instance, the "gradient" in plant ecology is a differential in the environment, while in physiology it is a differential in the activity of the organisms or parts of the organisms. Granting the assumption that there is necessary harmony between the organism and its habitat, the concept "gradient" still carries a difference of emphasis in the two disciplines. As will be shown later, human ecologists are more prone to employ the physiological concept of "gradient," at the same time, emphasizing environmental determinism.

The concept "dominance" human ecologists apply both as it is understood in plant ecology and as it is formulated in physiology. In plant ecology dominance is defined as

> the ability of the characteristic life-form to produce a reaction sufficient to control the community for a period. Dominance may mean the control of soil factors alone, primarily water-content, of air factors, especially light, or of both water and light.[47]

In physiology, on the other hand, Child finds that the "relation between a more active and a less active region appears to be the foundation of physiological dominance or control."[48] As examples of this relation between parts of differential activity, he gives the following:

> The growing tip of the plant represents the most active region of the axis and its dominance depends on its activity. In animals the head, that is, the region of the brain and the chief sense organs, arises from the most active region of the polar gradient, and out of the primitive dominance of the active region in the earlier stages develops nervous control.[49]

A peculiar combination results from the fact that human ecologists take the concept "dominance" from two separate disciplines and apply it to a third one. On the one hand, they conceive of the center of the city as the area of highest activity, speaking of this area as the center of "intelligence," or the "cerebral cortex" of the city "organism"; on the other, they regard the dominant center as the result of

[47] Clements, *Plant Succession: an Analysis of the Development of Vegetation,* p. 98.

[48] Child, "Biological Foundations of Social Integration," *Proceedings and Papers of the American Sociological Society,* XXII, 31.

[49] *Ibid.,* p. 31.

successive settlements, each displaced by a group which is ecologically higher and, therefore, according to the ecological principle, most in harmony with the environment—that is, stabilized. In both cases there is an implication that the central area is *more evolved,* in the one case biologically and in the other, ecologically.

Human ecologists designate the business district as the center of dominance in the city. The higher rate of activity which characterizes the center of dominance in the physiological organism has its counterpart in the more intensified activity in the city center, which human ecologists see reflected in high mobility. The relation between mobility and activity is described by Park as follows: "The stir, the bustle, and the vivacity of city life are but the reflections of that intenser social life, of which we have sought to make an abstraction and to measure in terms of mobility."[50] Human ecologists also relate high mobility to social and ecological instability and in this way separate stability from dominance. However, the similar concept "dominance" in plant ecology has stability as a definitive attribute, so that human ecologists give this concept a meaning quite different from that intended by plant ecologists. By doing this they have undermined their conception of the fundamental ecological process of succession, since, as will be shown, the general trend of succession is toward the stabilized "climax" formation where "the climax phase of community development corresponds with the adult phase of an individual's life."[51]

A similar result is seen in the application of the physiological concept of "axiate pattern" and the ecological concept of "zonal pattern." Although McKenzie and Burgess speak of the "axiate pattern," ecologists are primarily concerned with the "zonal pattern" and with the delimitation of

[50] Park, "Sociology," in *Research in the Social Sciences,* edited by Gee, p. 18.

[51] Park, *op. cit.,* p. 9.

the zones in terms of various social and ecological factors. In its original application, the axiate pattern defines a diminishing *rate of physiological activity* along specific axes of the organic structure, and the zonal pattern, in contrast, expresses the proportional decrease or increase of the quantitative distribution of environmental factors as revealed in successive concentric circles. The former is a feature attributed to the organism itself, the latter is a configuration of the environment. The former is a single radius of diminishing potency; the latter is a belt of smaller or larger circumference within which the quantity of a given phenomenon is roughly equal. Obviously, the two conceptions, one organismic and one environmental, cannot be identified. Equally obviously, it is important to know whether the subject under investigation belongs to one category or the other. A serious difficulty with regard to the human-ecological transference of concepts is precisely that, because they merge the two concepts and generally superimpose the physiological on the ecological, we are often at a loss to know whether the entity they deal with—the area or the zone, for example—is construed as itself organic or as the environmental counterpart of an organism. Consequently, there is a tendency to assume that certain social phenomena partake at the same time of the character of the physiological "axiate pattern" and of that of the ecological "zonal pattern." Finally, the lack of a clear distinction between the organismic and environmental factors inevitably creates a confusion in the causal interpretation of the social phenomena.

Since any scientific concept gains its peculiar significance from its relation to its own universe of discourse, the same terms acquire distinctive and variant conceptual characters in the different systems that employ them. Had the human ecologists, seeking squarely to represent some aspect or even some vision of social reality, adapted to this purpose the relevant concepts of other sciences, they would have related various appropriate elements and integrated them into a new concept, coherently related to their own system of thought. A concept such as "dominance" would have involved then a new combination of the relevant and applicable elements of the two original concepts, its adaptation to the subject matter of human ecology, and therewith a changed set of implications. In brief, a new concept would have been developed. However, human ecologists have not logically delimited the borrowed concepts nor have they co-ordinated these into a complementary relation to each other. Instead they apply them haphazardly to their own theory, now emphasizing the aspects of the ecological concept and now elaborating the implications carried within the physiological concept. They have thrown the emphasis upon the identity of the terms, usually neglecting to state and perhaps to apprehend the differences in the two concepts, so that the reader is left to interpret for himself the explicit or implicit meaning of such a concept in its particular context. This difficulty is further aggravated by the fact that the theoretical formulations, alike of the borrowed concepts and of the system in general within which they fall, are extremely meager and disconnected. While the ecologists' empirical researches may provide material for inference, these are seldom developed so as to bear out the full significance either of the whole ecological frame of reference or of any particular concept within it. Not only does this leave to the reader a considerable latitude of interpretation, but, in fact, ecologists themselves often deviate from one another in their interpretations of concepts and the use they make of these, both in statements of theory and in empirical investigations.

HURD'S THEORY OF LAND VALUES AND CITY GROWTH

If the form of the main ecological concepts has been borrowed from plant ecology, a good part of their content has been adapted from economic history, economic geography, studies made of city and regional planning, and more particularly of land values. At the beginning of the century Richard M. Hurd, a real-estate expert, published a penetrating monograph, *Principles of City Land Values,* in which he attempted to interpret land values in terms of economic, social, and geographic factors. Human ecologists adapted his theories of land values as fundamental to their thesis and have incorporated his principles concerning the growth of cities, the distribution and movement of population and utilities, and the relation of these factors to land values.

The ecologists' consideration of land values, based as it is upon the interaction between these land values and the spread and distribution of population and utilities in a growing city, on the whole follow Hurd's principles. However, the human ecologists concede greater importance to land values in this relation than does Hurd.

On the face of it, the ecologists' professed approach to physical as related to social facts seems to coincide with that of Hurd. To mention one instance, Hurd speaks of the "physical city being the reflex of the total social activities of its inhabitants,"[52] and Park, for one, agrees with him in saying that "the physical or ecological organization of the community, in the long run, responds to and reflects the occupational and the cultural."[53] However, there is a difference in the approach and in the emphasis which each accords to the different aspects under consideration. Whereas Hurd regards economic and social factors as indices to land values,

[52] R. M. Hurd, *Principles of City Land Values* (New York, 1911), p. 145.

[53] Park, "The Urban Community as a Spacial Pattern and a Moral Order," in *The Urban Community,* edited by Burgess, p. 9.

the human ecologists reverse the order and employ land values as indices and even causes of social and economic phenomena. Hurd's treatment gives social significance to the value of the land as well as to the physical entities which this value represents. He emphasizes social and psychological factors in the determination of distribution and land values:

> Underneath all economic laws, the final basis of human action is psychological, so that the last stage of analysis of the problems of the structure of cities, the distribution of utilities, the earnings of the buildings which house them, and the land values therefrom, turn on individual and collective taste and preference, as shown in social habits and customs.[54]

Human ecologists, on the other hand, abide by a rigid determinism, which attributes to physical elements, reflected in land values, causal importance in all human phenomena:

> It is because geography, occupation, and all the other factors which determine the distribution of population determine so irresistibly and fatally the place, the group, and the associates with whom each one of us is bound to live that spacial relations come to have, for the study of society and human nature, the importance which they do.[55]

We are told by Park that within the ecological community "the local populations and the local institutions will tend to group themselves in some characteristic pattern, dependent upon geography, lines of communication, and land values."[56] Zorbaugh emphasizes land values as the selective factor in the settlement of population, saying that: "Land values, characterizing the various natural areas, tend to sift and sort the population. At the same time segrega-

[54] Hurd, *op. cit.*, pp. 17–18; see also pp. 145–59.

[55] Park, *op. cit.*, pp. 17–18.

[56] Park, "Community Organization and the Romantic Temper," in Park, Burgess, *et al.*, *The City*, p. 115.

tion re-emphasizes trends in values."[57] Wirth also stresses the factor of land values as of primary importance in the distribution of various elements in the city:

> Land values are the chief determining influence in the segregation of local areas and in the determination of the uses to which an area is to be put. Land values also determine more specifically the type of building that is to be erected in a given area—whether it shall be a tenement house, an office building, a factory, or a single dwelling—what buildings shall be razed, and what buildings are to be repaired. . . Land values are so potent a selective factor that the human ecologist will find in them a very accurate index to many phases of city life.[58]

It is not that ecologists neglect the social, economic, political, and psychological factors which may be involved in determining land values; they probably take these for granted. It is rather that ecologists usually underestimate these same factors as determinants and conditions of distribution. For example, Park occasionally makes a statement to the effect that

> physical geography, natural advantages and disadvantages, including means of transportation, determine in advance the general outlines of the urban plan. As the city increases in population, the subtler influences of sympathy, rivalry, and economic necessity tend to control the distribution of population.[59]

But it is nevertheless true that these "subtler influences" are more commonly overlooked and the emphasis is laid upon the mechanical determination of distribution by physical entities which land value represents. In an attempt to give an inclusive generalization, ecologists assume, for example, that populations, like utilities, compete for a spatial

[57] Zorbaugh, "The Natural Areas of the City," in *The Urban Community*, edited by Burgess, pp. 222–23.

[58] Wirth, "A Bibliography of the Urban Community," in Park, Burgess, *et al., The City*, pp. 203–4.

[59] Park, "The City: Suggestions for the Investigations of Human Behavior in the Urban Environment," in Park, Burgess, *et al., The City*, pp. 5–6.

position[60] thus making the value of the land the essential basis for selection of population. In contrast, Hurd makes a distinction between the basis of distribution of utilities and that of populations, the first, according to him, being governed by economic and the second by social principles:

In general the basis of the distribution of all business utilities is purely economic, land going to the highest bidder and the highest bidder being the one who can make the land earn the largest amount. We may note that the better the location the more uses to which it can be put, hence the more bidders for it.

On the other hand, the basis of residence values is social and not economic—even though the land goes to the highest bidder—the rich selecting the locations which please them, those of moderate means living as near by as possible, and so on down the scale of wealth, the poorest workmen taking the final leavings, either adjacent to such nuisances as factories, railroads, docks, etc., or far out of the city.[61]

Human ecologists, too, make a distinction between the bases of the different types of distribution, as when Park states that "the distribution of industry and commerce is effected by forces relatively independent of those which determine the location of residential and retail business centers."[62] Obviously, however, this distinction does not follow that of Hurd, since Park classifies together the distribution of residences and of retail business. In isolated cases Park does consider residential sections separately with respect to distribution, but what the forces influencing this distribution are, Park does not explicitly state:

The struggle of industries and commercial institutions for a strategic location determines in the long run the main outlines of the urban community. The distribution of population, as well as the location and limits of the residential areas which they occupy,

[60] Zorbaugh, *op. cit.*, p. 222.

[61] Hurd, *op. cit.*, pp. 77–78.

[62] Park, "Sociology," in *Research in the Social Sciences,* edited by Gee, p. 22.

are determined by another *similar but subordinate* system of forces.[63]

Here Park concedes a predominant rôle to industries and commercial institutions in determining the distribution, as he does in the statement that "business and industry seek advantageous locations and draw around them certain portions of the population."[64]

In the ecologists' approach, social and psychological factors are necessarily reduced to the physical terms which may be a concomitant or indication of these and are conveniently measured by and attributed to the causal influence of land values. Hence, from the ecologists' point of view, land values "delimitate, so to speak, the cultural contour of the community" and also "offer a new device by which we may characterize the ecological organization of the community, the social environment, and the habitat of civilized man."[65]

In spite of the enumerated differences of emphasis and approach, on the whole, human ecologists adhere to Hurd's theory rather closely and take over his formulations of the various processes in the growth of the city, of the differentiation of its elements into areas, and of the relation of processes to topographical and other physical factors.

Hurd claims that in their growth all cities conform to biological laws and lays down two principles of city growth —the central and the axial:

In their methods of growth cities conform always to biological laws, all growth being either central or axial. In some cities central growth occurs first while in others it is axial growth, but all cities illustrate both forms of growth and in all cases central

[63] Park, "Human Ecology," *American Journal of Sociology,* XLII, 8; italics mine.

[64] Park, "The City: Suggestions for the Investigation of Human Behavior in the Urban Environment," *op. cit.,* p. 6.

[65] Park, "Sociology," in *Research in the Social Sciences,* edited by Gee, p. 24.

growth includes some axial growth, and axial growth some central growth.[66]

"Central growth" is what ecologists refer to as "radial expansion," while "axial growth" is sometimes spoken of as "axiate or axial growth" and sometimes referred to as growth in "star-like fashion."[67] Human ecologists are divided concerning the importance which they attribute to the two respective types of growth. Burgess and Park stress radial growth and regard it as the fundamental type, while McKenzie tends to emphasize axiate growth,[68] which, as has been seen, he relates to the organismic principle. Hurd finds that the two types of growth are interrelated and vary in importance in different cities:

> Central growth consists of the clustering of utilities around any point of attraction and is based upon proximity, while axial growth is the result of transportation facilities and is based on accessibility. A continual contest exists between axial growth, pushing out from the centre along transportation lines, and central growth, constantly following and obliterating it, while new projections are being made further out of the various axes. The normal result of axial and central growth is a star-shaped city, growth extending first along the main thoroughfares radiating from the centre, and later filling in the parts lying between. The modifications of the shape of cities comes chiefly from topography, the lesser influences being an uneven development of some one factor of growth or individual ownership of land.[69]

In his description of central growth Hurd speaks of subcenters which ecologists refer to as "satellite Loops."[70] He says:

[66] Hurd, *op. cit.*, pp. 58–59.

[67] See McKenzie, "The Scope of Human Ecology," in *The Urban Community*, edited by Burgess, p. 171.

[68] See McKenzie, "The Ecological Approach to the Study of the Human Community," p. 73, and "The Scope of Human Ecology," pp. 170–71, in Park, Burgess, *et al.*, *The City*.

[69] Hurd, *op. cit.*, p. 59.

[70] Burgess, "Urban Areas," in *Chicago: an Experiment in Social Science Research*, edited by Smith and White, pp. 127–28.

Turning to central growth, this has two aspects, first the main general growth in all directions from the point of origin, second the growth from various sub-centers within the city, such as—transportation termini, public buildings, exchanges, factories, hotels, etc.[71]

Hurd's analysis of the differentiation of the city into districts of utilities and those of residences suggests the ecological process of "segregation" and the concept of "natural areas." He describes the segregation and differentiation of utilities:

> As cities grow, external influences become constantly of less relative importance, while the original simple utilities develop into a multitude of differentiated and specialized utilities, tending constantly to segregate into definite districts.[72]

He adds that

> probably the most important movement within a city as it grows is the gathering together of those carrying on the same kind of business into special districts.[73]

These districts Hurd classifies according to the use of land: "that used for distribution—retail or wholesale stores and railroads—that used for administration—banking and office property—and that used for production—manufacturing property."[74] The ecologists' equivalent classification differs from Hurd's, referring to areas of commerce, industry, retail business and residences.[75]

Of the residential areas Hurd says:

> The main consideration in the individual selection of a residence location is the desire to live among one's friends . . . for which reason there will be as many residence neighborhoods in a city as there are social strata.[76]

Human ecologists make a manifold classification of the residential areas; first in terms of zones according to the eco-

[71] Hurd, *op. cit.*, p. 63. [72] *Ibid.*, p. 14. [73] *Ibid.*, p. 81.
[74] *Ibid.*, p. 75. [75] See Park, *op. cit.*, p. 22. [76] Hurd, *op. cit.*, p. 78.

nomic income and the social characteristics of the population, and second in terms of areas demarcated by any one or more of a great many factors, such as cultural and moral standards, nationality, race, type of living conditions, and so forth.

In his consideration of the processes of city growth Hurd indicates the various stages of occupation which human ecologists study under the processes of radial expansion and succession. Curiously enough, Hurd's conception of the regularity of sequence of populations and utilities and of the infringement of zones upon each other is reminiscent of the processes of succession which take place in the plant communities. It is this similarly that probably suggested to human ecologists the possibility of intermingling the principles of Hurd with those of biological ecology. In the following quotation Hurd describes the outward pressure of zones upon each other, suggesting a universal relationship between the different elements of the zones:

> The outward pressure of one zone upon another involves the slow advance of the banking and office section into the older retail or wholesale districts, the continual following along of the lighter wholesale houses into the buildings vacated by the retail shops, the close pursuit of the best residence sections by the best retail shops, with normally a mixed zone of institutions, etc., acting as a buffer between them, and the steady march of residences into the outlying country, first utilized for gardens or cottages. Whatever the size or shape of a city, the order of dependence of one district upon another remains the same, although many districts are not clearly defined but overlap others of different character.[77]

This regularity of sequence is emphasized by ecologists as representing a natural and inevitable order.[78]

Human ecologists, moreover, show remarkable similarity to Hurd's theory in their treatment of topographical factors as controlling the shape and direction of city growth, as

[77] Hurd, *op. cit.*, pp. 84–85. [78] See chaps. vi and vii.

facilitating or impeding movement, as influencing land values, and as partly determining the uses of the land. However, whereas Hurd emphasizes the diminishing influence of topographical factors with the growth of the city, human ecologists tend to give them a place of relatively unchanging importance. Hurd's analysis of the relation of systems of communication and transportation to growth of the cities, particularly to the axial growth and to land values, his descriptions of the association of the latter to mobility, correspond with only few variations to the ecologists' presentation of these factors. In fact, the following statement by Hurd gives almost verbatim the ecologists' formulations of the city growth:

> Growth in cities consists of movement away from the point of origin in all directions, except as topographically hindered, this movement being due both to aggregation at the edges and pressure from the centre. Central growth takes place both from the heart of the city and from each subcentre of attraction, and axial growth pushes into the outlying territory by means of railroads, turnpikes and street railroads. All cities are built up from these two influences, which vary in quantity, intensity, and quality, the resulting districts overlapping, interpenetrating, neutralizing and harmonizing as the pressure of the city's growth brings them in contact with each other. The fact of vital interest is that, despite confusion from the intermingling of utilities, the order of dependence of each definite district on the other is always the same. Residences are early driven to the circumference, while business remains at the centre, and as residences divide into various social grades, retail shops of corresponding grades follow them, and wholesale shops in turn follow the retailers, while institutions and various mixed utilities irregularly fill in the intermediate zone, and the banking and office section remains at the main business centre. Complicating this broad outward movement of zones, axes of traffic project shops through residence areas, create business subcentres, where they intersect, and change circular cities into star-shaped cities. Central growth, due to proximity, and axial growth, due to accessibility, are summed up in the

static power of established sections and the dynamic power of their chief lines of intercommunication.[79]

Although human ecologists make occasional references to Hurd, their usual claim is that those concepts of their theory which are borrowed depend upon organic ecology for their enrichment and elaboration. In McKenzie's words, "the structural growth of community takes place in successional sequence not unlike the successional stages in the development of the plant formation."[80]

[79] Hurd, *op. cit.*, pp. 14–15. For the ecological adaptation of these principles see McKenzie, "The Ecological Approach to the Study of Human Community," in Park, Burgess, *et al.*, *The City*, pp. 63–79. Park, "The City: Suggestions for the Investigation of Human Behavior in the Urban Environment," *op. cit.*, pp. 5–12, and "Sociology," in *Research in the Social Sciences*, edited by Gee, pp. 20–23. Burgess, in *Chicago: an Experiment in Social Science Research*, edited by Smith and White.

[80] McKenzie, *op. cit.*, p. 74.

CHAPTER SIX

ECOLOGICAL PROCESSES

THE RÔLE OF PROCESSES IN HUMAN ECOLOGY

THE QUEST for processes is typical of the ecological school, and, as we show elsewhere, their whole interpretation of human organization is far more in terms of process than in terms of structure. This is partly due to their analogical treatment of human organization with plant formations. Plant ecologists emphasize a "developmental approach," which envisages structures as stages of process, so that structure is a record of process, and at any one time it melts into process.[1] At the same time, ecologists hold an environmentalist point of view, in which process necessarily takes on a greater importance than structure.

This approach to human life in terms of process seems paradoxical when we consider that the majority of ecological monographs are preoccupied with the distribution of specific phenomena at a given time over a determinate area—in other words, with the pattern of data within a presumptive system. However, the system itself, that is, the structure which includes each particular pattern, whether of delinquency, of migration, of accommodation, or of disorganization, is not revealed. The data presented consist of geometric configurations within which some sort of social or economic structure is assumed to exist. The processes mainly represent physical movements within and between these configurations. Because of their physical aspect we would expect a description of the actual movement, of the flow, as it

[1] See pp. 190–203.

were, of these processes. Instead, we are given a series of external indices of each process in terms of space and time. We are left to infer the character of the process, of the impulses which dominate it, of the changing currents. Moreover, such physical movements could be easily subjected to mathematical measurements, but we have only general statements about them. The ecologists have not yet dealt with ecological processes beyond the descriptive phase. They are presented to us like a series of snapshots, from different angles, which can be given a mechanical animation, but which do not exhibit the real internal continuity of the process they represent. The continuity implies a structure within which change occurs, but as will be shown later the processes have not been related to the ecological pattern.

Consequently, the body of ecological theory depends to some extent for its treatment of processes upon a priori assumptions derived from studies of the city in other fields, such as economics and city planning, or arrived at by analogy from plant and animal ecologies. Specific studies of processes, such as McKenzie's "Ecological Succession in the Puget Sound Region,"[2] deal with conditions and resultant factors of the process of succession, but do not fundamentally treat of the process itself.

Nor have the processes been delimited in their theoretical significance. Apart from the fact that very scanty theoretical formulations have been made by ecologists with respect to processes, these seem to vary in their inclusiveness from one ecologist to another or even in the treatment by the same person in different contexts, as is evident in the discussion of "succession" which follows. Moreover, ecologists have a tendency to treat entities such as human beings, goods of various sorts, utilities, and physical structures as belonging to the same category. Thus, a particular process,

[2] *Publications of the American Sociological Society,* XXIII, 60–80.

such as centralization, is defined so as to be appropriate to social movements, such as population movements; and then we find that it is reapplied without discrimination to physical changes of quite disparate character, such as "movements" of buildings, utilities, and so forth. Ecologists do not differentiate between the kind and the rate of movement typical of living organisms and those of inanimate or abstract entities. Moreover, when they occasionally do differentiate between, for example, aggregation of populations and aggregation of interests they do not keep the distinctions and use both concepts interchangeably. In fact, this type of transference and identification is peculiarly characteristic of the school.

Furthermore, the same processes are referred to areas of variant extent, from the small "natural areas" to the regions including several cities and towns. The inference would be that a similar structure prevails in all the different types of areas. We shall see that this is not the case, and this reduction of categories does not help to clarify the ecological organization.

The scheme of ecological process is eclectically borrowed from plant ecology, which envisages the development of a plant formation in definite successive cycles. This cyclic conception coincides with the organismic point of view. Thus, the ecological processes are assumed to be stages in the cyclical changes of the ecological organism. "By ecological process is meant the tendency in time toward special forms of spatial and sustenance groupings of the units comprising an ecological distribution."[3] Ecologists regard such processes as a direct expression of the constant competition which they assume to occur between human beings, between services, and between physical structures, for the most ad-

[3] McKenzie, "The Scope of Human Ecology," in *The Urban Community*, edited by Burgess, p. 172.

vantageous position, namely, for "a point of equilibrium among competing forces."[4] According to Park and Burgess "competition means mobility,"[5] where mobility is interpreted as "all the movements, migrations, and changes of location that take place within the community, or in any way affect the routine of communal life."[6] It might be supposed that, in reference to physical structures and services, the use of the concept of competition is metaphorical, but in the thought of the school no such distinction is drawn. This may be attributable to the tendency of the school, to which we draw attention elsewhere, to hypostasize abstract types or at least to personify inanimate realities.

The Ecological Theory of Change.—Ecological processes are envisaged as being cyclical, both in terms of long trend and of short-span changes. This coincides with the general ecological conception of change. The ecologists adhere to Teggart's theory, to which they refer as "the catastrophic theory of history."[7] The cycles are thought of as initiated in a "catastrophic" manner, so that change takes place, not as a continuous, uninterrupted process, but rather as spasmodic upsets of the existing equilibrated pattern. Park speaks of this conception as

> the theory that each succeeding social order has its origin in the conditions created by the earlier; that society is continually reborn, but that now and then a new and fundamentally different society emerges. In that case, it emerges suddenly and abruptly with the accumulation of minor changes in the course of a long-term trend.[8]

A similar type of change is understood to take place in the ecological community. McKenzie states, for example, that:

[4] *Ibid.*, p. 169.

[5] Park and Burgess, *op. cit.*, p. 512.

[6] Park, *op. cit.*, p. 17.

[7] Park, "Succession, an Ecological Concept," *American Sociological Review*, I, 175.

[8] *Ibid.*

The community tends to remain in this condition of balance between population and resources until some new element enters to disturb the *status quo,* such as the introduction of a new system of communication, a new type of industry, or a different form of utilization of the existing economic base. Whatever the innovation may be that disturbs the equilibrium of the community, there is a tendency toward a new cycle of adjustment. This may act in either a positive or negative manner. It may serve as a *release* to the community, making for another cycle of growth and differentiation, or it may have a retractive influence, necessitating emigration and readjustment to a more circumscribed base.[9]

Park finds this type of change to be identical in both "society" and "community." He says that:

> Every now and then something occurs . . . to disturb the biotic balance and the social equilibrium, thus tending to undermine the existing social order. It may be the advent of a new insect pest, like the boll weevil, or the arrival of a newly invented and perfected artifact, like the automobile. Under these circumstances, forces and tendencies formerly held in check are released, and a period of intense activity and rapid change ensues which then continues until the cycle is completed and a new biotic and social equilibrium is achieved.[10]

The process which determines the cycles of variant types and extent is called "succession," after the basic process of plant ecology.

Thus, the ecological organization must be viewed in terms of intermittent cycles and as an organization which is relatively equilibrated and set until some factor disturbs it, at which point it is dominated by process. When an adjustment to the new factor is made, process takes a secondary place and the ecological pattern is relatively still for awhile.

Ecological Forces.—The forces which initiate change in the ecological organization are not identically conceived by

[9] McKenzie, "The Ecological Approach to the Study of the Human Community," in Park, Burgess, *et al., The City,* p. 68.

[10] Park, *op. cit.,* p. 177.

the ecologists. While most of them vaguely refer to ecological forces, Burgess and McKenzie have given a classified list. The former makes a distinction between factors, or "the elements that co-operate to make a given situation," and forces as "type-factors operative in typical situations."[11] The latter, however, overlooks this distinction and designates ecological forces as "ecological factors."[12] The general character of these factors, as employed by McKenzie, would tend to establish them as forces, when judged by Burgess' criterion. McKenzie distinguishes the ecological factors which have "a general significance throughout the entire cultural area in which they operate" from those which have "limited reference, applying merely to a specific region or location." He gives a sample list of these factors:

For instance, the shaft elevator, introduced in the seventies, and steel construction, introduced in the nineties, and the more recent advent of the automobile have acted as general factors in affecting the concentration of population and organization of communities. On the other hand, geographic factors, such as rivers, hills, lakes, and swamps, may have either general or limited significance with regard to ecological distribution, depending upon the peculiarities of local conditions. Certain factors, such as bridges, public buildings, cemeteries, parks, and other institutions or forces have only limited significance in attracting or repelling population.[13]

McKenzie then proceeds to enumerate ecological factors as being:

(1) geographical, which includes climatic, topographic, and resource conditions; (2) economic, which comprises a wide range and variety of phenomena such as the nature and organization of local industries, occupational distribution, and standard of living of the population; (3) cultural and technical, which include,

[11] Burgess, "Can Neighborhood Work Have a Scientific Basis?" Park, Burgess, *et al., The City,* p. 143.

[12] See McKenzie, "The Scope of Human Ecology," in *The Urban Community,* edited by Burgess, p. 171.

[13] *Ibid.,* p. 171.

in addition to the prevailing condition of the arts, the moral attitudes and taboos that are effective in the distribution of population and services; (4) political and administrative measures, such as tariff, taxation, immigration laws, and rules governing public utilities.[14]

Burgess' classification of forces is quite different from McKenzie's. He says that:

> The ecological forces are those which have to do with the process of competition and the consequent distribution and segregation by residence and occupation. Through competition and the factors which affect it, as trade centers, etc., every neighborhood in the city becomes a component and integral part of the larger community, with a destiny bound up by its relation to it.[15]

In this way, Burgess identifies ecological with economic forces and seems to include with them both the ecological patterning and the geographical factors. He then distinguishes cultural and political from ecological forces. He does say that "ecological or economic forces are naturally basic to the play of cultural forces,"[16] but nevertheless he does not designate geographic, economic, cultural, technical, and political factors as ecological forces. Hence, while there is some indication of the division between social and ecological organizations in Burgess' classification, there is not a vestige of it in the classification by McKenzie. For the latter, almost any factor in human organization is an ecological one. And yet it seems that McKenzie takes a broader view of human organization as representing the interdependence of all phases of life and consequently as involving the complex interactions of causal concomitances and sequences. He leaves no room, however, for the distinctions made by the ecologists between community and society.

Park gives no definite classification of ecological forces, but refers here and there to factors which are ecologically significant. He says, for instance:

[14] McKenzie, "The Scope of Human Ecology," *op. cit.*, pp. 171–72.

[15] Burgess, *op. cit.*, pp. 147–48.

[16] *Ibid.*, p. 150.

transportation and communication, tramways and telephones, newspapers and advertising, steel construction and elevators—all things, in fact, which tend to bring about at once a greater mobility and a greater concentration of the urban populations—are primary factors in the ecological organization of the city.[17]

He also adds to these physical geography, natural advantages and disadvantages, land values, occupation, personal tastes and convenience, vocational and economic interests, and so forth. Thus he states:

Physical geography, natural advantages and disadvantages, including means of transportation, determine in advance the general outlines of the urban plan. As the city increases in population, the subtler influences of sympathy, rivalry, and economic necessity tend to control the distribution of population. Business and industry seek advantageous locations and draw around them certain portions of the population. There spring up fashionable residence quarters from which the poorer classes are excluded because of the increased value of the land. Then there grow up slums which are inhabited by great numbers of the poorer classes who are unable to defend themselves from association with the derelict and vicious.[18]

It seems that Park's conception is somewhat similar to that of McKenzie, although he does not include such a wide range of forces. In the face of these variant and divergent classifications and approaches, it is difficult to say what underlying principle of ecological forces is held by ecologists.

Radial Expansion and Zones.—While ecological processes represent physical movements, the ecological structure is a geometric configuration of spatial units. The frame of the ecological data consists of physical elements, such as topographic variations, physical structures, and systems of communications. Each spatial unit is regarded as a "natural area" or an ecological community, and ecological processes

[17] Park, "The City: Suggestions for the Investigation of Human Behavior in the Urban Environment," in Park, Burgess, *et al., The City,* p. 2.

[18] *Ibid.,* pp. 5–6.

are repatternings of these areas, resulting from the constant growth of the city. This growth is specifically expressed in the process of "radial expansion," which describes the extension outward of the concentric circles or zones that make up the city.

The typical processes of the expansion of the city [says Burgess] can best be illustrated, perhaps, by a series of concentric circles, which may be numbered to designate both the successive zones of urban extension and the types of areas differentiated in the process of expansion.[19]

It is "radial expansion" which gives direction to the various ecological processes, the latter functioning either as conditions or concomitants of this centrifugal trend:

Every community as it grows expands outward from its center. This radial extension from the downtown business district toward the outskirts of the city is due partly to business and industrial pressure and partly to residential pull. Business and light manufacturing, as they develop, push out from the center of the city and encroach upon residence. At the same time, families are always responding to the appeal of more attractive residential districts, further and ever further removed from the center of the city.[20]

In the centrifugal tendency of city growth, each zone encroaches upon the next and pushes the outer rims into ever-widening circles. The displacement of various elements by the oncoming ones is termed succession:

the main fact of expansion . . . [is] the tendency of each inner zone to extend its area by the invasion of the next outer zone. This aspect of expansion may be called *succession,* a process which has been studied in detail in plant ecology.[21]

[19] Burgess, "The Growth of the City: an Introduction to a Research Project," in Park, Burgess, *et al., The City,* p. 50.

[20] Burgess, "Residential Segregation in American Cities," *The Annals of the American Academy of Political and Social Science,* Pub. No. 2180, November, 1928, pp. 1–2.

[21] Burgess, *op. cit.,* p. 50.

The completion of displacement represents a full cycle for the particular areas: "Ecological formations tend to develop in cyclic fashion. A period of time within which a given ecological formation develops and culminates is the time period for that particular formation."[22]

Human ecologists differentiate five distinct zones, formed in the process of "radial expansion." The central business district, which is usually given as the point of ecological dominance; the area of transition, invaded by light manufacturing and business; the zone of workingmen's homes; the residential zone; and the commuter's zone. These five zones seem to fall into two classes: the first two zones, which are classified mainly according to the use of land, and the next three zones, which appear to be distinguished by the type of occupants of the zones. The zones are claimed to differentiate the population of the city into "natural economic and cultural groupings."[23]

The subdivisions of the zones are smaller territorial units, referred to as "natural areas." These latter fall into numerous classes, as will be shown later, but are sometimes spoken of as areas of "function and selection," or as areas of "competitive co-operation."[24] They are assumed to have centers and rims and the boundaries which frame them are either physical and geographical factors or land values. It is within these zones and areas, as well as between them, that the cyclical processes are described as taking place.

Although human ecologists do not advance a standard classification of ecological processes, the categories suggested by McKenzie are the most thoroughly elaborated. We shall, therefore, take them as the basis of the following discussion,

[22] McKenzie, "The Ecological Approach," in Park, Burgess, *et al., The City,* p. 63.

[23] Burgess, *op. cit.,* p. 56.

[24] Park, "The Urban Community as a Spacial Pattern and a Moral Order," in *The Urban Community,* edited by Burgess, p. 12.

pointing out, where necessary, the differences between these and the classifications put forward by other members of the school.

McKenzie distinguishes five major ecological processes: concentration, centralization, segregation, invasion, and succession. The first three processes, concentration, centralization, and segregation, are regarded as occurring within a single continuum, as groups or services accumulate or become differentiated, while the last two, invasion and succession, refer to direct displacement or attempted displacement of one ecological grouping by another. McKenzie claims that each of the five processes has an opposite or negative aspect and that each has one or more subsidiary processes. Only a few of these have been dealt with theoretically.

CONCENTRATION

McKenzie defines concentration as "the tendency of an increasing number of persons to settle in a given area or region."[25] The process is analogous to the concept of "aggregation" used in plant and animal ecologies.[26] McKenzie refers to concentration as a "mere regional aggregation,"[27] which may be measured by the density of population and which is the product of immigration as well as of natural increase of population. As a demographic concept it has been extensively dealt with in sciences such as economic history and economic geography, and it is the interpretation of these disciplines that McKenzie has adopted. It is revealed in the following discussion that this also applies in varying degrees to his treatment of other ecological processes.

His initial assumption is that concentration today results

[25] McKenzie, "The Scope of Human Ecology," in *The Urban Community,* edited by Burgess, p. 172.

[26] Clements, *Research Methods in Ecology,* and W. C. Allee, *Animal Aggregations, a Study in General Sociology.* [27] McKenzie, *op. cit.,* p. 175.

from industrialism and modern forms of transportation and communication.[28] "This new type of regional community that is emerging from the former pattern of semi-independent units of settlement is . . . the direct result of motor transportation and its revolutionary effect upon local spatial relations."[29]

Regarding the location of areas of concentration, he states: "It may be assumed that population is always tending toward the most efficient spatial distribution for the utilization of natural resources under prevailing conditions of technological culture."[30] Local food supply plays an ever-decreasing part in the location of communities, and in modern times it is "industrialism [which] has created new regions of concentration."[31]

The size and stability of a community are "a function of the food supply and of the rôle played in the wider ecological process of production and distribution of commodities."[32] They are determined by the economic advantages enjoyed by the location of a community and its competitive status. "The limits of regional concentration of population . . . are determined by the relative competitive strength which the particular region possesses over other regions in the production and distribution of commodities,"[33] while the limits of new regions of concentration are defined "by the strategic significance of location with reference to commerce and industry."[34] At the same time, the primary activities define the territorial range of a community in terms of the "prevailing modes of local transportation and communica-

[28] *Ibid.*, p. 173. [29] McKenzie, *The Metropolitan Community*, p. 69.

[30] *Ibid.*, p. 9. [31] McKenzie, *op. cit.*, p. 172.

[32] McKenzie, "The Ecological Approach to the Study of the Human Community," in Park, Burgess, *et al.*, *The City*, p. 65.

[33] McKenzie, "The Scope of Human Ecology," in *The Urban Community*, edited by Burgess, pp. 173–74.

[34] *Ibid.*, p. 172.

tion"[35] so that the radius of a community has been greatly increased with motor transportation as compared with the earlier types of vehicular transportation.[36]

The above postulates make it clear that McKenzie's description of concentration is the commonly accepted economic interpretation of population aggregates. As points of concentration McKenzie distinguishes four types of ecological communities in terms of the economic base conforming to the elementary classification by economists. The first of these is the primary-service community, which "serves as the first step in the distributive process of the outgoing basic commodity and as the last stage in the distributive process of the product finished for consumption."[37] Agricultural, fishing, mining, or lumbering communities fall within this category. The size of these communties "depends entirely upon the nature and form of utilization of the extractive industry concerned, together with the extent of the surrounding trade area."[38]

The second type is the commercial community, "one that fulfills the secondary function in the distributive process of commodities. It collects the basic materials from the surrounding primary communities and distributes them in the wider markets of the world."[39] The "extent of its distributive functions" determines its size.

The third kind of community is the industrial town, which "serves as the locus for the manufacturing of commodities,"[40] but may also combine the functions of the two former types of community. Its size is not limited and "growth is dependent upon the scope and market organization of the particular industries which happen to be located

[35] McKenzie, *The Metropolitan Community,* p. 69.

[36] See Hurd, *op. cit.,* pp. 94–95.

[37] McKenzie, "The Ecological Approach," in Park, Burgess, *et al., The City,* p. 66.

[38] *Ibid.*

[39] *Ibid.*

[40] *Ibid.,* p. 67.

within its boundaries."[41] Unlike the first three types of community, which McKenzie considers basic, the fourth type is distinguished as having no specific economic base. This type includes recreational resorts, political, educational, defense, penal, or charitable communities. Because these communities draw their economic sustenance from other communities, their growth is not dependent upon their economic function, and they are said to be subject to different laws from the other three types of community. "They are much more subject to the vicissitudes of human fancies and decrees than are the basic types of human communities."[42] The laws governing this type of community are not discussed by McKenzie, but a possible inference might be that this type of community is not natural, but rather expresses the phenomena of "society."

Another process considered in conjunction with concentration is that of dispersion. "Concentration in one region usually implies dispersion in another."[43] McKenzie claims that dispersion results from factors which facilitate the transportation of people or hinder the transportation of commodities. Apparently there is a reciprocal relationship between concentration and dispersion: "The spread of population provides the economic foundation for urban living, and the city furnishes the market or economic stimulus for dispersion."[44] While, according to McKenzie, conditions during the last few years have been favorable to dispersion of populations, the long-term trend has been in the opposite direction.[45]

Regional specialization of production is included by McKenzie in the process of concentration and is said to be

[41] *Ibid.* [42] *Ibid.*, pp. 67–68.

[43] McKenzie, "The Scope of Human Ecology," in *The Urban Community*, edited by Burgess, p. 174.

[44] McKenzie, *The Metropolitan Community*, p. 50. [45] *Ibid.*

"the natural outcome of competition under prevailing conditions of transportation and communication."[46] It apparently serves as a correlative of regional concentration and results in economic interdependence between different regions and communities, which "changes the sustenance relations not only of the individuals within the community but also of the different communities to one another."[47] In addition, it produces regional "selection of population by age, sex, race, and nationality in conformity with the occupational requirements of the particular form of specialized production."[48] Thus, territorial specialization of production is said to condition the economic activities of the individuals already within the region and at the same time to attract a special kind of individuals into that region. We shall see later that this concept, inclusive of regional specialization, merges into another process, segregation, which is made the basis not only of regional economic divisions but also of smaller divisions of "natural areas" within the city.[49] Ecologists assume that certain laws and processes are equally applicable to entities of different types and variant inclusiveness. Just as the process of territorial specialization is said to apply to regions, cities, as well as small subdivisions of the city, so individuals within the community are in the same relationship with each other as are the larger groupings, and, also various other entities, such as utilities and territorial areas. They all compete with one another, and under the pressure of competition they all specialize their activities and consequently become interdependent.

In discussing the causal factors of concentration, McKenzie takes the point of view generally put forward by economists and geographers that "the spatial arrangement of the population is basically determined by the operation of

[46] McKenzie, *op. cit.*, p. 174.
[47] *Ibid.*
[48] *Ibid.*
[49] See below, pp. 157–66.

economic forces."[50] Of these, the different types of basic industries, the manufacturing industries, and commerce are considered the main factors of population concentration. The first of these, basic industries or "the field work at the sources from which the basic materials are procured from nature,"[51] have a progressively diminishing importance in modern population concentration; the second, the manufacturing industries, while showing a general tendency to concentration, have apparently tended to spread out during the past ten years. So that, on the whole, McKenzie regards commerce as the most important factor of population concentration. Other factors which he considers of importance in concentration are increase in importance of service occupations of the public, professional, domestic, and personal type, growth of college population, and increase of leisure activities which result in concentration of population in resorts. It is apparent here that, with the exception of the increase of service occupations, the factors of concentration correspond to the four types of community described. What we are given is in effect a rearrangement of economic commonplaces in terms of ecological classification.

CENTRALIZATION

Centralization as one of the five major ecological processes is described as "a temporary form of concentration,"[52] the latter being "a mere regional aggregation." Centralization implies a congregation of people in a locality for a definite purpose, for a satisfaction of specific interests:

Centralization is an effect of the tendency of human beings to come together at definite locations for the satisfaction of specific common interests, such as work, play, business, education. The

[50] McKenzie, *The Metropolitan Community*, p. 51. [51] *Ibid.*, p. 50.

[52] McKenzie, "The Scope of Human Ecology," in *The Urban Community*, edited by Burgess, p. 174.

satisfaction of each specific interest may be found in a different region. Centralization, therefore, is a temporary form of concentration, an alternate operation of centripetal and centrifugal forces. Centralization implies an area of participation with center and circumference. *It is the process of community formation.* The fact that people come together at specific locations for the satisfaction of common interests affords a territorial basis for group consciousness and social control. Every communal unit, the village, town, city, and metropolis, is a function of the process of centralization.[53]

Centralization, then, refers to territorial concentration of specific activities and services or to concentration of people within a locality for the satisfaction of interests. This involves associational activities, but McKenzie does not directly consider the social aspect of this coming together of people. Instead, centralization, according to him, describes the physical process of movement of people, services and structures, their location and relocation. However, it is considered a "community-making" process, so that civilization is said to be a product of centralization.[54] The focal point of centralization in a modern community is, he says, the retail shopping center, and it is the trade area which he asserts to be of more community-making significance than the cultural institutions, such as the school, the church, the theater, and other types of "interest center."[55]

Since centralization refers to both a specific type of activities and a specific location in which these activities take place, territorial specialization is thought of as a necessary corollary of centralization: "The urban area becomes studded with centers of various sizes and degrees of specialization, which is a magnet drawing to itself the appropriate age, sex, cultural, and economic groups."[56] There is specialization not only in terms of location but also in point

[53] McKenzie, "The Scope of Human Ecology," *op. cit.*, p. 175; italics mine.
[54] *Ibid.*, p. 177. [55] *Ibid.*, p. 175. [56] *Ibid.*, p. 177.

of time: "At different hours of the day and night the waves of selective centralization ebb and flow."[57] We are told that centralization implies "an area of participation with center and circumference"[58] and that the distance from the center to the edge of this area depends upon "the degree of specialization which the center has attained and on the conditions of transportation and communication."[59] He describes two ways in which centralization may come about: "first, by an addition to the number and variety of interests at a common location, as, for instance, when the rural trade center becomes also the locus of school, church, postoffice, and dance hall; second, by an increase in the number of persons finding satisfaction of a single interest at the same location."[60] Obviously the first type of centralization would preclude territorial specialization, while the second would increase it. The inference in this text is that the second type of centralization is predominant in the modern community and that the larger the "community," the greater the specialization of centers.[61]

The author states that the "focal points of centralization are invariably in competition with other points for the attention and patronage of the inhabitants of the surrounding area,"[62] and subsequently centralization represents "but a temporary stage of unstable equilibrium within a zone of competing centers. The degree of centralization at any particular center is, therefore, a measure of its relative drawing-power under existing cultural and economic conditions."[63]

He suggests a classification of centers according to "(1) size and importance as indicated by land values and concentration; (2) the dominant interest producing the centralization, such as work, business, amusement; (3) the distance or area of the zone of participation."[64] The location and re-

[57] *Ibid.* [58] *Ibid.*, p. 175. [59] *Ibid.*, pp. 175–76. [60] *Ibid.*, p. 176.
[61] *Ibid.*, p. 177. [62] *Ibid.*, p. 176. [63] *Ibid.* [64] *Ibid.*, p. 177.

distribution of different types of center depend upon lines of transportation and communication and in general follow the distribution of local populations, with local business centers leading in this trend, the retail shopping districts tending to move in the direction of the higher economic residential areas, and the financial centers showing more stability of location.

> Work centers [we are told] are controlled by forces which frequently transcend the bounds of community; those of the basic manufacturing type tend to move out to the fringe of the community, thus making for decentralization. Leisure-time centers, not associated with trade centers, are comparatively unstable, as is indicated by the dynamic changes in land values.[65]

The two subprocesses of centralization are those of recentralization and decentralization. "By decentralization is meant the tendency for zone areas of centralization to decrease in size, which of course implies a multiplication of centers, each of relatively less importance."[66] McKenzie asserts that both centralization and decentralization are constantly taking place with regard to different interests. He states a general law that

> the centralization of any interest varies directly with the element of choice involved in the satisfaction of the interest.* Standardization of commodities, both in quality and in price, minimizes the element of choice, with the result that all primary standardized services, such as grocery stores, drug stores, soft-drink parlors, are very widely distributed. On the other hand, the more specialized services tend to become more and more highly centralized.[67]

[65] *Ibid.*, p. 178. For a comprehensive analysis of these kinds of distribution see Hurd, *Principles of Land Values*, pp. 16–20, 70–97.

[66] *Ibid.*, p. 179. Park refers to this process as "devolution." See Park, "Urbanization as Measured by Newspaper Circulation," *American Journal of Sociology*, XXXV, 65–67.

[67] McKenzie, "The Scope of Human Ecology," in *The Urban Community*, edited by Burgess, p. 179. * Choice here obviously does not mean volition, but the range of selection as opposed to standardization.

In comparing the two processes of concentration and centralization, it appears that concentration refers to an aggregation in larger regions, while centralization more often describes an aggregation within a smaller territory. Also that, while concentration implies a more permanent grouping, centralization is only temporary when considered from the point of view of population which congregates for the satisfaction of specific interests; this point loses its significance, however, if centralization refers to utilities and physical structures. Furthermore, while concentration describes a simple demographic grouping, centralization is given here in terms of sociological data, since it is the process of "community-making," which provides "a territorial basis for group consciousness" and signifies the coming together of groups "for the satisfaction of common interests." However, none of these distinctions are usually taken into consideration by ecologists, and even McKenzie, who makes the theoretical distinctions, loses sight of them in practice. For instance, he describes two identical processes in terms of both concentration and centralization. "This business centralization . . . is not accompanied by a corresponding concentration of industry,"[68] and "up to 1920, the leading factor making for population concentration was the centralization of industry. In other words, the population followed the factories."[69] He also speaks of "geographic concentration of many commercial functions,"[70] of the tendency of "retail trade to concentrate in the larger towns and cities,"[71] and at the same time refers to industry in terms of centralization and decentralization: "Any attempts to measure centralization or decentralization tendencies in in-

[68] McKenzie, "Ecological Succession in the Puget Sound Region," *Publications of the American Sociological Society,* XXIII (1928), 79.

[69] McKenzie, *The Metropolitan Community,* p. 311.

[70] *Ibid.,* p. 60.

[71] *Ibid.,* p. 61.

dustry by statistics relating to the size of the community in which the industry happens to be located are apt to be misleading."[72] Again, he states: "Thus a stationary or even a declining industrial population located in a rapidly growing city would in time show a tendency toward centralization as measured by the size of the community in which it is located."[73] McKenzie also speaks of concentration of both "center" activities or functions and of population.[74] Burgess, too, minimizes the distinction between these processes when he considers decentralization as the obverse process of concentration.[75]

This confusion of the two processes is probably due to the fact that both concentration and centralization are indiscriminately referred to in relation to populations as well as utilities, as may be seen in the above quotations, so that the two processes tend to merge. Centralization, which, as a temporary grouping, is time bound, loses this quality when looked at from the point of view of centralization of the specific interests or structures, such as industry, theaters, and so forth. In this case, there is simply a concentration either of physical structures or of services, although one may still speak of centralization of the population in those sections where the services are concentrated. Furthermore, since ecologists tend to treat districts of variant sizes as belonging to the same category, what applies to a larger unit also generally applies to a smaller one, and thus the processes of concentration and centralization are not differentiated on the basis of size.

Finally, the distinction between concentration as a mere population aggregate and centralization as a process of community-making is completely overlooked, as is shown in the

[72] McKenzie, *The Metropolitan Community,* p. 54. [73] *Ibid.* [74] *Ibid.,* p. 51.

[75] See Burgess, "The Determination of Gradients in the Growth of the City," *Publications of the American Sociological Society,* XXI (1927), 9.

interchangeable use of these processes in reference to industry, business, and population.

SEGREGATION

Of particular importance to human ecologists is the process of segregation. McKenzie describes it as the "'concentration of population types within the community."[76] It is the process by which the population in a community becomes geographically differentiated into specific groups with certain characteristics distinct from those of other groups. "Every change in the conditions of social life manifests itself first and most obviously in an intensified mobility and in movements which terminate in segregation."[77]

Although McKenzie defines segregation essentially in terms of population differentiation, the concentration of particular types of services and physical structures is also included by him in this process, closely following Hurd's description of the differentiation and movements of the different elements of the growing city. McKenzie presents the process of segregation and its effects as follows:

> As the community grows there is not merely a multiplication of houses and roads but a process of differentiation and segregation takes place as well. Residences and institutions spread out in centrifugal fashion from the central point of the community, while business concentrates more and more around the spot of highest land values. Each cyclic increase of population is accompanied by greater differentiation in both service and location. There is a struggle among utilities for the vantage-points of position. This makes for increasing value of land and increasing height of buildings at the geographic center of the community. As competition for advantageous sites becomes keener with the growth of population, the first and economically weaker types of

[76] McKenzie, "The Scope of Human Ecology," in *The Urban Community*, edited by Burgess, p. 179.

[77] Park, "Sociology," in *Research in the Social Sciences*, edited by Wilson Gee, p. 33.

utilities are forced out to less accessible and lower-priced areas. By the time the community has reached a population of about ten or twelve thousand, a fairly well-differentiated structure is attained. The central part is a clearly defined business area with the bank, the drugstore, the department store, and the hotel holding the sites of highest land value. Industries and factories usually comprise independent formations within the city, grouping around railroad tracks and routes of water traffic. Residence sections become established, segregated into two or more types, depending upon the economic and racial composition of the population.[78]

It can be seen that two ideas are involved in the process of segregation, one of which is quantitative and the other qualitative. The first is the separation from the wider community and the subsequent grouping together of population, services or physical structures into spatially distinct units; the second, the selection of the particular types which go to constitute these units.[79]

Ecologists assume that segregation is territorial and that, therefore, these "natural" groupings according to one or more specific characteristics correspond to geographic units called "natural areas": "The natural areas into which the urban community—and every other type of community, in fact—resolves itself are, at least in the first instance, the products of a sifting and sorting process which we may call segregation."[80] Also "social selection and segregation, which create the natural groups, determine at the same time the natural areas of the city."[81]

It is the qualitative aspect of segregation with which the

[78] McKenzie, "The Ecological Approach," in Park, Burgess, *et al., The City,* pp. 73–74. See also Hurd, *Principles of City Land Values,* pp. 15–17.

[79] Although both these ideas are ordinarily implied in the concept of segregation, sometimes the terms "selection" and "sorting and sifting" are used in addition to segregation, thus stripping segregation of its qualitative significance.

[80] Park, *op. cit.,* p. 33.

[81] Park, "The Urban Community as a Spacial Pattern and a Moral Order," in *The Urban Community,* edited by Burgess, p. 9.

ecologists are particularly concerned, because in the process of segregation the factors of selection are made to serve either as the attractive agents or the unifying principle for the "natural area." As the ecologists most commonly describe segregation, the factors of selection operate from within the "natural area" itself: "From the mobile competing stream of the city's population each natural area of the city tends to collect the particular individuals predestined to it."[82]

The factors of selection are difficult to classify since they include a varied range of physical, social, economic, psychological, and other types of phenomena. Not only this but also the particular types of segregation are not classified in a logical form any more than are the motivating forces and the conditioning factors of segregation. Therefore the discussion of the factors of selection will be only touched upon here and taken up more fully in the treatment of natural areas.

Most ecologists speak of economic factors as the basic attribute of selection. However, these are variantly understood by the different members of the school, receive different degrees of emphasis, and are sometimes considered only in an indirect way. Burgess, for example, emphasizes physical elements as the ecological factors of selection. To him, the area itself, its topography, and "all its other external and physical characteristics, as railroads, parks, types of housing," condition and exert a determining influence upon the distribution and movements of the inhabitants. It is this physical area which selects, sifts, and sorts individuals and families by "occupation, nationality, and economic or social class."[83] Economic factors are possibly implied in his con-

[82] Zorbaugh, "The Natural Areas of the City," in *The Urban Community*, edited by Burgess, p. 223.

[83] Burgess, "Can Neighborhood Work Have a Scientific Basis?" in Park, Burgess, *et al.*, *The City*, p. 144.

ception, but they necessarily assume a secondary place.

McKenzie, on the other hand, stresses the economic factors of selection. His reference to economic segregation apparently signifies a segregation according to various economic levels of the population and the economic types of service, as is suggested by the following quotation:

> Economic segregation is the most primary and general form. It results from economic competition and determines the basic units of the ecological distribution. Other attributes of segregation, such as language, race, or culture, function within the spheres of appropriate economic levels.[84]

Wirth considers land values the most important factor of differentiation and segregation of groups in the city and, in general, speaks of the economic factors in terms of values. He says that of the selective factors "the more fundamental . . . is probably that of economic values, for the sentiments of the people tend ultimately to bow before this criterion which is the expression of the competitive process."[85] The thesis then is that the agent of selection is the value of the land, which ecologists occasionally suggest correlating with rent. It is assumed that different land values define the "natural areas" and their boundaries, so that the economic differentiation of the areas no less than the economic leveling of the inhabitants and the types of service take place through comparative land values. To Wirth, "land values are so potent a selective factor that the human ecologist will find in them a very accurate index to many phases of city life."[86] Thus, if land values determine the location as well as the function of the areas and the buildings, by implication they also determine the type of popula-

[84] McKenzie, "The Scope of Human Ecology," in *The Urban Community,* edited by Burgess, p. 180.

[85] Wirth, Louis, *The Ghetto,* p. 285.

[86] Wirth, "A Bibliography of the Urban Areas," in Park, Burgess, *et al., The City,* p. 204.

tion that will either inhabit these areas or work in them. But, if Burgess' statement is taken into consideration, land values are secondary, and the physical factors in themselves determine the allocation of the population.

One might raise the question as to whether land values are not in this respect largely an index of the economic selective factors and the physical elements of relevance only in so far as they acquire a social significance. In this case the attribution to them, as such, of so determinant a rôle may be doubtful. However, in their use of the term "selection," ecologists do not so much imply volition on the part of the individuals as their automatic apportionment to the physical structures, which are determined by the value of the land. This conception of selection is of importance in the ecological approach. It is the basis of their tendency to animate entities such as areas and their physical elements, as well as factors such as land values. It is these that do the selecting, because they are conceived of as natural entities following the unswerving laws of nature. Moreover, the various physical elements are to them by nature more set, more permanent, and less mobile than the populations; these physical elements come into existence before the bulk of the population is allocated to them and hence serve as the limiting basis of distribution. It is also in this sense that land values acquire for ecologists a causal significance.

The exact rôle of land values is not always clearly distinguished. For example, Zorbaugh says that "land values, characterizing the various natural areas, tend to sift and sort the population"[87] and then adds that "cultural factors also play a part in this segregation, creating repulsions and attractions."[88]

On the whole, Park advances a like point of view, but

[87] Zorbaugh, *op. cit.*, pp. 222–23. [88] *Ibid.*, p. 223.

with a less consistently mechanical interpretation. Physical factors, whether expressed in terms of land values or considered directly, are still for him the determinants of distribution and segregation of population; but when it comes to the explanation of human behavior in general, Park seems to give almost as much importance to social as to economic factors. He emphasizes the importance of land values by saying that "land values, which are themselves in large measure a product of population aggregates, operate in the long run to give this aggregate, within the limits of the community, an orderly distribution and a characteristic pattern."[89] He further points out that "land values contribute something like a third dimension to our human geography";[90] that, besides occupying a position "which can be described in distance measured in terms of space or time . . . we also occupy a position which is determined by the value of the space we occupy and by the rent we pay" and that land values are "indications of social status, buying power, and general commercial credit."[91] But he also says:

> Population movements are usually initiated by economic changes, and a new equilibrium is achieved only when a more efficient economy has been established. Society, however, is something more than an economy, and human nature is always animated by motives that are personal and social as well as economic.[92]

And again:

> Personal tastes and convenience, vocational and economic interests, infallibly tend to segregate and thus to classify the populations of great cities.[93]

This incoherent classification or enumeration of causes of segregation is somewhat bewildering. Park lays great em-

[89] Park, "Sociology," in *Research in the Social Sciences,* edited by Gee, p. 21. [90] *Ibid.,* p. 24. [91] *Ibid.* [92] *Ibid.,* p. 34.

[93] Park, "The City," in Park, Burgess, *et al., The City,* p. 5.

phasis upon land values as selective factors and then decides that there are also personal motives for individuals' settlement in any one area. He does not distinguish between inner motives and the external basis of allocation nor between causes and conditioning factors. Personal tastes may be the basis of selection of an area by an individual, and yet the land values may be a limiting condition to his settling in a district. In fact, none of the ecologists seem to differentiate between motivating factors and external conditions. This confusion is partly the outcome of a deterministic conception where the volitional factors of human beings are secondary to external conditions. However, even this point which is basic to ecological theory is not clearly and consistently formulated by ecologists, as will be shown in the discussion on causal interpretation.

The confusion results in such statements as Park's to the effect that, within the natural areas "segregation [is] based upon vocational interests, upon intelligence, and personal ambition,"[94] and at the same time that within the community "the local populations and the local institutions will tend to group themselves in some characteristic pattern, dependent upon geography, lines of communication, and land values."[95] Again, the same author claims that

> the city cannot fix land values, and we leave to private enterprise, for the most part, the task of determining the city's limits and the location of its residential and industrial districts. Personal tastes and convenience, vocational and economic interests, infallibly tend to segregate and thus to classify the populations of great cities. In this way the city acquires an organization and distribution of population which is neither designed nor controlled.[96]

[94] Park, "The Urban Community . . ." in *The Urban Community,* edited by Burgess, p. 9.

[95] Park, "Community Organization and the Romantic Temper," in Park, Burgess, *et al., The City,* p. 115.

[96] Park, "The City," *op. cit.*, p. 5.

Wirth likewise states that "land values, rentals, accessibility, and the attitude of its inhabitants and owners determine, in the last analysis, what type of area it shall become."[97] Although this author has already been quoted as emphasizing land values as the basic factor of segregation, elsewhere he refers to natural areas as groupings "according to selective and cultural characteristics."[98]

McKenzie, however, indicates a definite relation between the economic and cultural factors determining segregation. He states:

> Economic segregation decreases in degree of homogeneity as we ascend the economic scale; the lower the economic level of an area, the more uniform the economic status of the inhabitants, because the narrower the range of choice. But as we ascend the economic scale each level affords wider choice, and therefore more cultural homogeneity.[99]

Bearing in mind the assumption that people are segregated into those areas in which the land values and rents correspond to their particular income levels, we are told that economic segregation is universal in the lower economic strata, but that it progressively decreases as it applies to the higher income levels. The conclusion that McKenzie draws from this is that the range of the factors of selection widens as we ascend the economic scale; so that a wider margin is conceded to the play of cultural factors in the higher income brackets, whereas they almost lose their significance in the poorer areas:

[97] Wirth, *The Ghetto,* p. 285.

[98] Wirth, "A Bibliography of the Urban Community," in Park, Burgess, *et al., The City,* p. 188.

[99] McKenzie, *op. cit.,* p. 180. Although McKenzie finds different degrees of economic homogeneity in areas with inhabitants of different economic levels, he also says that "it is customary to find a considerable degree of economic homogeneity in all established residential districts." In Park, Burgess, *et al., The City,* p. 77.

The slum is the area of minimum choice. It is the product of compulsion rather than design. The slum, therefore, represents a homogeneous collection as far as economic competency is concerned, but a most heterogeneous aggregation in all other respects. Being an area of minimum choice, the slum serves as the reservoir for the economic wastes of the city.[100]

It is possible to generalize from this statement and to assume that all areas which represent economic homogeneity necessarily show cultural heterogeneity and areas which reveal many economic levels or types are endowed with cultural unity or homogeneity. Hence segregation does not result in culturally unified areas in the poorer sections of the city. This, however, is a direct contradiction of the burden of the ecological thesis. One of the laws both stated and implied by the majority of ecologists is that natural areas tend to become cultural areas. "Natural areas and cultural groups tend to coincide."[101] In fact, this universal hypothesis is the foundation of the numerous ecological studies of natural areas. Developing more fully this law, Park says:

Every natural area is, or tends to become in the natural course of events, a cultural area. Every natural area has, or tends to have, *its* own peculiar traditions, customs, conventions, standards of decency and propriety, and, if not a language of its own, at least a *universe of discourse,* in which words and acts have a meaning which is appreciably different for each local community.[102]

The process of segregation is not only the resultant of concentration and centralization, but it is also implicit in them. Regional concentration, we are told, corresponds to the selection of population by age, sex, and nationality "in conformity with the occupational requirements of the particular form of specialized production,"[103] while segregation within a community designates a selection by the above-

[100] McKenzie, *op. cit.,* p. 180.

[101] Zorbaugh, *op. cit.,* p. 223.

[102] Park, "Sociology," in *Research in the Social Sciences,* edited by Gee, p. 36.

[103] McKenzie, *op. cit.,* p. 174.

mentioned factors, as well as numerous other factors. In both cases there is an assumption of attractive forces of selection which work to differentiate one group or one area from another. Similarly with the growth of the city, centralization of interests is said to become more specialized and thus more territorially differentiated. Thus similar or complementary types of interests tend to group within particular districts; that is, the process of segregation takes place. Ecologists state that centralization generally resolves itself into territorial specialization, and they also imply that territorial concentration is selective, in which case both the processes of centralization and concentration are tantamount to the process of segregation.

The loss of the clear distinction between these processes is seen in the terminology of the school; often the term "centralization" is virtually abandoned and "concentration" is used in two senses—as the equivalent of either aggregation or segregation. This interchangeability of terms is evident in the fact that ecologists do not clearly distinguish between segregation of people by residence and the centralization of population by interest, any more than they differentiate between the segregation of people and the segregation of services. All these processes are most commonly grouped under the concept "segregation." In fact, McKenzie loses sight of his assumed distinctions and in some cases uses the three processes synonymously. For instance:

> The effect of these and many other forms of recent business amalgamation has been to make Seattle the financial and business center of the region and to increase its dominance in the communal constellation. This business *centralization,* however, is not accompanied by a corresponding *concentration* of industry. On the contrary manufactures are distributed rather widely over the region and show but little tendency to *segregate.*[104]

[104] McKenzie, "Ecological Succession in the Puget Sound Region," *Publications of the American Sociological Society,* XXIII (1928), 79; italics mine.

INVASION

The process of invasion is defined by McKenzie as "a process of group displacement."[105] Although this definition refers explicitly to population displacement only, invasion, like other ecological processes, is applied to any type of factor.[106] In plant ecology invasion is conceived of as "the movement of plants from an area of a certain character into one of a different character, and their colonization in the latter."[107] It involves two ideas, that of movement and that of the establishment of the plants in the new area. "From the nature of invasion, which contains the double idea of going into and of taking possession of, it usually operates between contiguous formations, but it also takes place between formational zones and patches."[108] In human ecology, too, invasion usually takes place between adjacent areas. Invasion "implies the encroachment of one area of segregation upon another, usually an adjoining, area."[109] As in the case of other processes, invasion, whatever its ultimate causes may be, is considered as the expression of the growth of the city. Most commonly, it refers either to the encroachment of a concentric circle or zone upon the next outer one or to that of the smaller natural areas within the zones upon each other.

Although in plant ecology invasion may concern an individual, a species, or a group of species,[110] in human ecology it pertains to group displacement only, the term "atomatization" being employed in the case of individual migra-

[105] McKenzie, *op. cit.*, p. 180.

[106] McKenzie, "The Ecological Approach to the Study of the Human Community," in Park, Burgess, *et al.*, *The City*, p. 72, and "The Concept of Dominance and World Organization," *The American Journal of Sociology*, XXXIII (1927), 37.

[107] Clements, *Research Methods in Ecology*, p. 210.

[108] *Ibid.*, p. 210.

[109] McKenzie, "The Scope of Human Ecology," in *The Urban Community*, edited by Burgess, p. 180.

[110] Clements, *op. cit.*, p. 210.

tions. "Invasion should be distinguished from atomatization; the latter is a consequence of individual displacement without consciousness of displacement or change in cultural level."[111] From this statement it also follows that invasion implies a consciousness of displacement or a change in cultural level:

The term "invasion," in the historic sense, implies the displacement of a higher by a lower cultural group. While this is perhaps the more common process in the local community, it is not, however, the only form of invasion. Frequently a higher economic group drives out the lower-income inhabitants, thus enacting a new cycle of the succession.[112]

McKenzie distinguishes two main classes of invasion: "those resulting in change in use of land, and those which introduce merely change in type of occupant."[113] Evidently the first type is the more general class within which the second type takes place. By the invasion which results in change in the use of land is meant "change from one general use to another, such as of a residential area into a business area or of a business into an industrial district."[114] Ecologists do not specifically define the categories of "general uses." The second type of invasion, which introduces "merely change in type of occupant," takes place within the general type of use areas. It embraces "all changes of type within a particular use area, such as the changes which constantly take place in the racial and economic complexion of residence neighborhoods, or of the type of service utility within a business section."[115] This type of invasion, according to McKenzie produces successional stages of qualitative significance, "that is, the economic character of the district may rise or fall as the result of certain types

[111] McKenzie, *op. cit.*, p. 180. [112] *Ibid.*

[113] McKenzie, "The Ecological Approach," in Park, Burgess, *et al.*, *The City*, p. 74.

[114] *Ibid.*, pp. 74–75. [115] *Ibid.*, p. 75.

of invasion."[116] He also distinguishes between invasions into territories of various degrees of occupancy.[117]

According to McKenzie, there are three stages in the development of an invasion: the initial stage, the secondary or developmental stage, and the climax stage. The initial stage, he says, "has to do with the point of entry, the resistance or inducement offered the invader by the prior inhabitants of the area, the effect upon land values and rentals."[118] The point of entry is specified as the point of greatest "mobility," usually in the proximity of the business center of the city:

> It is a common observation that foreign races and other undesirable invaders, with few exceptions, take up residence near the business center of the community or at other points of high mobility and low resistance. Once established they gradually push their way out along business or transportation thoroughfares to the periphery of the community.[119]

Like Hurd, McKenzie correlates the initial stage of invasion with changes in land values:

> If the invasion is one of change in use the value of the land generally advances and the value of the building declines. This condition furnishes the basis for disorganization. The normal improvements and repairs are, as a rule, omitted, and the owner is placed under the economic urge of renting his property to parasitic and transitory services which may be economically strong but socially disreputable and therefore able and obliged to pay higher rentals than the legitimate utilities can afford.[120]

Evidently McKenzie refers here to the increase in land values due to the influx of new utilities and population and the consequent actual or anticipated increase of building in the area. As a corollary of this, the decline in the value of the pre-existing buildings would result from their dimin-

[116] *Ibid.* [117] *Ibid.*, p. 76. [118] *Ibid.*, p. 75.
[119] *Ibid.*, p. 76. [120] *Ibid.*

ished suitability to the new invading utilities or population. Hurd explains that, if new buildings are erected

> in a built-up section . . . old buildings are removed to make place for the new ones, public attention is attracted to the locality and the prices of surrounding land stiffen. The new buildings are quite certain to draw some tenants from the older surrounding buildings, so that their rents and value will diminish, while the land being suitable for better buildings will increase in value.[121]

An area in the first stage of invasion is described by McKenzie as a "transitional area."[122] Clements also speaks of "transition areas" in plant formations which are the result of mutual invasion. This kind of area, according to him, "epitomizes the next stage in development."[123]

The secondary or developmental stage of invasion is the period of displacement and selection determined by the character of the invader and of the area invaded:

> The early stages are usually marked by keenness of competition which frequently manifests itself in outward clashes. Business failures are common in such areas and the rules of competition are violated. As the process continues, competition forces associational groupings. Utilities making similar or complementary demands of the area tend to group in close proximity to one another, giving rise to subformations with definite service functions. Such associations as amusement areas, retail districts, market sections, financial sections, and automobile rows are examples of this tendency.[124]

Thus, within the area, the secondary stage of invasion is marked by intense competition and a geographical differentiation of groups and services; in other words, by the process of centralization and segregation.

The "climax" is the final stage of invasion and results

[121] Hurd, *op. cit.*, p. 112.

[122] McKenzie, *op. cit.*, p. 76.

[123] Clements, *Plant Succession: an Analysis of the Development of Vegetation*, p. 75.

[124] McKenzie, *op. cit.*, pp. 76–77.

in the dominance of a particular type of occupants or of a particular type of land utilization, either of which is, for the time being, able to resist further invasions. When a particular type of utilities or population segregation is said to be dominant, it is assumed to be in a position to resist further invasion on account of the lessening of competition and the development of control:

> In the process of development [of a residental district], a uniform cost type of structure tends to dominate, gradually eliminating all other types that vary widely from the norm, so that it is customary to find a considerable degree of economic homogeneity in all established residential districts. The same process operates in areas devoted to business uses, competition segregates utilities of similar economic strength into areas of corresponding land values, and at the same time forces into close proximity those particular forms of service which profit from mutual association such as financial establishments or automobile display-rooms. Once a dominant use becomes established within an area, competition becomes less ruthless among the associational units, rules of control emerge, and invasion of a different use is for a time obstructed.[125]

McKenzie also refers to "climax" as the point of culmination or as a condition of balance between population and resources.[126] His assumption is that the size and structure of a community tends to increase to the point at which the population is adjusted to the economic base and that this equilibrium tends to persist "until some new element enters to disturb the *status quo,* such as the introduction of a new system of communication, a new type of industry, or a different form of utilization of the existing economic base."[127] This, of course, resolves itself into the obvious and universal principle that, granted the relationship between the existing population and the economic resources, the *status quo* will remain unless a new, disturbing factor enters.

[125] *Ibid.,* p. 77. [126] *Ibid.,* p. 68. [127] *Ibid.*

SUCCESSION

There is a logical confusion in McKenzie's treatment of the final process—succession, as distinguished from the process of invasion. The latter is defined as the process of group displacement, while he says of succession: "The thing that characterizes a succession is a complete change in population type between the first and last stages, or a complete change in use."[128] However, McKenzie has already defined invasion in terms of this same change in use or in population type when tracing the three stages of invasion. Consequently it would seem that the two concepts, which he seeks to distinguish, run confusedly into one another.

His earlier description of invasion fits into the following illustration of the process of succession:

> The process of obsolescence and physical deterioration of buildings makes for a change in type of occupancy which operates in a downward tendency in rentals, selecting lower and lower income levels of population, until a new cycle is commenced, either by a complete change in use of the territory, such as a change from residence to business, or by a new development of the old use, the change, say, from an apartment to a hotel form of dwelling.[129]

McKenzie also speaks of "stages" in succession. What they are he does not specify, although by implication they are the stages of invasion. In plant ecology these two processes are closely bound together, but a distinction is made between them:

> Succession is the phenomenon in which a series of invasions occurs in the same spot. It is important, however, to distinguish clearly between succession and invasion, for, while the one is the direct result of the other, not all invasion produces succession. The number of invaders must be large enough, or their effect must be sufficiently modifying or controlling to bring about the gradual decrease or disappearance of the original occupants, or

[128] McKenzie, "The Scope of Human Ecology," in *The Urban Community*, edited by Burgess, p. 181.

[129] *Ibid.*

a succession will not be established. . . Succession depends in the first degree upon invasion in such quantity and of such character that the reaction of the invaders upon the habitat will prepare the way for further invasion. The characteristic presence of stages in a succession, which normally correspond to formations, is due to the peculiar operation of invasion with reaction.[130]

Burgess differs from McKenzie in that he defines succession as the generic process of which invasion is a specific sub-process.

Succession as a process has been studied and its main course charted as (1) *invasion,* beginning often as an unnoticed or gradual penetration, followed by (2) *reaction,** or the resistance mild or violent of the inhabitants of the community, ultimately resulting in (3) the *influx* of newcomers and the rapid abandonment of the area by its old-time residents, and (4) *climax* or the achievement of a new equilibrium of communal stability.[131]

On comparing the four stages of succession as given by Burgess with the three stages of invasion put forth by McKenzie, it is evident that the initial stage of invasion, which "has to do with the point of entry, the resistance or inducement offered the invader by the prior inhabitants of the area, the effect upon land values and rentals,"[132] compares with the first two stages of succession proposed by Burgess, namely, invasion and reaction. McKenzie's secondary or developmental stage of invasion, which refers to "a process of displacement and selection determined by the character of the invader and of the area invaded,"[133] cor-

[130] Clements, *Research Methods in Ecology,* pp. 239–40.

[131] Burgess, "Residential Segregation in American Cities," *The Annals of the American Academy of Political and Social Science,* Publication No. 2180, November, 1928, p. 8. * The term "reaction," although used by both the plant and the human ecologists, has a different meaning in each case. In plant ecology, it means "the effect which a plant or a community exerts upon its habitat" ("Succession," Clements, p. 79), while in human ecology it represents the resistance of the inhabitants to the invaders.

[132] McKenzie, "The Ecological Approach to the Study of the Human Community," in Park, Burgess, *et al., The City,* p. 75. [133] *Ibid.,* p. 76.

responds to influx in Burgess' classification of succession. And finally, "climax" is both the last stage of invasion as described by McKenzie and the final stage of succession as suggested by Burgess. Thus, it is evident that succession as interpreted by Burgess and invasion as understood by McKenzie are synonymous. Nevertheless, McKenzie does attempt to differentiate between invasion and succession by saying that invasions enact successions[134] and that, in plant communities, "successions are the products of invasion."[135] In these statements succession may be interpreted as standing for the final stage of invasion—the "climax." However, his treatment of these two processes does not leave any basis for the differentiation between them. Instead, each of the two processes is confusedly introduced into the consideration of the other.

Burgess' classification of ecological processes differs from that of McKenzie's in other respects. For instance, he speaks of the process of aggregation, which McKenzie does not include in the ecological processes and which, although not defined, is apparently equivalent to concentration. He also employs the process of "radial expansion" as the generic process of which succession is a sub-process. Burgess names three other processes which are involved in the process of "radial expansion": the first is extension, which apparently signifies the spread of technical services;[136] second, concentration, which seems to be the equivalent of centralization as defined by McKenzie, although at the same time Burgess uses the two concepts "concentration" and "centralization" synonymously;[137] finally, decentralization, which is said to be the obverse as well as the complementary process of

[134] McKenzie, "The Scope of Human Ecology," in *The Urban Community*, edited by Burgess, p. 180.

[135] McKenzie, *op. cit.*, p. 74.

[136] Burgess, "The Growth of the City," in Park, Burgess, *et al.*, *The City*, p. 52.

[137] *Ibid.*

concentration and which refers to the growth of new subcenters within the city.[138]

The same overlapping is seen in the treatment of the causal factors which initiate invasion and those which bring about succession. Although only some of the conditioning factors of invasion are given by McKenzie, his is the fullest classification, since none of the other ecologists consider them to any degree.

> The conditions which initiate invasions are legion. The following are some of the more important: (1) changes in forms and routes of transportation; (2) obsolescence resulting from physical deterioration or from changes in use or fashion; (3) the erection of important public or private structures, buildings, bridges, institutions, which have either attractive or repellent significance; (4) the introduction of new types of industry, or even a change in the organization of existing industries; (5) changes in the economic base which make for the redistribution of income, thus necessitating change of residence; (6) real estate promotion creating sudden demands for special location sites, etc.[139]

In other words, as in the case of segregation,[140] almost any type of change in the physical, economic, and, to a lesser extent, social factors within the city will condition or cause a movement of the population or utilities. At the same time, the obsolescence of the physical structures will move services and population, while the movement of services will be followed by population migration.

In reference to succession, McKenzie maintains that new cycles of growth or decline are initiated by the disturbance of the equilibrium of the community. The determining factors of these successive cycles in modern times are "changes in forms and routes of transportation and communication and the rise of new industries."[141] These factors are among those given as conditions initiating invasion, so that in terms

[138] *Ibid.*

[139] McKenzie, *op. cit.*, p. 75.

[140] See Park, *op. cit.*, p. 33.

[141] McKenzie, *op. cit.*, p. 69.

of forces the two concepts "invasion" and "succession" are not differentiated.

Succession as an Historical Process.—Among ecologists Park has the broadest conception of the process of succession. He conceives of it from the organismic point of view and applies it not only to the physical expansion of areas of various types but also to social changes in an historical perspective. Although it is only recently that he has developed the conception of succession in relation to "society," there is a suggestion of it in the *Introduction to the Science of Sociology,* where he and Burgess state that:

> Civilizations are born, grow, and decay. We may see the phenomenon in its simplest form in the plant community, where the very growth of the community creates a soil in which the community is no longer able to exist. But the decay and death of one community creates a soil in which another community will live and grow. This gives us the interesting phenomenon of what the ecologists call "succession." So individuals build their homes, communities are formed, and eventually there comes into existence a great city. But the very existence of a great city creates problems of health, of family life, and social control which did not exist when men lived in the open, or in villages. Just as the human body generates the poisons that eventually destroy it, so the communal life, in the very process of growth and as a result of its efforts to meet the changes that its growth involves, creates diseases and vices which tend to destroy the community.[142]

But on the whole Park's preoccupation with the idea of succession has been confined to the cyclical displacement of people or utilities resulting from the growth of communities.[143]

His more recent interpretation of succession, while still embracing his earlier definitions in terms of spatial factors, is extended to cover "any orderly and irreversible series of events, provided they are to such an extent correlated with

[142] Pages 956–57.

[143] Park, *op. cit.*, pp. 3–49.

other less obvious and more fundamental social changes that they may be used as indices of these changes."[144] Or, stated in another way:

> Changes, when they are recurrent, so that they fall into a temporal or spatial series—particularly if the series is of such a sort that the effect of each succeeding increment of change reënforces or carries forward the effects of the preceding—constitute what is described in this paper as succession.[145]

Thus Park extends the process of succession beyond its exclusively territorial connotation, so that the spatial definition of succession becomes only a particular type within a larger concept.

Apparently succession in its new meaning stands for three types of change, all of which are conceived to be orderly and "irreversible." The first is a series of successive events in which "each succeeding event is more or less completely determined by the one that preceded it."[146] This type of succession he illustrates by a series of inventions such as the alphabet, the printing press, the newspaper, and the radio. Presumably the implication is that the process in question occurs within a "closed system."

The second type of succession is, according to Park, a series of recurrent events appearing as the manifestations of a more permanent condition. As an example of this, Park cites "the recurrent manifestations, the periodic risings and subsidings, of discontents" in agrarian movements, which he describes as "the periodic outbreaks of a disease that was endemic in the country."[147]

The third type is a succession which represents "not a casual sequence of events but the consequences of an inexorable historical process."[148] Park sees as representative

[144] Park, "Succession, an Ecological Concept," *American Sociological Review,* I (April, 1936), 172. [145] *Ibid.,* p. 177.

[146] *Ibid.,* p. 173. [147] *Ibid.* [148] *Ibid.,* p. 174.

of this type the sequence of settlers in South Africa, from the wild Bushmen hunters to the civilized and industrial English, showing a succession from a simple to a complex economy in regular stages.

Having defined the three types of succession in this manner, Park proceeds, however, to extend still further the process of succession to "include within the perspective and purview of the concept, and of the studies of succession, every possible form of orderly change so far as it affects the interrelations of individuals in a community or the structure of the society of which these individual units are a part."[149]

The extension of succession to correspond to all orderly change may or may not be of theoretical or practical use. One might question the necessity for substituting new terms for old, and one might doubt the value of such an all-inclusive and vague concept as Park proposes. However, it appears that orderly social change and succession are not equivalent. The fact of importance here is that a certain type of rigid one-way causal interpretation is inherent in the concept "succession," and it is this that gives the concept its peculiar connotation.

As we have already seen, the first type of succession Park describes as "an irreversible series in which each succeeding event is more or less completely determined by the one that preceded it,"[150] and he illustrates it by the succession of the inventions of the alphabet, the printing press, the newspaper, and the radio. The underlying assumption here is that the sequence is irreversible and that it takes place in an inevitable order; or, to express it in ecological terminology, these events occur in their "natural" sequence.

[149] Park, "Succession," *op. cit.*, p. 177. This is another instance of the tendency of ecologists to expand the definition of their special terms so that they lose their distinctiveness and become elusive or even bewildering to the interpreter.

[150] *Ibid.*, pp. 172–73.

The validity of this assumption is open to question. For example, the invention of the printing press in China in 867 preceded, not only the use of the alphabet, but probably even the awareness of its existence. Furthermore, the printing press, in defiance of this ecological assumption, has persisted in China without the benefit of the alphabet. The same may be said concerning the sequence of the newspaper and the radio. There is no a priori reason to postulate this rigid causal order of precedence, even though the time sequence is in accord with historical fact. Nor can it be said that the invention of the newspaper was the exclusive determinant of the invention of the radio. This is not to deny that the same or similar factors have conditioned both inventions and that there is a nexus of interaction between the two. Nevertheless it is possible to conjecture a reversal of the order of the two inventions, as well as of their widespread adoption.

The second type of succession, described as recurrent cycles within a secular trend or within a more enduring condition, does not seem to raise the question of irreversibility or inevitability and in that case might be predicated of any sequence of change. However, even here there is an indication of an underlying direction. Citing the "granger movements," Park says:

> Although each wave of utopianism was incontinently followed by a corresponding period of depression and disillusionment, there was, nevertheless, evidence with each recurring wave of a growing realism in the attitudes of the leaders at least. This was manifest in the character of the programs and in the methods for putting them into effect.[151]

In the third type of succession proposed by Park and illustrated by the procession of different peoples in South Africa, this irreversible sequence is defined in terms of the

[151] *Ibid.*, p. 173.

stages of the economy that each succeeding group has brought with it to a particular area:

> First came the Bushmen; they were hunters who have left in caves in the mountains, as records of their presence, interesting rock pictures. The Hottentots followed. They were hunters, to be sure, but herdsmen also, and they had a great deal of trouble with the Bushmen who killed their cattle with poisoned arrows. So the Hottentots drove the Bushmen into the Kalahari desert. The Bantu were next. They were hunters and herdsmen but they were more. They cultivated the soil and raised Kaffir corn.
>
> Later still came the Boers, particularly the *voortrekkers,* who settled the Transvaal and the Orange Free State, conquered and enslaved the natives, settled on the land, raised large families, and lived on their wide acres in patriarchal style. Although they were descendants, for the most part, of the earlier Dutch immigrants, with a sprinkling of Huguenots and other Europeans, they had become, as a result of their isolation and their long association with the country, an indigenous folk, having their own language, their own customs and culture.
>
> Then, finally, came the English. They were a sophisticated city folk, and they came in force only after diamonds were discovered in Orange Free State in 1867 and gold was discovered in the Transvaal in 1884. They built Johannesburg, a cosmopolitan city —a world city, in fact, like Calcutta, and Shanghai, and London. In this way they drew South Africa out of its isolation into the current of international trade and the new world civilization.[152]

Although this illustrates a recapitulation of an evolutionary economic process in a specific situation, there is an assumption that such a sequence has a universal application. "The thing that makes the settlement of South Africa relevant and significant, as an example of succession, is the fact that it seems to represent not a casual sequence of events but the consequences of an inexorable historical process."[153] The general principle which this succession is said to express is that "the land eventually goes to the race or people that can get the most out of it."[154]

[152] Park, "Succession," *op. cit.,* pp. 173–74. [153] *Ibid.,* p. 174. [154] *Ibid.*

Whether the reversal of this type of sequence, such as the succession of Barbarians in ancient Rome or the Tartar invasion of Europe, could also be termed as part of an "orderly and irreversible series of events" and as "the consequences of an inexorable historical process," or whether these would lie outside the process of succession, we have no way of telling. No more reason is there to maintain that the order of sequence described above is of universal validity. There are numerous historical instances in which groups with the most evolved type of modern economy have directly displaced primitive hunting or pastoral groups, thus obviating the intermediary stages described in the South African succession. Alexander Goldenweiser advances an effective argument against the rigid conception of regularity of stages, part of which may relevantly be quoted here:

> The triumphal phase of evolutionism was . . . of short duration. With the accumulation of adequate anthropological material the concept of uniformity and of stages was shaken and then collapsed altogether. . . Eduard Hahn and his followers attacked the dogma of the three stages in economics and succeeded in showing that wherever man was a hunter women gathered wild plants; that a pastoral stage did not necessarily follow hunting for there were agricultural tribes in North America and elsewhere who had never known domestication; that the agricultural stage, finally, required an analytical restatement, since two forms of agriculture were to be distinguished which were very different in their cultural status. These were primitive agriculture without domestication, with the hoe as its only tool and mostly practiced by women; and historic agriculture with domestication and the use of the plow, practiced by the male, whose labors as tiller of the soil were shared by the domesticated cattle and later the horse.[155]

[155] Alexander Goldenweiser, "Social Evolution," in *Encyclopaedia of the Social Sciences*, edited by Edwin R. A. Seligman and Alvin Johnson (New York, 1931), pp. 659–60.

CHAPTER SEVEN

SOME IMPLICATIONS OF THE TREATMENT OF PROCESSES BY HUMAN ECOLOGISTS

HISTORICAL VERSUS LOGICAL SEQUENCE

WHILE there is no reason to doubt the existence of orderly processes in social change, or, for that matter, of specific and, in certain cases, of irreversible sequences, the discussion in the previous chapter was directed toward the fact that the ecological conception of processes is conditioned by a specific ideology which involves a rigidly set pattern of both process and structure.

The most questionable aspect of the examples of succession given by Park is the confusion of historical with logical sequence. Actuality merges here with inevitability. Park apparently takes for granted that the mere historical occurrence of a series of events logically establishes between these events a deterministic relation which may then be universalized. This tendency was revealed in the discussion of the concept "natural." We found that most phenomena exhibited in actuality within the human groupings turned out to be "natural"—natural in so far as they were assumed to reveal tendencies inherent within the object, occurring apart from design and even in spite of it. These phenomena are regarded as inevitable for the very reason that they come into existence. Consequently that which occurs is natural in that it occurs.

The confusion of historical with logical sequence is further explained by the philosophical postulates of the school, which are in keeping with the mechanistic interpretation of biological evolution. This they apply to human groupings by analogy from plant ecology, in which the evolutionary trend is assumed to be marked by definite and generally irreversible stages. Clements expresses this view in defining succession as "a series of invasions, a sequence of plant communities marked by the change from lower to higher life-forms."[1] This same meaning is given to succession by Warming. "Forest," he says, "is in all places the last natural stage of evolution of vegetation, excepting where the development of trees is checked by a substratum of rock, lack of nutriment, water, cold or drought."[2] This ascending order of change is related by human ecologists to the organismic analogy held by plant ecologists. Clements states, for example, that "the developmental study of vegetation necessarily rests upon the assumption that the unit or climax formation is an organic entity."[3] Paralleling the organismic conception of the human community, "as an organism the [plant] formation arises, grows, matures, and dies . . . The life-history of a formation is a complex but definite process, comparable in its chief features with the life-history of an individual plant."[4] Upon this thesis is based the analogical application, by both plant and human ecologists, of evolution as it pertains, not to the whole of the organic world, nor to a species, but to a single organism.

In his analysis of the evolutionary process, MacIver draws the following distinction:

There are many unities or systems which reveal a process of differentiation, but the process itself varies with the nature of the

[1] F. E. Clements, *Plant Succession: an Analysis of the Development of Vegetation,* p. 6.

[2] Eugenius Warming, *Oecology of Plants* (Oxford University Press, 1909), p. 365.

[3] Clements, *Research Methods in Ecology,* p. 199.

[4] Clements, *op. cit.,* p. 3.

subject which undergoes it. Thus differentiation occurs (*a*) where the subject is the whole organic world, branching into its genera and species, (*b*) where the subject is a particular species, revealing *either* a modification of its type in this direction *or* the emergence of several varieties from an earlier type, (*c*) where the subject is an individual organism, in the course of its development from the germ to the full-grown being, and (*d*) where the subject is any unity or system which comes to assume a more determinate form or a variety of forms through the operation of inherent forces.[5]

According to MacIver, society comes under the last type, but "there has been a constant danger of confusing it with one—or all at the same time—of the other three." He points out, for instance, that "group (*b*) exhibits an evolutionary process which has no determinate limits, whereas the process in group (*c*) is bounded by the life of the individual organism."[6] By placing society in the last group MacIver is in fact eliminating the necessity of analogical treatment and is suggesting that society has its own principles and means of differentiation, in terms of which it can be studied.

Just as the evolution of a single organism lays itself open to a patently deterministic interpretation, so social change, when interpreted in terms of this analogy, is apt to be seen in a more rigid and deterministic light, in which the complicating volitional factors may be neglected. Also, just as the individual organism has "determinate limits" and therefore may be dealt with in terms of the definite cycles of its birth, growth, and death,[7] so ecologists are led by this analogy to an interpretation of social change in terms of such definite, predetermined cycles. It is in this perspective that the process of succession must be comprehended.

It is within the frame of an analogy with an individual

[5] Robert M. MacIver, *Society, Its Structure and Changes*, p. 404, New York. Copyright 1931. Reprinted by permission of the publishers, Farrar & Rinehart, Inc.

[6] *Ibid.*

[7] *Ibid.*, pp. 403–6.

organism that succession represents an irreversible evolutionary trend, subdivided into definite cyclic trends, these in turn assumedly revealing further subsidiary and minor cycles. In other words, the process of succession moves in a particular and definite direction. This is also revealed by the inner content of the process. According to plant ecologists,

> Succession is inherently and inevitably progressive. As a developmental process, it proceeds as certainly from bare area to climax as does the individual from seed to mature plant. While the course of development may be interrupted or deflected, while it may be slowed or hastened, or even stayed for a long period, whenever movement does occur it is always in the direction of the climax.[8]

Among human ecologists Park finds that "the climax phase of community development corresponds with the adult phase of an individual's life."[9] McKenzie acknowledges the same point of view in saying that "while there is not the intimate connection between the stages in a plant succession, nevertheless there is an economic continuity which makes the cycles in a human succession quite as pronounced and as inevitable as those in the plant succession."[10]

McKenzie further emphasizes the predetermined character of the long-term range of succession: "Certain specialized forms of utilities and uses do not appear in the human community until a certain stage of development has been attained, just as the beech or pine forest is preceded by successional dominance of other species."[11]

For this conception of succession, human ecologists also

[8] Clements, *op. cit.*, p. 145.

[9] Park, "Human Ecology," *American Journal of Sociology,* XLII, 9.

[10] McKenzie, "The Scope of Human Ecology," in *The Urban Community,* edited by Burgess, p. 181.

[11] McKenzie, "The Ecological Approach to the Study of the Human Community," in Park, Burgess, *et al., The City,* p. 74.

draw upon Hurd's description of city growth. Hurd advances a general principle that "the growth of cities leads normally to the ultimate conversion of residence land into business land."[12] He indicates the general stages of the process of succession in their relation to land values:

> The unfolding of a city, with its change in land utilization, shows normally in the case of any lot a slow increase in value up to a high point, after which a gradual decline takes place, with occasional fluctuations varying the main movement. Thus where good residences take the place of small suburban homes, a higher utility supplants the lower, and when these good residences become old-fashioned and are converted into boarding houses a drop in value will ordinarily occur. Moreover, property of this class having the prospect of being overtaken by business buildings has an anticipated value in advance of its yield. When retail stores arrive and become firmly established the high level of value is usually reached, this period lasting possibly thirty to sixty years. As the retail stores move on a lower utility succeeds—and usually a lower value unless the city's increase in population more than offsets the drop in utility—wholesale houses being followed by storage warehouses, cheap tenements, dilapidations, etc., until sometimes land formerly the best in the city becomes so remote from the active business centre as to have little or no value.[13]

On the whole Burgess abides by Hurd's conception of this orderly sequence, applying it to the series of successions in any one neighborhood. He distinguishes eight successive stages through which an area passes and refers to them as the "general cycles of the life-history of the neighborhood":

> In the decline of a neighborhood the following stages of deterioration have been worked out: first, the stage of residential home ownership, with a high degree of community spirit; second, the stage of tenancy, with a decline of neighborhood loyalty; third, the invasion of business; fourth, rooming-house stage; fifth, entrance of a racial or nationality group of imputed inferior cultural status; sixth, the intrusion of vice and crime; seventh, the stage of social chaos; and eighth, the final stage, when business

[12] Richard M. Hurd, *op. cit.*, p. 53.

[13] *Ibid.*, pp. 87–88.

or industry takes full possession of the area. This is the general cycle of the life-history of the neighborhood. There are, of course, certain variations in this pattern, as when a residential area of single homes is transformed into an apartment house or residential hotel, area.[14]

Because of this set, deterministic conception of process, the ecological configuration, too, is propounded as a rigid pattern. For instance, Park tells us that the "natural areas" within the city organism "seem to find, in some natural and inevitable manner, their predetermined places."[15] From his point of view, it is "as if the position of every form of business and building in the area were somehow fixed and determined by its relation to every other."[16]

Plant ecologists have explicitly defined the direction in succession. To them the final climax is the dominance of the most ecologically evolved form of vegetation, the forest, which assumedly represents a more "permanent" stabilization, an equilibrium between the plant covering and the habitat.[17] The course of succession is thus a progress toward a stabilized harmony between the life-forms and the environment: "In one sense, succession is only a series of progressive reactions by which communities are selected out in such a way that only that one survives which is in entire harmony with the climate."[18]

Human ecologists, on the other hand, while adhering to the idea of specific direction in succession, have nowhere fully developed its implications or treated it to specific analysis. We may gather a more coherent idea of their conception of evolutionary change if we weave into one pattern several of the various presentations of succession. In the

[14] Burgess, "The Natural Area as the Unit for Social Work in the Large City," *Proceedings of the National Conference of Social Work,* Chicago, 1926, p. 509.

[15] Park, "The Urban Community as a Spacial Pattern and a Moral Order," in *The Urban Community,* edited by Burgess, p. 10.

[16] *Ibid.,* p. 10. [17] See Clements, *op. cit.,* pp. 3, 6. [18] *Ibid.,* p. 80.

previous discussion of succession, it was found that Park refers to change as development from the less evolved to the more evolved types; that he sees succession in one aspect as the change from a simple to an industrial economy; and in another, from less to more advanced technical achievements; and, finally, on the subjective side, from the less to the more realistic approach to problems. Park also discerns a transition from juvenile to adult and senile phases in the community. McKenzie, for his part, finds a trend in the structure of the city organism from a symmetrical to an axiate pattern, from a homogeneous to a differentiated configuration with the development of central dominance. He also sees a shift of emphasis from "political to economic or ecological dominance"[19] in more recent times, and states that "in the process of community growth there is a development from the simple to complex, from the general to the specialized; first to increasing centralization and later to a decentralization process."[20] Burgess advances a general principle of succession from an initial stage of residential home ownership to a final stage of occupation by business and industry (with six intermediate stages), and from a high degree of community spirit to the absence of it. All human ecologists speak of the trend from the absence of specialization to division of labor. We are told that succession culminates in a climax condition of an equilibrium between the groups as well as between these and the habitat.[21] Competition diminishes and stability prevails. And finally, in the city, succession takes place radially from the center outward.

[19] McKenzie, "The Concept of Dominance and World Organization," *American Journal of Sociology,* XXXIII (July, 1927), 33.

[20] McKenzie, "The Ecological Approach," in Park, Burgess, *et al., The City,* p. 73.

[21] See Park, "Human Ecology," *The American Journal of Sociology,* XLII, 9.

By the same token ecologists assume a change from the predominance of the natural order to the dominance of the social order, from "community" to "society," from the less conscious to the more conscious organization, from competition to co-operation, and so forth. From Park's point of view all these changes would come under succession and therefore would be regarded within the scope of human ecology. Moreover, since we are not given a classification into spatial and historic types of succession, it is apparent that ecologists regard all these trends as within the same continuum, in most cases one implying the other.

If we accept the ecologists' claim that the natural and less evolved order is the subject matter of human ecology, then the study of the axiate and differentiated city pattern, of the modern divisions of labor and economic relations, as well as of the social organization, should be, in strict logic, regarded as non-ecological. But for the inclusion of the various economic factors or the presumably more complex spatial pattern of the modern world, we have the claim that they are the less evolved aspects, the more "natural" factors, no matter how evolved or differentiated in themselves. It is probably this thought that underlies McKenzie's assertion that the modern trend is toward "economic or ecological dominance." Yet it is difficult to reconcile this statement with the more general ecological assumption that the evolutionary trend is from ecological to social "dominance" or control, from competition and "community" to co-operation and "society."

McKenzie also holds that the more common type of displacement is that of a higher cultural group by a lower one.[22] Park, on the other hand, claims that the subsequent stages of succession are marked by the more evolved economic

[22] See McKenzie, "The Scope of Human Ecology," in *The Urban Community*, edited by Burgess, p. 180.

base.[23] Hence, either culture is assumed to be correlated inversely with the advance of the economic base (and with the ecological conception of the more evolved conditions), or the two statements are contradictory. Although these authors are of one mind that the stages of succession lead toward some fulfillment, they are not consistent regarding the specific direction in which it lies.

In spite of such contradictions, superficially it would appear that the processes enumerated above generally coincide with some of the trends frequently presented in the social sciences. But, besides these, the ecological school envisages changes in terms of spatial succession and of a particularistic view of the "natural order" involving competition and freedom. As spatial succession is the process most relevant to the ecological theory, we shall attempt to examine its coherence with other ecological concepts and more specifically with the trend of which it is an aspect.

DEGREE OF STABILITY VERSUS DEGREE OF DEVELOPMENT OR DOMINANCE

The plant ecologists conceive of structure as a "developmental" scheme. This scheme is mainly concerned with processes exhibiting a continuous trend generally irreversible, so that the structural character revealed at any one time is regarded as a stage in development:

> In both individual and community the clue to development is function, as the record of development is structure. Thus, succession is preeminently a process the progress of which is expressed in certain initial and intermediate structures or stages, but is finally recorded in the structure of the climax formation.[24]

This point of view emphasizes process, except in relation to the final stage of a formation when the emphasis is given to a somewhat static type of structure.

[23] See Park, "Succession, an Ecological Concept," *American Sociological Review*, I, 173–74.

[24] Clements, *op. cit.*, p. 7.

The outcome of succession is zonation: "The nature of succession as a sequence of communities from extreme to median conditions determines that its major and universal expression in structure will be zonation."[25] The zones are

> due to the gradual increase or decrease in a basic factor, typically water, from an area of deficiency or excess. Successional stages are produced by the slow change of a bare area from one of deficiency, *e.g.*, rock, or one of excess, water, to more or less median conditions. In the case of water, for example, the bare area of excess is the starting-point for the series of zones, as it is for the series of stages. In short, zones are stages.[26]

Hence, "zonation is the epitome of succession."[27] In this case, "potential climaxes stand in a zonal relation to a particular formation, and this relation is that of the sequence of successional stages."[28] Consequently, spatial sequence corresponds to temporal sequence:

> The intrinsic relation between zones and stages is best proved by zonation about water. . . Such seres furnish the complete demonstration of the identity of zones and stages, and also serve to emphasize the fact that every zone has a temporal as well as a spatial relation, and hence is the result of development.[29]

Therefore, the zones most distant from the climax area are also the earliest and least ecologically evolved. The less evolved zones are thus marked by more frequent invasions, while the nearer to the dominant area, the more stable the communities.

Human ecologists not only adopt the process of succession and the pattern of zonation but also conceive of the zones as stages of succession. A fundamental concept in plant ecology, succession is so well knit into the general framework of this system that its incorporation into human ecology must of necessity mean the acceptance of all its implications and its related concepts.

[25] *Ibid.*, p. 111.
[26] *Ibid.*
[27] *Ibid.*
[28] *Ibid.*, p. 107.
[29] *Ibid.*, p. 112.

The direction of succession in plant ecology is prescribed by three principles: (1) the determined stages of development inhering in the process itself—the sequential change from initial to stabilized climax stages; (2) the determined sequence in the relation and the order of the moving elements—the evolutionary succession of plants in relation to the environmental conditions, the trend being from the extreme to median conditions; and (3) the spatial direction of movement. Human ecologists subsume all three principles in their conception of the borrowed category "succession." However, they exhibit some slight variations in their formulation of the process. For example, whereas in plant formations the relation of successive elements is fairly rigid, the order may vary according as the conditions of the soil change from excess to median or deficiency to median conditions. Human ecologists, while adopting this idea of the trend toward harmony between habitat and environment, assume a more rigid, a one-way order of succession, as well as a rigid relation between successive elements. The trend here is from a residential to a business occupation, from a less to a more efficient utilization of the land, from a natural to a social order, and so forth. This is in part due to the more rigid formulation of the third principle. While the spatial direction is determined in plant ecology by the gradient pattern, it is not a one-way course—zones may succeed one another from the center outward or vice versa, or again, in a linear sequence with bilateral symmetry.[30] In human ecology, on the other hand, the direction of succession is irreversible and rigidly determined by the principle of radial expansion from the center to the periphery. Whatever movements may take place in opposition to the radial direction are processes apart, since they do not undermine or essentially deflect the course of expansion of the zones

[30] Clements, *op. cit.*, p. 276.

from the center. In this way the zones are set both spatially and temporally, and they necessarily represent historic records of the central dominant area. This dominant center is conceived of as a culminating point of the process, at which the pattern of growth is fulfilled in a definitive type, the climax of the series of development stages, the *societas perfecta,* as it were, marking the final symmetry of the forces of "natural" change.

As in plant ecology, succession is a developmental process from the less to the more stable and permanent stage. Park, for instance, defines succession as "that orderly sequence of changes through which a biotic community passes in the course of its development from a primary and relatively *unstable* to a relatively permanent or climax stage."[31] Likewise, Park's conception of territorial succession, as illustrated in the succession of peoples in South Africa, suggests a trend toward progressive adjustment to the habitat and increasing harmony with the environment. Moreover, the sequence of populations is predetermined in the light of the principle that "the land eventually goes to the race or people that can get the most out of it."[32]

As in plant ecology, too, this fixed course of succession determines the set pattern of the areas (in this case of the city) and the relation of the dominant center to the series of concentric zones, revealing decreasing dominance in regular gradients with increasing distance. As in plant ecology, dominance is related to equilibrium or stabilization, and hence to the climax stage: "The climax stage is reached in the invasion process, once the dominant type of ecological organization emerges which is able to withstand the intrusions of other forms of invasion."[33] Moreover the dom-

[31] Park, "Human Ecology," *American Journal of Sociology,* XLII, 9.

[32] Park, *op. cit.,* p. 174.

[33] McKenzie, "The Ecological Approach," in Park, Burgess, *et al., The City,* p. 77.

inant area is the later, the more developed or evolved stage: "the climax phase of a community development corresponds with the adult phase of an individual's life."[34]

Burgess suggests a trend in human succession parallel to plant succession when he refers to the movements of population groups and the growth of the city as "forces making for community change" and as "tending toward equilibrium and adjustment."[35] McKenzie likens the center of dominance to the most evolved part of the human organism—the "cerebral cortex."[36] By analogy with plant ecology he ascribes more evolved characteristics to the central dominant zone: "Certain specialized forms of utilities and use do not appear in the human community until a certain stage of development has been attained, just as the beech or pine forest is preceded by successional dominance of other plant species."[37]

Hence, the dominant area, or the climax stage, which is the fulfillment of the trend of succession, reveals the more advanced or evolved type of occupants and exhibits to a maximum degree the characteristics of stabilization, permanence, and equilibrium between the occupants and the habitat. As a corollary of this, the periphery or the outer zone should be the least evolved, the least stabilized, the least permanent, and the most subject to invasions.

Since the central area of the city represents the "adult" type of organization, it may be assumed that all the other zones will, in time, tend to approximate the same type. This is confirmed by Burgess' principle of the trend from residential to business occupancy. The more general restatement

[34] Park, "Human Ecology," *American Journal of Sociology,* XLII, 9.

[35] Burgess, "Urban Areas," in *Chicago: an Experiment in Social Science Research,* edited by T. V. Smith and Leonard White, p. 123.

[36] McKenzie, "The Concept of Dominance and World Organization," *American Journal of Sociology,* XXXIII (July, 1927), 29.

[37] McKenzie, *op. cit.,* p. 74.

of this assumption is that the evolutionary trend within ecological succession is toward the type of area represented by the central zone.

Ecologists, however, do not consistently fit their general conceptual framework to their descriptive particulars, so that we find that the outer zones are in actuality more stable and hence less subject to invasions than the dominant area. Thus, discussing the succession of immigrant groups, Park declares that:

> Immigrant peoples ordinarily settle first in or near the centers of cities. . . From there they are likely to move by stages (perhaps one might better say, by leaps and bounds) from an area of first to areas of second and third settlement, generally in the direction of the periphery of the city and eventually into the suburban area—in any case, *from a less to a more stable section* of the metropolitan region.[38]

McKenzie makes a similar observation in pointing out that the areas are more subject to invasions at the center and more stable ecologically at the periphery: "It is a common observation that foreign races and other undesirable invaders, with few exceptions, take up residence near the business center of the community or at other points of high mobility and low resistance."[39] The same apparently applies to social stability: "Measured by almost any index, the city shows a tendency toward increasing wholesomeness [*sic*] and social stability with distance from the center."[40]

That the central area of dominance is not stable is also shown by the high "mobility" in the dominant center: "the area of greatest mobility, *i. e.*, of movement and change of

[38] Park, "Succession," *American Sociological Review,* I, 171; italics mine.

[39] McKenzie, *op. cit.*, p. 76.

[40] McKenzie, *The Metropolitan Community,* p. 185. The correlation between spatial and social stability is inherent in the more general ecological principle of the relationship between spatial and social phenomena.

population, is naturally the business center itself."[41] Since "mobility may be taken as an index of social change,"[42] the central area is characterized also by an intensity and rapidity of social change and by a lack of permanence. This state ecologists refer to as disorganization, and it is difficult to conceive of equilibrium or stability as being a concomitant of disorganization.

If dominance is thus found to be concomitant with instability, disorganization, high mobility, and frequency of invasions, then, contrary to the ecological thesis, it is not the outcome of succession and cannot possibly represent its point of culmination. In keeping with ecological theory, dominance would be a process concurrent with freedom of competition, the least degree of social control and (by implication) the relative absence of conscious behavior and rational organization.

Thus to deny the definitive attributes to the concept of dominance (based as it is upon equilibrium and stability) and to the process of succession, of which dominance is both the indirect determinant[43] and the fulfillment, is to undermine both concepts. It is not only that a discrepancy inheres in the theoretical formulations, but the latter, apparently, in no way coincide with the factual observations. Whatever relation exists between the ecologists' theoretical conception of dominance and succession and their factual statements in regard to the area of dominance, is at best spasmodic and imperfectly apprehended.

Other questionable conclusions may be drawn in regard to the criteria of direction of succession in relation to the

[41] Park, "The Urban Community as a Spacial Pattern and a Moral Order," in *The Urban Community*, edited by Burgess, p. 10.

[42] Park, "Sociology," in *Research in the Social Sciences*, edited by Gee, p. 16.

[43] See Park, "Human Ecology," *American Journal of Sociology*, XLII, 9.

spatial ecological pattern. Thus we have zones showing less and more evolved characteristics, zones marked by less and more specialization, populations with a less or more evolved economic base, subject in varying degrees to the cultural dominance of the center, zones showing gradient stages of equilibrium between the group and the environment, and so forth.

Undoubtedly, one of the pitfalls the ecologists set for themselves is the indiscriminate application of concepts from different disciplines. Granted the rigid regularity of sequence in both time and space, the two necessarily coincide, so that the trend of succession is expressed in the pattern of the concentric zones. Whereas succession in plant ecology tends toward stabilization and is expressed in the climax area with the dominance of the more evolved life-form, in physiology, where no equivalent process of succession takes place, the higher rate of activity rather than stability is the basis of dominance. Ecologists try to reconcile these two principles and to fit both into a system alien to them, with the result that the concepts "dominance" and "succession" lose their logical coherence.

Ecologists also tend to relate ecological processes, without qualifications, to categories of variant qualities as well as of variant extent. For instance, we are not given any specific basis for differentiating between the types of succession which may be said to take place within a zonal pattern in the city and those which may occur in a larger region. Nor are we presented with distinctions between territorial successions over a short span of time and the series of successions which may represent an evolutionary trend over a long period. At the same time ecologists offer no specific qualitative distinction between historical succession, such as is said to occur, for instance, in technological development or cultural sequences, and the successions represented by movements of populations within the "natural areas" of variant extent.

Not only does this reduction to the same denominator run counter to the ecologists' own division of process in "community" and "society," but it is impossible to conceive of any logical basis for the inclusion of such disparate, such incongruous phenomena within a single universe of discourse. Park's definition of succession presumably makes a distinction between historical and spatial succession when he states that "changes, when they are recurrent, so that they fall into a temporal *or* spatial series—particularly if the series is such that the effect of each succeeding increment of change reënforces or carries forward the effects of the preceding—constitute what is described . . . as succession."[44] However, we saw that, for instance, the relation of succession to the zonal pattern and "radial expansion," involves both the spatial and the temporal sequences, the former as historical records of the latter. Moreover, the second part of Park's definition applies equally to both spatial and historical succession as conceived by ecologists. The very attempt to term both types of change, succession, indicates the unitary treatment of the two.

We may, furthermore, question the interpretation of social and technological and again economic changes in terms of one concept. Any one of these facets of human organization may show recurrent changes, but are they all governed by identical or even similar principles? Does one master key fit all the gateways leading from problems to their solutions?

The essential difficulty is that the historical data nowhere fall within a single closed system with determinate frontiers of space or of time. Systems, of course, abound; political systems, economic systems, class systems, community systems, technological systems, religious systems, language systems, thought systems,

[44] Park, "Succession," *American Sociological Review,* I, 177.

mode of living systems. These systems are interwoven and interdependent, but their indeterminate and changing frontiers are bewilderingly non-coincident except perhaps in some rare fastnesses where small tribes still live remote from contacts—and from history. There alone, if anywhere, is the dream of totalitarianism realized in our present world. Elsewhere the various systems refuse the measure of any Procrustean bed devised by race fanatics or culture purists, who would make the world conform to the simplicity of their own thoughts. It has been so ever since what we name civilization began. In this fact . . . we find one main reason for rejecting the notion that societies or civilizations on any scale whatever, are organic wholes, all of whose elements and systems are bound together in indissoluble unity, grow together, flourish together, and at length die together.[45]

In human ecology the concepts "succession," "dominance," and "natural area" are so all-inclusive and general that their application results in distortion as well as confusion. Surely no scientific method requires such straining of interpretation in the interests of simplification. While elasticity of general concepts may be desirable, any concept serves a purpose within a particular framework only so long as it succinctly describes either a reality or an ideal representation of that reality and thereby serves to provide a distinction between different categories. Once a concept assumes a connotation which neither delimits it nor particularizes it, whether in its own content or by relation to cognate categories, it loses its value as a scientific tool.

Thus ecologists speak of succession as taking place in relation to all kinds of "natural areas"—the world, the region, the city, the zone, or the subdivisions of the zone. Yet, surely the process of succession takes on a different meaning, not only in terms of the dimension of the area, but also in terms of the very organization of that area. What technological succession may mean for a large region may not be

[45] MacIver, "The Historical Pattern of Social Change," *Journal of Social Philosophy*, II, 38.

identical with what it means for a local area within the city. The trend of settlements on a continent does not necessarily parallel the trend of settlements in a local area. Topographical features, such as the Carpathian Mountains and the Great Lakes, may serve as obstructions to movements and to succession, as well as to contacts of populations, but do elevations of topography and artificial lakes serve as identical or equivalent barriers to these processes in the city or in its areas?

Similarly, ecological dominance involves not only ecological factors, but also economic, social, cultural, and so forth. McKenzie regards ecological dominance as synonymous with economic dominance, while Park claims that, because trade areas "coincide with the cultural,"[46] the cultural and political organizations of the community tend to conform to the economic, so that ecological dominance is said to reveal all types of dominance. Thus, for instance, dominance pertains to control of the more evolved type of economy, to technical and technological influence or control over populations and physical structures, to the diffusion of social and psychological phenomena.

The degree of dominance of any of these is measured in terms of physical or geometric distance from its center, this usually following a similar pattern for all factors, since the Central Business District of the city is "the focus of its commercial, social, and civil life."[47] Burgess tells us that "quite naturally, almost inevitably, the economic, cultural, and political life centers here."[48]

Although in the distinction between "community" and "society" we were led to understand that distinct (even

[46] Park, "Urbanization as Measured by Newspaper Circulation," *American Journal of Sociology,* XXXV, 62.

[47] Burgess, *op. cit.,* p. 114.

[48] Burgess, "The Growth of the City: an Introduction to a Research Project," in Park, Burgess, *et al., The City,* p. 52.

though related) laws govern the two categories, it now appears that the factors included in each come under the same ecological principles. Nor are we given the specific content of the concept dominance. No distinction is made between control, such as is exemplified in the central management of chain stores, and the diffusion of specific cultural traits or social characteristics, such as delinquency. If ecologists limited themselves to the study of dominance of a center in terms of, for example, economic control, one might conceivably see a pattern in which the central portion of the city serves as a directing focus or, in McKenzie's words, the "cerebral cortex," which dominates the economic aspect of the city life. But even here it would be essential to know whether this type involved the economic status or the economic efficiency of the populations in the different zones, the type of utilities, and so forth. The general formulations given to dominance leave a great many questions unanswered. Since the influence of the dominant focus "is greatest at the center, and diminishes as it radiates,"[49] the inference is that the outer zones of the city are less subject to this dominance than are the areas in the vicinity of the dominant center. If, as McKenzie asserts, the intelligence is concentrated in the dominant center, would this mean that the control which this intelligence exercises is less in the better residential district, which is more distant from the dominant area, than in the workingmen's home zone which is nearer to it? How is this principle related to the decreasing gradient pattern of such factors as delinquency, suicide, and insanity, which represents patterns of diffusion from the focal center? Or again, does dominance, with its regular gradient pattern, equally apply to such factors as delinquency, attendance at theaters, fashions, influence of the newspaper, intensity of interest in economic conditions,

[49] Park, *op. cit.*, p. 65.

technological improvements, cultural influence, and so forth? The general formulations of dominance and the factual researches would both imply that dominance pertains to any and all factors. The ecological premise is, as we have seen, that ecological dominance reveals cultural and social dominance, so that the central area is likewise the point of social dominance, and the radius of the ecological dominance determines that of the cultural.[50]

Inherent in the ecological treatment here is the fact that physical distances are the indices of the social categories. The logical basis for this procedure is explained clearly by Park in his treatment of newspaper *distribution* as an index of the social and economic *organization:*

> The existing distribution of newspaper circulation in the metropolitan region, since it seems to have arisen in response to the same forces which have brought about the existing territorial distribution of social and economic function, is an index of the existing social and economic organization of the region.[51]

Thus the operation of the same or similar causes upon the distribution of two factors establishes the distribution of one as the index to the organization of the other. Two questions may be raised here: (1) Does the operation of "the same forces" upon two factors establish one as the index of the other? (2) Does this warrant the use of the territorial extent of one factor as the index of the structure of the other?

The method of reasoning employed by Park in this conjunction may be contrasted with that of Durkheim in his study of suicide.[52] Finding that Protestants reveal a higher rate of suicide than do Catholics, he used Protestant affiliation as an index to suicide; not because the "same forces"

[50] Park, *op. cit.*

[51] Park and Newcomb, "Newspaper Circulation and Metropolitan Regions," in McKenzie, *Metropolitan Community,* p. 105.

[52] Emile Durkheim, *Le Suicide,* Paris, 1897.

operate upon both suicide and Protestant ideology, but because social isolation, which was found to be a determinant of suicide, was also found to be inherent in the Protestant ideology. It is quite obvious that the processes of reasoning in the two cases are substantially different.

Furthermore, Park's statement leads to a *reductio ad absurdum*. Ecologists claim that "competition is the process through which the distributive and ecological organization of society is created";[53] that "competition determines the distribution of population, territorially and vocationally";[54] and, again, that the "spatial pattern of the community—the typical arrangement of population and institutions—is . . . conceived to be a function of competition and competitive-coöperation."[55] From all of which the only inference is that the distribution of any factor whatever can be taken as the index of the organization of all factors.

[53] Park and Burgess, *op. cit.*, p. 508. [54] *Ibid.*

[55] McKenzie, "Demography, Human Geography, and Human Ecology," in *The Fields and Methods of Sociology*, edited by L. L. Bernard, p. 59, New York. Copyright 1934. Reprinted by permission of the publishers, Farrar & Rinehart, Inc.

CHAPTER EIGHT

NATURAL AREAS

THE ECOLOGICAL "STRUCTURE"

WHILE ecological processes are essentially expressions of physical movement, ecological structure involves physical factors. The different ecologists deviate from this physical interpretation in varying degrees, Park being the most notable dissentient; McKenzie, however, represents the typical point of view when he defines the ecological structure in terms of roads and buildings:

> Ecological processes always operate within a more or less rigid structural base. The relative spatial fixity of the road and the establishment furnishes the base in which the ecological processes function. The fact that the movements of men and commodities follow narrow channels of rather fixed spatial significance gives a structural foundation to human spatial relations which is absent in the case of plant and animal communities.[1]

When Park designates "natural areas" as the units of the structure of the city,[2] the question arises whether he, too, conceives of this structure and its elements in exclusively physical terms. In other respects, however, his definition and that of McKenzie are divergent and incompatible.

From the various formulations of "natural areas" it can be seen that there is no consistent adherence to the physical conception of the ecological structure. For the concept is also defined in terms of population groupings and the dis-

[1] McKenzie, "The Scope of Human Ecology," in *The Urban Community*, edited by Burgess, pp. 181–82.

[2] See Park, "Sociology," in *Research in the Social Sciences*, edited by Gee, p. 29.

tribution patterns of various institutions, or again in terms of the distribution of social and economic factors. In the latter usage the "ecological structure" in McKenzie's sense becomes merely a conditioning or limiting factor. Thus the physical set-up is treated both as the ecological structure and as the conditioning or limiting factor of the ecological structure.

Finally, the ecological structure is thought of in terms of the definitive attributes of the natural "community." Here, the conception of the different "natural areas" takes on a less tangible form involving as it does biotic competition, symbiosis, and "natural" behavior.

The last-mentioned approaches to the ecological structure raise the question as to what the term "area" signifies: whether it is a unit of physical territory, a grouping of tangible elements, such as physical structures, commodities, and living organisms, or again a system of specific relations, biotic or otherwise.

Park refers to "natural areas" as "communities." Yet he obviously thinks of them not only as "natural" ecological units but also as *cultural* units, which are to him, in some way, products of natural forces and thus natural communities:

> The urban community turns out, upon closer scrutiny, to be a mosaic of minor communities, many of them strikingly different one from another, but all more or less typical. Every city has its central business district; the focal point of the whole urban complex. Every city, every great city, has its more or less exclusive residential areas or suburbs; its areas of light and of heavy industry, satellite cities, and casual labor mart, where men are recruited for rough work on distant frontiers, in the mines and in the forests, in the building of railways or in the borings and excavations for the vast structures of our modern cities. Every American city has its slums; its ghettos; its immigrant colonies, regions which maintain more or less alien and exotic culture. Nearly every large city has its bohemias and hobohemias, where

life is freer, more adventurous and lonely than it is elsewhere. These are the so-called *natural areas* of the city. They are the products of forces that are constantly at work to effect an orderly distribution of populations and functions within the urban complex. They are "natural" because they are not planned, and because the order they display is not the result of design, but rather a manifestation of tendencies inherent in the urban situation; tendencies that city plans seek—though not always successfully—to control and correct. In short, the structure of the city, as we find it, is clearly just as much the product of the struggle and efforts of its people to live and work together collectively as are its local customs, traditions, social ritual, laws, public opinion, and the prevailing moral order.[3]

The term "area," then, denotes a system of relationships, which involves a regularity of distribution and a unitary ecological character. Although some of these areas are cultural, yet for some reason they are all products of natural forces and reveal the "natural order" as distinct from the "social order," which, as we have already seen, is the result of conscious planning and communication. As such, they are indiscriminately included in the concept "natural area." "Natural areas" are, moreover, areas of function:

A region is called "a natural area" because it comes into existence without design, and performs a function, though the function, as in the case of the slum, may be contrary to anybody's desire. It is a natural area because it has a natural history. The existence of these natural areas, each with its characteristic function, is some indication of the sort of thing the city turns out upon analysis to be—not as has been suggested earlier, an artifact merely, but in some sense, and to some degree an organism.[4]

McKenzie, too, thinks of these "natural areas" as communities, and, like Park, includes cultural characteristics as definitive of them:

[3] Park, "Sociology," *op. cit.*, pp. 27–29.

[4] Park, "The City as a Social Laboratory," in *Chicago: an Experiment in Social Science Research,* edited by Smith and White, p. 9.

The general effect of the continuous processes of invasions and accommodations is to give to the developed community well-defined areas, each having its own peculiar selective and cultural characteristics. Such units of communal life may be termed "natural areas," or formations, to use the term of the plant ecologist. In any case, these areas of selection and function may comprise many subformations or associations which become part of the organic structure of the district or of the community as a whole.[5]

Burgess likewise regards "natural areas" as communities, but classifies these as ecological, cultural, and political. To him, these are not spatially coincident, and each reveals a different sort of unity. Of these the ecological area is thought of "almost exclusively in terms of location and movement," and is regarded as a basis of determination of social selection.[6]

Whatever the contradictions and divergences in these points of view, if we accept Burgess' generic concept of "natural area" as being equivalent to Park's and McKenzie's, then it appears that the term "area" generally signifies a system of some kind of relationships and involves a distribution of concrete elements as well as of social and economic factors. Consequently, McKenzie's definition of ecological structure in terms of roads and buildings does not coincide either with his own definition of "natural areas" as units of the ecological organization, nor with the formulations of other ecologists. It is with this understanding that the discussion of the "natural areas" will be undertaken.

CHARACTERIZATION OF THE ZONES

Ecologists apply the term "natural area" to units of varying sizes and comprehension, which range all the way from

[5] McKenzie, "The Ecological Approach to the Study of the Human Community," in Park, Burgess, *et al., The City,* p. 77.

[6] See Burgess, "Can Neighborhood Work Have a Scientific Basis?" in Park, Burgess, *et al., The City,* p. 144.

the small local subdivisions of a city to the "world community," each of the smaller units being included in the larger one. Although various different areas are mentioned by this school, only five types have been made the subject of investigation. These are the broad economic regions including several cities and towns; the smaller district of the city and its hinterland; the city apart from its hinterland; the zones within the city; and finally the smallest ecological units of the city, which are most generally referred to as "natural areas." Some ecologists speak of the subdivisions of these small "natural areas," *viz.*, neighborhoods, as "natural areas," but the prevailing usage is to regard these as constituent parts of the "natural areas" and to refer to them as such.

Although the zonal pattern was first explicitly formulated by Burgess, he based his assumption upon a study made by McKenzie, *The Neighborhood, a Study of Columbus, Ohio.*

> Following the lead of Hurd, he [McKenzie] observed that the city expands radially from the central business area, and, depending upon topography, this area tends to be the geographic center of the city. It is surrounded by a more or less disintegrated area inhabited by migratory groups with low buying power. Out from these areas range other residential and industrial districts. Population elements are sifted to these areas in terms of their economic status and racial sentiments. These outlying sections maintain business centers at strategic transportation points which are subsidiary to the central business area.[7]

Upon these findings and upon the data of plant ecology and physiology, Burgess based his first formulations of the successive zones or "concentric circles." Subsequent ecological investigations gave him material for fuller definition of the

[7] Dawson, "Sources and Methods of Human Ecology," in *The Fields and Methods of Sociology*, edited by L. L. Bernard, p. 291, New York. Copyright 1934. Reprinted by permission of the publishers, Farrar & Rinehart, Inc.

zones, not only in terms of the economic level of the populations and of the economic use of the land in each zone, but

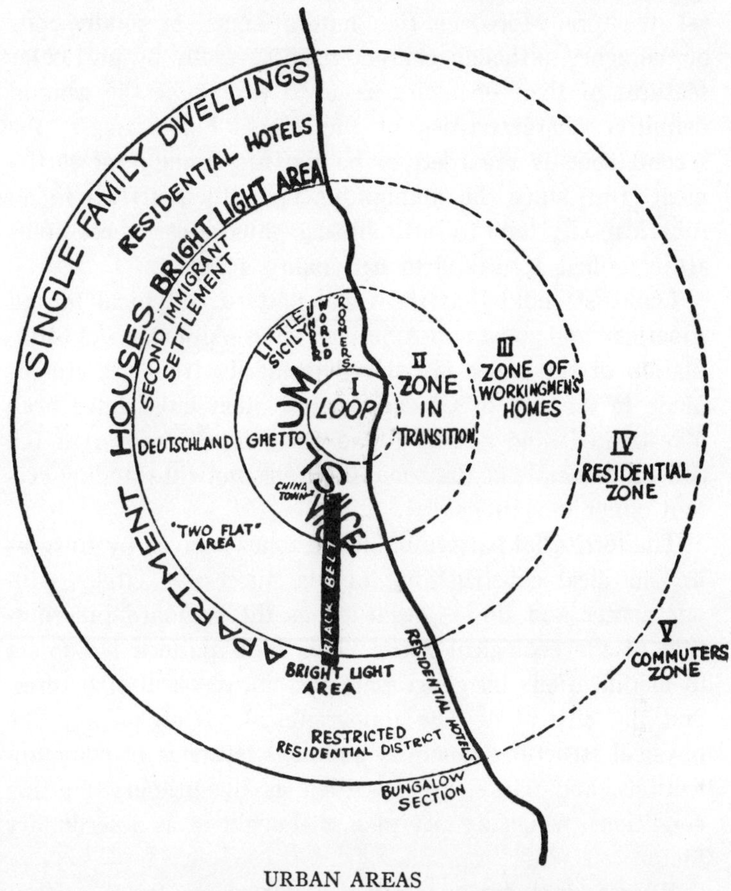

URBAN AREAS

From Park, Burgess, *et al.*, *The City,* p. 55.

also in terms of physical, cultural, social, psychological, and political factors, and, indeed, in terms of almost any arbitrarily selected characteristic.

Thus, the definition of the zones came to include more

and more elements, until now human ecologists find it possible to treat them as well differentiated units in the ecological structure. Moreover, the "natural areas" or subdivisions of the zones, although characterized severally by particular features of their own, are assumed to exhibit the general definitive characteristics of the zones. For example, the second zone is regarded to be the first immigrant settlement. But, since the immigrants upon their arrival in an American city tend to settle in segregated areas, these areas are classified according to nationality groups.

Ecologists hold that the zonal pattern is typical for all American and some non-American cities. Although the formulation of the zones is derived primarily from the studies made in the city of Chicago, a few other cities have been investigated, and it was found that these conform to the general principle of the zonal divisions, notwithstanding certain minor deviations.

The territorial patterning of the zones is given by Burgess in "an ideal construction" of five successive circles with one center and this is regarded as the standard presentation of the ecological zones. This ideal pattern is subject to modifications by geographic factors, physical structures, and the city plan. The topographical variations and the physical structures, such as buildings, systems of communications, and parks, are regarded as the primary limiting conditions, while the city plan is thought of as a secondary factor.

Burgess includes the following factors under the variations of topography which distort the zonal pattern: (*a*) Elevation in topography forming sections which attract for residence the higher income levels of populations. (*b*) A site on a lake front such as that which, for instance, modifies the concentric circles in Chicago to semi-circles and which tends to attract the wealthier residents to its shores. (*c*)

Natural barriers, like rivers which divide a city into sections and serve as obstacles to movement. Thus:

The north and south branches of the Chicago River divide the city into three parts, the North Side, the West Side, and the South Side. These parts of the city have developed to a considerable extent independently, have specialized functions, are the habitat of more or less divergent racial and cultural groups, and possess a certain degree of sectional consciousness as in part indicated by the South Park Board, the West Park Board, and the Lincoln Park Board, and by the customary territorial recognition of these sections in political action.[8]

Banks of rivers are said to be "the location of early industrial establishments, but consequently the place of residence of the first immigrants."[9] (*d*) Artificial barriers like elevated railroads, influencing "community organization" and preventing "to a greater or less degree the free movement for business, industry, and population in accordance with the principle of radial extension outward to the peripheries from the Central Business District."[10]

Burgess points out that "the elevation of the complicated system of railroad lines in Chicago has had the effect of dividing large areas by artificial barriers into more or less isolated and self-sufficient local communities. These 'walled-in' communities in consequence of this derived economic and social solidarity tend to resist the changes involved in the pressure of radial extension outward from the center."[11]

The second condition limiting and modifying the zonal pattern is the "checkerboard street plan" including the structure of the local transportation system. According to Burgess, if the factor of the checkerboard plan "were operating alone, community growth would not be radial but

[8] Burgess, "Urban Areas," in *Chicago: an Experiment in Social Science Research,* edited by Smith and White, p. 120.

[9] *Ibid.*

[10] *Ibid.*, pp. 119–20.

[11] *Ibid.*, pp. 120–21.

at right angles outward from the center of the city." In Chicago, for instance, he says:

A natural tendency under the checkerboard plan has been to lay out the local system of street railroads and rapid transportation on or near the main arterial streets running north and south, east and west. The result has been to accelerate the force of radial expansion on arterial streets running at right angles to the Central Business District, but to retard and even impede the tendency to radial expansion on the oblique angles which ran across rather than with the checkerboard street formation. The total effect of the superimposition of the square pattern of the checkerboard street plan upon the circular pattern of urban zones is to give the typical American city, like Columbus, Ohio, or Fort Worth, Texas, the form of a Maltese cross.[12]

In spite of the distortions occasioned by these factors, the ecologists find that they are not of sufficient significance to undermine the regularity of the zonal pattern, so that the regular circles presented in Burgess' "ideal construction" are used as bases of generalization. Zorbaugh, in his description of the zonal pattern, says, for example:

Ideally, this gross segregation may be represented by a series of concentric circles, and such tends to be the *actual fact* where there are no complicating geographical factors.

Such is a generalized description of the gross anatomy of the city—the typical structure of a modern American commercial and industrial city. Of course, no city quite conforms to this ideal scheme. Physical barriers such as rivers, lakes, and rises of land may modify the growth and structure of the individual city, as is strikingly demonstrated in the cases of New York, Pittsburgh, and Seattle. Railroads, with their belts of industry, cut through this generalized scheme, breaking the city up into sections; and lines of local transportation, along the more travelled of which grow up retail business streets, further modify the structure of the city.

The structure of the individual city, then, while always exhibiting the generalized zones described above, is built about this

[12] Burgess, "Urban Areas," *op. cit.*, p. 121.

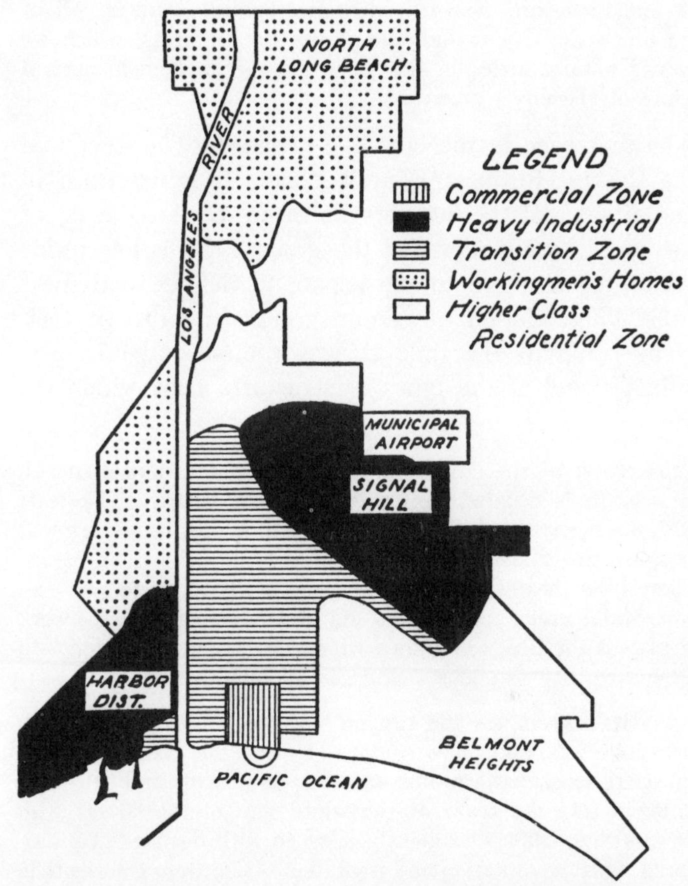

LAND USAGE MAP, LONG BEACH, CALIFORNIA

"The fundamental concept of city growth as developed by E. W. Burgess is applicable to the city of Long Beach, although the form of radial expansion in concentric circles from the center outward, as presented by him, is somewhat distorted, due to the natural contour of the ground and the natural fixed boundaries." Elsa Schneider Longmoor and Erle Fiske Young, "Ecological Interrelationships of Juvenile Delinquency, Dependency, and Population Mobility: A Cartographic Analysis of Data from Long Beach, California," *The American Journal of Sociology*, XLI, 601–2.

framework of transportation, business organization and industry, park and boulevard systems, and topographical features. All of these break the city up into numerous smaller areas, which we may call natural areas, in that they are the unplanned, natural product of the city's growth.[13]

The first zone in the city is designated "The Loop" or "The Central Business District Zone." It is described in terms of some of the interests which are centered in it; of some of the occupations of the groups who either reside there or come there to participate in definite activities; of the differentiation of certain groups in terms of their activities and of the time at which these activities predominate; and of the types of structures built within the zone.

At the center of the city as the focus of its commercial, social, and civic life is situated the Central Business District. The heart of this district is the downtown retail district with its department stores, its smart shops, its office buildings, its clubs, its banks, its hotels, its theaters, its museums, and its headquarters of economic, social, civic, and political life. Encircling this area of work and play is the less well-known wholesale Business District with its "market," its warehouses, and storage buildings.[14]

By day its skyscrapers and canyon-like streets are thronged with shoppers, clerks, and office workers. During the evening, crowds of pleasure seekers swarm into theaters, restaurants and cafés and out again into the blaze of the white way of the streets with their towering edifices brilliantly adorned with displays of multicolored signs of salutation and invitation. Aside from transients in hotels, homeless men as hoboes and "home guards" (Casual resident workers), and dwellers in Chinatown, the central business district has few inhabitants.[15]

[13] Zorbaugh, "The Natural Areas of the City," in *The Urban Community*, edited by Burgess, pp. 221–22; italics mine. See map, p. 213.

[14] Burgess, *op. cit.*, p. 114.

[15] Burgess, "Residential Segregation in American Cities," *The Annals of the American Academy of Political and Social Science*, Pub. No. 2180, November, 1928, p. 2.

The second zone is called the "Zone in Transition" or the "Zone of Deterioration," and it is usually alluded to as an interstitial area, being in a state of transition from a residential to a business and industrial area. This zone is described in terms of types of structures and utilities. It is thought of as being in a state of physical deterioration and social disorganization, the latter being revealed in high rates of such factors as delinquency, crime, mental and physical disease, bootlegging, and sexual vice. It is further delimited in terms of the race, the nationality of the residents, and the status of the immigrants; in terms of certain aspects of personalities, aspirations, and ideals of the population—their cultural and religious, economic, occupational and social status; in terms of certain aspects of their mode of life and the degree of family integration; in terms of the composition, mobility, and growth of the population; and finally it is described in terms of the prevailing institutions of the area.

> Surrounding the Central Business District are areas of residential deterioration caused by the encroaching of business and industry from Zone I . . . with a factory district for its inner belt and an outer ring of retrogressive neighborhoods, of first-settlement immigrant colonies, of rooming-house districts, of homeless-men areas, of resorts of gambling, bootlegging, sexual vice, and of breeding-places of crime. In this area of physical deterioration and social disorganization our studies show the greatest concentration of cases of poverty, bad housing, juvenile delinquency, family disintegration, physical and mental disease. As families and individuals prosper, they escape from this area into Zone III beyond, leaving behind as marooned as residium of the defeated, leaderless, and helpless.[16]

Here in the rooming-house districts—"the purgatory of 'lost souls' "—are the "mobile and mixed population of youth

[16] Burgess, "Urban Areas," in *Chicago: an Experiment in Social Science Research,* edited by Smith and White, pp. 114–16.

and old age, aspiring and defeated individuals, pleasure-seeking Bohemians and hard-working students, rural Fundamentalists and radical freethinkers, and of law-abiding citizens and professional criminals."[17]

Near by is the Latin Quarter, where creative and rebellious spirits resort. The slums are . . . crowded to overflowing with immigrant colonies—the Ghetto, Little Sicily, Greektown, Chinatown—fascinatingly combining old world heritages and American adaptations. Wedging out from here is the Black Belt, with its free and disorderly life. The area of deterioration, while essentially one of decay, of stationary or declining population, is also one of regeneration, as witness the mission, the settlement, the artists' colony, radical centers—all obsessed with the vision of a new and better world.[18]

The third zone is designated as "The Zone of Workingmen's Homes" or "The Zone of Independent Workingmen's Homes," and it is defined in terms of the types of houses, population composition, the occupation and certain social aspects of the life of the residents, and their motives in selecting this zone for residence.

In American cities the zone of workingmen's homes is generally an area of second immigrant settlement. Its inhabitants are constantly being recruited from those making their escape from the zone of transition, but at the same time are being depleted by those who are seeking more desirable residences in the zone beyond.[19]

Its residents are those who desire to live near but not too close to their work. . . Its boundaries have been roughly determined by the plotting of the two-flat dwelling, generally of frame construction, with the owner living on the lower floor with a tenant on the other. While the father works in the factory the son and daughter typically have jobs in the Loop, attend dance halls and

[17] Burgess, *op. cit.*, p. 2.

[18] Burgess, "The Growth of the City: an Introduction to a Research Project," in Park, Burgess, *et al.*, *The City*, p. 56.

[19] Burgess, "Residential Segregation," *The Annals of the American Academy of Political and Social Science,* Pub. No. 2180, p. 2.

motion pictures in the bright-light areas, and plan upon marriage to set up homes in Zone IV.[20]

The residents here are said to be predominantly "factory and shop workers, but skilled and thrifty."[21]

The fourth zone is characterized as "The Zone of Better Residences" or "The Residential Zone." Its distinctive characteristics are given in terms of types of houses, the nationality and class of the residents, their occupation, sex distribution, social types, political, social, and intellectual interests, education, ideals, and status of women. And finally it is marked by certain local centers of economic and social institutions called "satellite Loops."

Extending beyond the neighborhoods of second immigrant settlements, we come to the Zone of Better Residences in which the great middle-classes of native-born Americans live, small business men, professional people, clerks, and salesmen. Once communities of single homes, these are becoming in Chicago apartment-house and residential-hotel areas. Within these areas at strategic points are found local business centers of such growing importance that they have been called "satellite Loops." The typical constellation of business and recreational units includes a bank, one or more United Cigar Stores, a drug store, a high class restaurant, an automobile display row, and a so-called "wonder" motion-picture theater. With the addition of a dancing palace, a cabaret, and a smart hotel, the satellite Loop also becomes a "bright-light area" attracting a city-wide attendance. In this zone men are outnumbered by women, independence in voting is frequent, newspapers and books have wide circulation, and women are elected to the state legislature.[22]

The residents are said to

have had high school if not college education. Their intellectual status is manifested by the type of books and magazines in the

[20] Burgess, "Urban Areas," in *Chicago: an Experiment in Social Science Research,* edited by Smith and White, p. 116.

[21] Burgess, "The Growth of the City," in Park, Burgess, *et al., The City,* p. 56.

[22] Burgess, *op. cit.,* pp. 116–17.

home, by the prevalence of women's clubs and by independence in voting. This is the home of the great middle class with ideals still akin to those of rural American society. In this zone are also located apartment and residential hotel areas with their urbanized and sophisticated tenants.[23]

The last zone considered in the city proper, "The Commuters' Zone," is differentiated in terms of the types of houses, degree of segregation of the communities within it, its "atmosphere," the economic and social status of the residents and their mode of life.

> The commuters' zone comprises the suburban districts of the city which combine the atmosphere of village residence with access by rapid transit or by automobile to the downtown metropolitan center for work, shopping, and entertainment. Residence in restricted suburban communities implies an economic rating sufficient to acquire a bungalow costing more than a stipulated minimum figure and an automobile of commensurate rank.[24]

This zone is apparently made up of "small cities, towns, and hamlets," which are mainly

> dormitory suburbs, because the majority of men residing there spend the day at work in the Loop . . . returning only for the night. . . Thus the mother and the wife become the center of family life. . . The communities in this Commuters' Zone are probably the most highly segregated of any in the entire metropolitan region, including in their range the entire gamut from an incorporated village run in the interests of crime and vice, such as Burnham, to Lake Forest, with its wealth, culture, and public spirit.[25]

The ecologists supplement these general classifications by differentiating the various zones with respect to specific criteria, both qualitative and quantitative. An example of the qualitative distinction of the zones is the division accord-

[23] Burgess, "Residential Segregation," *The Annals of the American Academy of Political and Social Science,* Pub. No. 2180, pp. 2–3.

[24] *Ibid.,* p. 4.

[25] Burgess, "Urban Areas," *Chicago: an Experiment in Social Science Research,* edited by Smith and White, p. 117.

ing to family types by Ernest R. Mowrer in his studies *Family Disorganization* and *The Family, Its Organization and Disorganization.* The author states that:

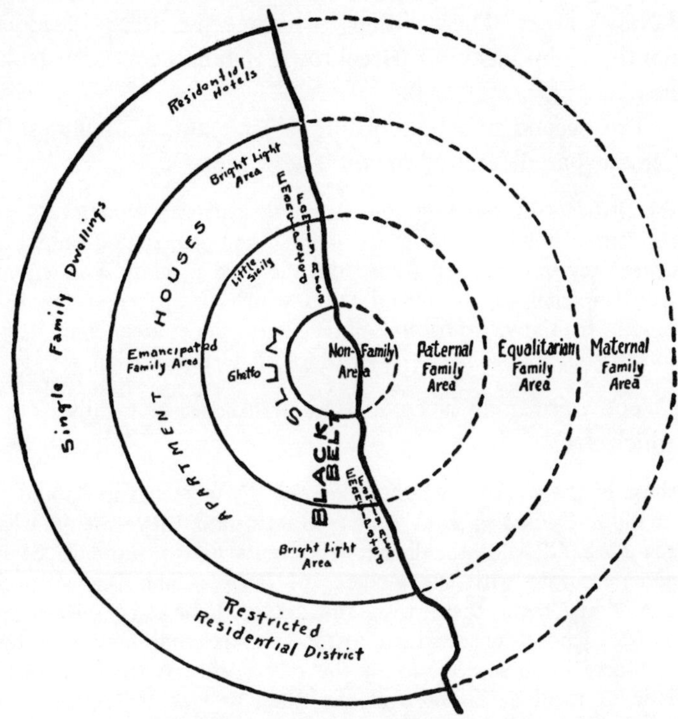

FAMILY AREAS IN CHICAGO, 1920

From E. R. Mowrer, *Family Disorganization; an Introduction to a Sociological Analysis,* p. 113.

Areas of the city may be classified with reference to the type of family life found in each community. Chicago, from this point of view, may be divided into five types of areas: (1) non-family areas, (2) emancipated family areas, (3) paternal family areas, (4) equalitarian family areas, and (5) maternal family areas.[26]

[26] Mowrer, *Family Disorganization,* p. 110.

He visualizes these areas as falling into a zonal pattern which he superimposes upon that evolved by Burgess and described above. He finds that the Central Business District Zone and the immediately adjoining districts are the "non-family" areas. These "tend to be one-sex areas—predominantly male—such as Greektown, Chinatown, and Hobohemia."

The second zone, according to the author includes the "emancipated family" areas. These are:

> the districts of rooming-houses and kitchenette apartments and residential hotels. These areas attract the emancipated family because they offer the isolation from the local primary contacts and freedom from group control upon which this type of family is based. In the organization of the city these areas tend to be interstitial, following the lines of rapid transportation.

The third zone is comprised of "paternal family" types which are:

> those of the workers, characteristic of the tenement areas and the immigrant colonies, such as the Ghetto and Little Sicily, where the husband rules the home. Low rents and a standard of life commensurate with the incomes of laborers and the culturally unadjusted make these areas the natural habitat of the working classes, whose conservatism fosters the paternal family pattern. Contacts in these sections of the city approach those characteristic of rural areas more closely than any of the other of the family areas.

The fourth zone is characterized by the "equalitarian family" and is explained as follows:

> Residence within the community tends to extend over a considerable period of time in the interests of contacts with friends and relatives. Since there are children, though families tend to be small, this also makes for less movement in an effort to stabilize school contacts. Greater interest is therefore taken in the neighborhood institutions than is characteristic of the emancipated family.

Regarding the fifth zone, Mowrer says:

> The maternal family areas are those of the commuter, primarily the neighborhoods of the upper bourgeoisie. . . Contacts in these areas are largely primary as far as the wife and children are concerned, though less so for the husband. Neighborhood opinion and conformity to the accepted patterns of social intercourse are rigidly held to. Family prestige is largely a matter of family connections and the type of home which is maintained.[27]

Although Mowrer's "family type" zones are charted upon the original zonal pattern laid down by Burgess, it is seen upon analysis that the two zonal patterns do not coincide. In fact, Mowrer's zones cut across and overlap Burgess' zonal arrangement. For instance, in his first, or "non-family" zone are also included the Chicago areas of Chinatown, Greektown, and Hobohemia, which according to Burgess are in the second or transitional zone. On the other hand, other areas within this transitional zone, such as Little Sicily and the Ghetto fall into Mowrer's third zone —that of the "paternal family." Furthermore, although Mowrer's description of the "equalitarian family" area corresponds to Burgess' definition of the fourth or "better residential" zone, Mowrer apparently bisects this fourth zone identifying the outer half of it with his fifth, or "maternal family," area of the commuter.[28] Finally, although Mowrer gives five types of family area only four of them fall into a distinctly zonal pattern. The second, or "emancipated family," type is interspersed within the zones of the "paternal family" and the "equalitarian family": "The areas of the emancipated family tend to be *interstitial,* in the sense that they spread across other areas, following the lines of rapid transportation."[29]

Whether Mowrer's classification of these areas of the city

[27] Mowrer, *The Family, Its Organization and Disorganization,* pp. 188–90.

[28] See maps, pp. 209, 219.

[29] Mowrer, *op. cit.,* p. 112; italics mine.

according to family types contributes to the concept of the zonal pattern as developed by Burgess and accepted by other ecologists is a moot point. However, Burgess does present this family differentiation as a confirmation of the zonal differentiation of the areas within the city. He further quotes Mowrer's figures for divorce rates as related to family types, to bear out his own conception of the zonal pattern.[30] The discrepancy between the spatial disposition of family types and that of the numerous factors in terms of which Burgess territorially delimits the zones indicates that either (*a*) the two zonal arrangements are not of the same universe; or (*b*) one general zonal pattern does not hold good for all factors and therefore more than one zonal arrangement is possible. In the latter case, zones should be treated, not as entities, but as arbitrary abstractions in terms of any one factor. This, however, would contradict Burgess' definitive delimitation of the zones. Needless to say, it would vitiate seriously the ecological concept of the "natural area" as a territorially delimited unit.

THE CONCEPT OF THE "GRADIENT"

For the delimitation of the zones on quantitative lines, the *fundamentum divisionis* employed by ecologists is the "gradient," defined by Burgess as: "the rate of change of a variable condition like poverty, or home ownership, or births, or divorce, from the standpoint of its distribution over a given area."[31] The principle here is that in a growing city rates of various phenomena vary directly or inversely with the distance from the center of dominance, the central business district zone. In this way the "gradations" in the rates are said to measure the degree of dominance

[30] See Burgess, "The Determination of Gradients in the Growth of the City," *Publications of the American Sociological Society*, XXI (1927), 178–83.

[31] *Ibid.*, p. 178.

which the center exercises over the areas of the city. The principle underlying the gradient pattern is that a great many physical, sociological, and economic characteristics are correlated, whether directly or inversely, and that, moreover, these numerous characteristics are spatially arranged in an orderly fashion.

Several ecological studies deal with the determination of gradients. For example, E. Mowrer establishes the gradients for divorce and desertion in the city of Chicago in his monograph *Family Disorganization*. In *Delinquency Areas*, Clifford Shaw, in collaboration with F. M. Zorbaugh, H. D. McKay, and L. S. Cottrell, presents one of the most thorough studies of the gradient pattern of juvenile delinquency in the same city. He set out to show that, with certain exceptions, the rates of juvenile delinquency vary inversely with the distance from the dominant center. R. Clyde White has worked out the gradients of adult felonies in Indianapolis[32] and found that, in general, they conform to the gradient pattern of juvenile delinquency in Chicago as computed by Shaw.[33] White also found a correlation between the distribution of adult felony rates and that of family welfare cases, of percentage of land used for business, and of mortality rates.

Such studies of the determination of "gradients" are based upon rates of any one factor computed for areas ranging from one-quarter to one square mile and constituting combinations or divisions of the official U. S. census tracts. The procedure is to include either all areas in the city or only a selected group of areas.

In describing a procedure employed in the city of Chicago, Burgess states that the ecologists selected a particular

[32] See White, "The Relation of Felonies to Environmental Factors in Indianapolis," *Social Forces,* X (May, 1932), 498–509.

[33] Shaw, *Delinquency Areas.*

series of census tracts which cut across the zones from the first to the fifth, in a line which was thought to have "experienced the full force of radial expansion."[34]

> This line of tracts running west along West Madison Street starts in the central business district with the intersection at State Street which 200,000 people pass daily, and extends through the zone in transition, the zone of second immigrant settlement, the middle-class residential district zone, and ends in the higher-class residential district zone of Oak Park.[35]

The twenty census tracts which fall along this nine-mile line were broken into thirty-six units, each one-quarter of a mile wide. Rates within these unit districts were computed for various factors, such as home ownership, poverty, divorce, desertion, and juvenile delinquency, as well as the percentages of the total population of males, of persons of twenty-one and over, and of the foreign-born. These units were further combined into one-mile unit districts and averages of the rates for various factors found for each, giving equal weight to each sub-unit district. Thus, rates were ascertained for a variable condition for the inner and outer mile of each zone.

As is evident from the Table, pages 226, 227, the rates of various factors, whether calculated for the smaller, quarter-mile or for the larger, one-mile area, exhibit a gradient pattern. That is, a relatively continuous progression or regression of rates is manifested along radial lines that cut the successive zones. In other words, the five zones, as presented by Burgess, cease to be sharply demarcated from each other, as they appear to be when described in terms of qualitative factors, such as economic and educational standards or types of profession, and so forth. The standard zonal boundaries do not serve as demarcations in respect of the ecological or social phenomena they circumscribe, but are arbitrary divi-

[34] Burgess, *op. cit.*, p. 179. [35] *Ibid.*

sions. They can be treated only as convenient methodological devices for the classification of data under smaller divisions than the total area included in a particular study. The zone can have significance only if it marks a distinction of gradients or between gradients. Otherwise, if the gradients are as continuous as the name implies, the zonal lines can be drawn indifferently at any radius from the center.

Yet Burgess' description of the five zones clearly indicates that ecologists envisage these zones as distinct units, differentiated in terms of numerous factors. This conception is inherent in the process of succession, which implies a sequence of distinct forms or types. If succession, as an aspect of radial expansion,[36] comprises "the tendency of each inner zone to extend its area by the invasion of the next outer zone,"[37] then each zone must show characteristics which are so distinct that this encroachment of one zone upon the other constitutes succession. For we saw that succession signifies the sequence not only of distinct physical features, but also of distinct economic and cultural characteristics;[38] in fact, "the thing that characterizes a succession is a *complete change* in population type . . . or a complete change in use."[39] Also implicit in this thesis is the fact that the zonal factors in terms of which the succession takes place remain relatively constant.

Furthermore, the division into five zones represents "the natural organization of the city,"[40] and the zones are "num-

[36] Burgess, "The Growth of the City," in Park, Burgess, *et al., The City,* p. 50.

[37] *Ibid.,* p. 50.

[38] See McKenzie, "The Scope of Human Ecology," *The Urban Community,* edited by Burgess, p. 180, and Park, "Succession, an Ecological Concept," *American Sociological Review,* Vol. I, No. 2, April, 1936.

[39] McKenzie, *op. cit.,* p. 181; italics mine.

[40] Walter C. Reckless, "The Distribution of Commercialized Vice in the City: a Sociological Analysis," in *The Urban Community,* edited by Burgess, p. 195.

TABLE

Poverty, Divorce, Juvenile Delinquency, and Home Ownership Rates in Chicago

(Poverty and Divorce Rates per 1,000 Population, Boy-Delinquency Rates per 1,000 Boys of the Juvenile Court Age in the Population [11–17 Years, Inclusive], and Home Ownership Rates [Percentage of Families Owning Their Homes], by Unit Districts)[a]

Urban Area	Unit District	Cases per 1,000 Population: Males and Females, All Ages: Poverty, ¼-mile unit	Poverty, 1-mile unit	Divorce, ¼-mile unit	Divorce, 1-mile unit	Males, 11–17 Years: Boy Delinquency, ¼-mile unit	Boy Delinquency, 1-mile unit	Percentage of Families Owning Their Homes: Home Ownership, ¼-mile unit	Home Ownership, 1-mile unit
Central business district zone	A 1	1.9		2.6		539		0	
	2	1.9	2.0	2.6	2.0	539	443	0	0.5
	3	2.0		1.3		346		1	
	4	2.0		1.3		346		1	
Zone in transition (area of first immigrant settlement)	B 5	3.9		2.9		57		4	
	6	3.9	3.2	2.9	2.9	57	58	4	5.5
	7	2.5		2.9		58		7	
	8	2.5		2.9		58		7	
	C 9	1.5		4.8		20		7	
	10	1.5	2.1	4.9	4.3	37	27	12	12.3
	11	2.2		3.3		38		15	
	12	3.1		4.0		12		15	

	D 13	3.0	1.3	3.0	3.4	16	15	15	17.3
	14	0.8		4.2		7		18	
	15	1.0		2.7		13		18	
	16	0.3		3.2		25		18	
Zone of second immigrant settlement (workingmen's homes)	E 17	0.2	0.1	2.6	2.0	4	4	17	19.8
	18	0.2		2.6		4		16	
	19	0.0		1.4		4		23	
	20	0.0		1.4		4		23	
Middle-class residential district zone	F 21	0.0	0.1	0.7	1.3	0	0	29	33.3
	22	0.0		1.9		0		30	
	23	0.3		1.4		0		31	
	24	0.1		1.2		0		40	
	G 25	0.1	0.1	1.2	1.2	0	0	40	40.0
	26	0.1		1.2		0		40	
	27	0.1		1.2		0		40	
	28	0.1		1.2		0		40	
Higher-class residential district zone	H 29	n.d.		n.d.		n.d.		40	51.0
	30							40	
	31							62	
	32							62	
	I 33	n.d.		n.d.		n.d.		62	62.0
	34							62	
	35							62	
	36							62	

[a] Burgess, "The Determination of Gradients in the Growth of the City," *Publications of the American Sociological Society*, XXI, 180, 183, Table I and Table III. (Numbers bracketed were derived from the same census tract. Poverty rates derived from *Map of the Distribution of Philanthropy and Poverty, 1920–21*, by Fay B. Karpf and Erle F. Young; divorce rates obtained from *Divorce Map of Chicago, 1919*, by Ernest R. Mowrer; boy-delinquency rates secured from *Map of Cases of Boys in the Cook County Juvenile Court, 1923–24*, by Clifford R. Shaw; home ownership rates from United States Census, 1920.)

bered to designate both the successive zones of urban extension and types of areas differentiated in the process of expansion."[41] As successive zones and as differentiated areas, then, they must show distinct characteristics in all or most of the factors in terms of which succession takes place. McKenzie's criterion of succession is a complete change of population type or change in use. Because ecologists do not state precisely what constitutes a population *type,* it is left to us to surmise that succession of population is a displacement in terms of any and all factors which may be regarded as comprising a type. The more general change in use is usually use of land. This type of succession also implies a change of population type, since it refers to changes such as those "of a residential area into a business area or of a business into an industrial district."[42]

As we have seen, this approach also carries with it the idea of the differentiation of the zonal pattern in terms of ecological development or evolution, in terms of the degree of equilibrium, stability, and dominance—ecological, economic, and social—and of varying degrees of susceptibility to invasion.

The very concept "natural areas" is presumed to define an actual entity in terms of "natural" attributes. In fact, ecologists set the "natural areas" over against administrative areas, such as political wards or city limits, established by governmental authorities and said to be *arbitrary delimitations* which do not coincide with the *actual divisions* of the "natural communities."[43] Hence, for ecologists the five zones are *ipso facto* ecological entities.

If such be the case, the gradient principle is incompatible with the zonal hypothesis, unless we take refuge in some un-

[41] Burgess, *op. cit.,* p. 50.

[42] McKenzie, "The Ecological Approach," in Park, Burgess, *et al., The City,* p. 75.

[43] See Zorbaugh, "The Natural Areas of the City," in *The Urban Community,* edited by Burgess, pp. 224–28.

specified factors which give each zone a unitary character and which represent a gradient pattern entirely coincident with the five zones. Of the so-called ecological factors, land values, for instance, do not seem to show such a bias, varying from the center outward on their own account and apart from the standard zonal pattern. Land values, in turn, are used as an index to mobility, so that assumedly mobility, too, follows the same pattern.[44] The type and condition of the physical structures are claimed to coincide with the zonal pattern, but if, as ecologists hold, they reflect the economic and social organization and strata, then these would also be expected to fall in with the zonal pattern. However, as we saw, they follow the continuous gradient pattern of "dominance."

THE SUBDIVISIONS OF THE ZONES

Of the different types of areas, ecologists have accorded the most thorough and extensive study to the subdivisions of the zones which they designate simply as "natural areas." Perhaps no other concept of the ecological theory has been subject to such divergence of interpretation, such a variety of classifications. Partial definitions, contradictory and vague statements, differences in approach, and the absence of a single rounded-out and inclusive definition make this concept almost impossible to analyze.

Its designations alone are a maze of words. McKenzie speaks of "natural areas" as segregations on the basis of

[44] In spite of this obvious deduction Park tells us that a different degree of mobility marks the zones: "Within the area bounded on the one hand by the central business district and on the other by the suburbs, the city tends to take the form of a series of concentric circles. These different regions, located at different relative distances from the center, are characterized by different degrees of mobility of the population." Park, "The Urban Community as a Spacial Pattern and a Moral Order," in *The Urban Community*, edited by Burgess, p. 10.

"such factors as race, language, income, and occupation."[45] Wirth considers them to be groupings "according to selective and cultural characteristics."[46] Park refers to them as areas of "competitive co-operation," each with "its own characteristic milieu, each performing its specific function in the urban economy as a whole."[47] He also speaks of business, residential, industrial, and racial areas, as well as moral regions.[48] Nels Anderson defines them as occupational units of the city and classifies them as areas of "residence, commerce, industry, transportation, recreation, administration, etc."[49] Burgess classifies them into ecological, cultural, and political areas or communities.[50] According to Dawson, the "concentric zones divide into smaller subsidiary natural areas in which are segregated, not by design, the economic and cultural groups with their own appropriate configuration of institutions and divisions of labor."[51] Vivien Palmer distinguishes two types of "natural areas," the ecological and the social, the latter falling into three classes: cultural, political, and marginal or interstitial areas.[52] Finally, Eubank suggests a definition of the "natural area" as "a section within a larger territory (usually within a city) in which there is some characteristic so outstanding and distinctive

[45] McKenzie, *The Metropolitan Community,* p. 240.

[46] Wirth, "A Bibliography of the Urban Community," in Park, Burgess, *et al., The City,* p. 188.

[47] Park, "The City as a Social Laboratory," in *Chicago: an Experiment in Social Science Research,* edited by Smith and White, p. 9.

[48] See Park, "Sociology," in *Research in the Social Sciences,* edited by Gee, p. 29.

[49] Anderson, "The Trend of Urban Sociology," in *Trends in American Sociology,* edited by Lundberg, Anderson, Bain, p. 272.

[50] Burgess, "Can Neighborhood Work Have a Scientific Basis?" in Park, Burgess, *et al., The City,* pp. 144–47.

[51] Dawson, "Sources and Methods of Human Ecology," in *The Fields and Methods of Sociology,* edited by L. L. Bernard, p. 292, New York. Copyright 1934. Reprinted by permission of the publishers, Farrar & Rinehart, Inc.

[52] Vivien Palmer, *Field Studies in Sociology.*

that it constitutes a designation by which the vicinity may be tersely and graphically designated and to some extent described."[53]

In one place McKenzie defines "natural areas" as "biological and cultural subdivisions of a city's population"[54] and in another as segregations of populations according to "their economic efficiency and their rôle in the life of the community."[55] Park constantly refers to "natural areas" as "communities,"[56] while Zorbaugh warns us not to confuse "communities" with "natural areas," the latter being usually "trade areas": "These natural areas, which are usually 'trade areas,' are not to be confused with communities. They are the result of the economic rather than of the cultural process."[57] To Zorbaugh, then, communities are the result of the cultural process, while "natural areas" are the result of the economic process.

Zorbaugh, furthermore, tells us that "natural areas" do not necessarily coincide with "communities" or, by his interpretation, with "cultural groupings." "Communities may or may not conform to natural areas, and natural areas may exist without corresponding communities as the Near North Side clearly illustrates."[58] However, elsewhere he makes a statement in complete contradiction to the above, saying that:

> From the mobile competing stream of the city's population each natural area of the city tends to collect the particular individuals predestined to it. These individuals, in turn, give to the area a peculiar character. And as a result of this segregation, the *natural areas of the city tend to become distinct cultural areas as well*—

[53] Earle Eubank, *The Concepts of Sociology*, p. 376.

[54] McKenzie, "The Ecological Approach," in Park, Burgess, *et al.*, *The City*, p. 78.

[55] McKenzie, *op. cit.*, p. 245.

[56] See, for example, Park, *op. cit.*, p. 29.

[57] Zorbaugh, *The Gold Coast and the Slum*, p. 231 n.

[58] *Ibid.*, pp. 231–32 n.

a "black belt" or a Harlem, a Little Italy, a Chinatown, a "stem" of the "hobo," a rooming-house world, a "Towertown," or a "Greenwich Village," a "Gold Coast," and the like—each with its characteristic complex of institutions, customs, beliefs, standards of life, traditions, attitudes, sentiments, and interests. The physical individuality of the natural areas of the city is reemphasized by the cultural individuality of the populations segregated over them. *Natural areas and natural cultural groups tend to coincide.*

A natural area is a geographical area characterized both by a physical individuality and by the cultural characteristics of the people who live in it.[59]

Zorbaugh further tells us that

natural areas, moreover, are not always so well defined as this ideal scheme might seem to indicate. In a city like Chicago, where natural barriers are few, a natural area may be defined almost wholly in terms of land values, as is the case of the area occupied by the Gold Coast in the Near North Side.[60]

Yet Burgess tells us that, in a study made of Chicago, it was found that

the lines of physical separation, with some few exceptions, were also the dividing lines between local communities. It was also found that while these local communities were in a state of change, more or less rapid as the case might be, the changes taking place were more or less localized by the effects of these permanent physical barriers.[61]

The only possible extenuation of such contradictions would be that the progress of empirical studies revealed new conditions which called for theoretical reformulations. However, the ecologists have not admitted this necessity, nor do they actually and explicitly repudiate their earlier formulations.

[59] Zorbaugh, "The Natural Areas of the City," in *The Urban Community,* edited by Burgess, p. 223; italics mine.

[60] Zorbaugh, *op. cit.,* p. 232.

[61] Burgess, "Basic Social Data," in *Chicago: an Experiment in Social Science Research,* edited by Smith and White, p. 59.

Zorbaugh is not alone in such internal inconsistencies. Burgess, for example, classifies the "natural areas" into three types of community—the ecological, the cultural, and the political. He bases this upon an assumption that "markedly different social relationships may have their roots in the conditions of a common territorial location." He adds:

> Indeed, it is just these outstanding differences in communal activities, viewed in relation to their geographic background, which have caused much of the confusion in the use of the term "community." For community life, as conditioned by the distribution of individuals and institutions over an area, has at least three quite different aspects.[62]

These three aspects (the ecological, cultural, and political) correspond to the types of areas:

> First of all, there is the community viewed almost exclusively in terms of location and movement. How far has the area itself, by its very topography and by all its other external and physical characteristics, as railroads, parks, types of housing, conditioned community formation and exerted a determining influence upon the distribution of its inhabitants and upon their movements and life? To what extent has it had a selective effect in sifting and sorting families over the area by occupation, nationality, and economic or social class? To what extent is the work of neighborhood or community institutions promoted or impeded by favorable or unfavorable location? How far do geographical distances within or without the community symbolize social distances? This apparently "natural" organization of the human community, so similar in the formation of plant and animal communities, may be called the "ecological community."[63]

Here the physical factors assume primary importance, and the ecological community resolves itself into a physical category, which apparently determines the selection, location, and movement of populations and institutions, and hence conditions the formation, growth, and mode of life

[62] Burgess, *op. cit.*, p. 144.

[63] *Ibid.*, pp. 144–45.

of the community. Burgess describes the cultural community as follows:

> The community may be conceived in terms of the effects of communal life in a given area upon the formation or the maintenance of a local culture. Local culture includes those sentiments, forms of conduct, attachments, and ceremonies which are characteristic of a locality, which have either originated in the area or have become identified with it. This aspect of local life may be called "the cultural community."[64]

If "communal life" is taken in the specifically ecological sense, then the cultural community signifies a local social organization as it is conditioned by physical and geographical factors.

The political community is explained in the following words:

> There remains a third standpoint from which the relation of a local area to group life may be stated. In what ways and to what extent does the fact of common residence in a locality compel or invite its inhabitants to act together? Is there, or may there be developed upon a geographical basis, a community consciousness? Does contiguity by residence insure or predispose to cooperation in at least those conditions of life inherent in geographic location, as transportation, water supply, playgrounds, etc.? Finally, what degree of social and political action can be secured on the basis of local areas? This is the community of the community organization worker and of the politician, and may be described as "the political community." It is upon this concept of the community as a local area that American political organization has been founded.[65]

The political community, then, represents corporate action and community consciousness, based upon common territory or pertaining to the physical factors of the area.

[64] Burgess, *op. cit.*, p. 145.

[65] *Ibid.*, p. 146. Here Burgess apparently uses the term "community" in a sense different from the ecological formulation of this concept.

Of these types of community, Burgess says:

These three definitions of the community are not perhaps altogether mutually exclusive. They do, however, represent three distinctly different aspects of community life that will have to be recognized in any basic study of the community and of community organization.[66]

Burgess then tells us that "the boundaries of local areas determined ecologically, culturally, and politically *seldom, if ever, exactly coincide*."[67] He illustrates this principle by the following example:

A given local area, like Hyde Park in Chicago, may at the same time constitute an ecological, cultural, and political community, while another area like the lower North Side in the same city, which forms a distinct ecological unit, falls apart into several cultural communities and cannot, at any rate from the standpoint of a common and effective public opinion, be said to constitute a going political community. The Black Belt in Chicago comprises one cultural community but overflows several ecological areas and has no means of common political action except through ward lines arbitrarily drawn.[68]

However, Burgess presents a direct contradiction to his statement when he says that "these cultural areas, these states of mind, whether those of immigrant groups, or of economic classes, or of all the other social groupings, in the long run *coincide*, or fall within these areas that are marked off so strikingly by the physical structure of the city,"[69] and that "in the long run the movement and the distribution of nationality and other cultural groups in the city is *determined by the natural units of its physical pattern*."[70]

Thus it turns out that ecological areas both do and do not coincide with cultural areas. What is particularly perplexing to the reader is that such statements as the above are given

[66] *Ibid.*, pp. 146–47. [67] *Ibid.*, p. 147; italics mine. [68] *Ibid.*

[69] Burgess, "The Natural Area as the Unit for Social Work in the Large City," *Proceedings of the National Conference of Social Work*, 1926, pp. 508–9; italics mine. [70] *Ibid.*, p. 510; italics mine.

without the slightest qualification or reference to other statements which so obviously contradict them. The fact that the different implications which the two contradictory statements carry are of grave methodological importance is also overlooked. If these areas do not coincide, then surely the ecological area ceases to be a factor basic to and determining the cultural structure of an area; and, too, the ecological and the social categories cannot be regarded as two aspects of the same whole. Yet Burgess, in the very article in which he asserts that the ecological and the cultural areas do not coincide, says that "ecological or economic forces are naturally basic to the play of cultural forces."[71]

Park holds a more consistent point of view in this respect. He asserts that "every natural area is, or tends to become, in the natural course of events, a cultural area."[72] He, too, presents a classification of the several aspects of community organization, albeit a somewhat different one from that of Burgess. First, we have the ecological organization:

> Within the limits of any community the communal institutions—economic, political, and cultural—will tend to assume a more or less clearly defined and characteristic distribution. For example, the community will always have a center and a circumference, defining the position of each single community to every other. Within the area so defined the local populations and the local institutions will tend to group themselves in some characteristic pattern, dependent upon geography, lines of communication, and land values. This distribution of population and institutions we may call the ecological organization of the community.[73]

The second is the economic organization:

> Within the limits of the ecological organization, so far as a free exchange of goods and services exists, there inevitably grows

[71] Burgess, "Can Neighborhood Work Have a Scientific Basis?" in Park, Burgess, *et al., The City*, p. 150. [72] Park, *op. cit.*, p. 36.

[73] Park, "Community Organization and the Romantic Temper," in Park, Burgess, *et al., The City*, p. 115.

up another type of community organization based on the division of labor. This is what we may call the occupational organization of the community.

The occupational organization, like the ecological, is a product of competition. Eventually every individual member of the community is driven, as a result of competition with every other, to do the thing he *can do* rather than the thing he *would like to do.* Our secret ambitions are seldom realized in our actual occupations. The struggle to live determines finally not only where we shall live within the limits of the community, but what we shall do.[74]

Finally there is the cultural and political organization:

Competition is never unlimited in human society. Always there is custom and law which sets some bounds and imposes some restraints upon the wild and wilful impulses of the individual man. The cultural and political organization of the community rests upon the occupational organization, just as the latter, in turn, grows up in, and rests upon, the ecological organization.

It is this final division or segment of the communal organization with which community-center associations are mainly concerned. Politics, religion, and community welfare, like golf, bridge, and other forms of recreation, are leisure-time activities, and it is the leisure time of the community that we are seeking to organize.[75]

These different aspects of "community" organization, however, do not demarcate the different types of area, since, according to Park, the cultural areas, for instance, tend to coincide with the "natural areas," the latter (it may be assumed) meaning the "ecological areas." Park substantiates this assumption in the following analysis:

Every natural area has, or tends to have, *its* own peculiar traditions, customs, conventions, standards of decency and propriety, and, if not a language of its own, at least a *universe of discourse,* in which words and acts have a meaning which is appreciably different for each local community. It is not difficult to recognize this fact in the case of immigrant communities which still pre-

[74] *Ibid.,* p. 116.

[75] *Ibid.,* pp. 116–17.

serve more or less intact the folkways of their home countries. It is not so easy to recognize that this is true in those cosmopolitan regions of the city where a miscellaneous and transient population mingles in a relatively unrestrained promiscuity. But in these cases the very freedom and the absence of convention is itself, if not a convention, at least an open secret. Even in regions where custom no longer reinforces conscience, public opinion and fashion exercise a powerful external control.[76]

Consequently, each "natural area" of the city is distinguished by its own local customs, conventions, and, in fact, represents what ecologists have defined as "society." Thus the cohesive principles of each would be "consensus" based upon communication. But it is Park again who tells us that the relations within the "natural areas" are symbiotic rather than social:

It does not follow . . . that the populations in the different natural areas of the city can be described as homogeneous. People live together on the whole, not because they are alike, but because they are useful to one another. This is particularly true of great cities, where *social distances are maintained in spite of geographical proximity,* and where every community is likely to be composed of people who live together in relations that can best be described as *symbiotic rather than social.*[77]

If, then, the relations between the individuals within a "natural area" are symbiotic, that is, independent of communication—external and unconscious relations which are "physical and vital rather than customary and moral"[78]—what mystical forces act upon these individuals so that they abide by the same "traditions, customs, conventions, standards of decency and propriety," which are distinct from the customs and traditions of an adjacent "natural area"? By

[76] Park, "Sociology," in *Research in the Social Sciences,* edited by Gee, pp. 36–37.

[77] Park, "The City as a Social Laboratory," in *Chicago: an Experiment in Social Science Research,* edited by Smith and White, p. 10; italics mine.

[78] Park, "Human Ecology," *American Journal of Sociology,* XLII, 15.

what mechanism is it that "every natural area is, or tends to become, in the the natural course of events, a cultural area"?[79]

Having stated that the relations within a "natural area" are symbiotic, Park then asserts that

> it is assumed, in short, partly as a result of selection and segregation, and partly in view of the contagious character of cultural patterns, that people living in natural areas of the same general type and subject to the same social conditions will display, on the whole, the same characteristics.[80]

But if the population in an area is not "homogeneous"[81] and if the relations between the individuals in an area are "symbiotic rather than social," then by what manner or means do these complex cultural patterns become a common heritage? There remains only one interpretation of Park's words: namely, that selection alone determines that the individuals in any area have similar traditions, customs, conventions, standards of decency, and so forth; that these are not preserved by reciprocal communication of ideas, by social interrelationship, but rather in the social isolation of these selected individuals; and that these individuals are, moreover, selected not on the basis of likeness, but "because they are useful to one another." This, however, still does not solve the problem of the social or cultural unity of the "natural area."

Again, Park's assertion of the maintenance of social distance in geographical proximity, "social distances are maintained *in spite* of geographical proximity,"[82] should be set alongside his further statement that "it is because social relations are *so frequently* and *so inevitably* correlated with

[79] Park, "Sociology," in *Research in the Social Sciences,* edited by Gee, p. 36.

[80] *Ibid.*, p. 30.

[81] See Park, "The City as a Social Laboratory," in *Chicago: an Experiment in Social Science Research,* edited by Smith and White, p. 10.

[82] *Ibid.*, p. 10; italics mine.

spacial relations; because physical distances, so frequently are, or seem to be, the indexes of social distances, that statistics have any significance whatever for sociology."[83] We need scarcely point out how sadly reduced would be the rôle of statistics in sociology if this assumption held, even more so, since the author himself repudiates the assumption upon which, according to him, statistics in sociology must depend.

Thus, the concept "natural area," so fundamental to human ecology, has not as yet been consistently defined and logically classified. The ecologists have adopted toward it no unity of approach, nor have they presented an adequate theoretical case for the preëminent position which they have accorded the concept. To a great extent this is due to the lack of coherence in the ecologists' conception of "community" and to the failure to delimit this concept adequately from that of "society." From the ecological point of view, the subdivision of the zone, the "natural area," is a specific type of "community," its content enriched by empirical investigations, which presumably substantiate its theoretical formulations. However, the concept "natural area" suffers from the same shortcomings as the more general category "community." No amount of empirical investigation can rectify the inconsistencies inherent in the theoretical statements pertaining to it. These must be met on the theoretical level as well as resolved through factual investigations. Apparently, however, the two, theory and fact, have not been reconciled by ecologists but have been treated as if meeting at separate points here and there.

It is surprising, therefore, that notwithstanding the nebulous character of the concept, the school has produced such capable studies (presumably of the "natural areas") as

[83] Park, "The Urban Community as a Spacial Pattern and a Moral Order," in *The Urban Community*, edited by Burgess, p. 18; italics mine.

Frederick Thrasher's *The Gang,* Ruth Cavan's *Suicide,* or Nels Anderson's *The Hobo.* Such studies, however, stand on their own merits as general sociological rather than specifically ecological works; as was mentioned earlier, they are very little concerned with the fundamental presuppositions of the theory of human ecology.

CHAPTER NINE

CONSPECTUS OF THE ECOLOGICAL APPROACH

THROUGHOUT this discussion it has been indicated that human ecologists approach both "biotic" and "cultural" manifestations from an environmentalist point of view. McKenzie gives a formal definition of human ecology as "the study of the spatial and temporal relations of human beings as affected by the selective, distributive, and accommodative forces of the environment."[1] A fundamental question arises here as to the meaning of the term environment as used in this definition. We have seen earlier that human ecologists conceive of "community" as an organism. Although they adapt some of Child's ideas to their organismic principle, they lean more upon animal and particularly plant ecologies for this conception. We have seen, too, that the basic process of "succession" and the idea of "natural area" are adaptations of the concepts of plant ecology. Moreover, the designation of their discipline as human "ecology" would lead one to associate it with biological ecologies.

The central idea of plant and animal ecologies is that of specific accommodation of organisms (be they individuals or communities) in terms of sustenance relationships. Ecology is concerned with the adaptational effects on organisms of variant geographical environments. To that extent the determinant factor in variation is thought of as the

[1] McKenzie, "The Ecological Approach to the Study of the Human Community," in Park, Burgess, *et al., The City,* pp. 63–64.

environmental one.[2] The effective factors, in short, are conceived as lying mainly, not within the primary activities of the organism itself, but in the environmental changes or new environmental factors which are the stimuli of organic change.

Human ecologists lay a similar emphasis upon environment, but with the difference that to them it is an extremely elastic concept. If the ecological "community" is an organism, the environment can be only the geographical one. Had ecologists adequately distinguished "community" from "society" and consistently adhered to this distinction, then perhaps "society" (even though the latter, too, is regarded as an organism) could be treated as a phenomenon external to "community" and therefore as environmental to it. Park tells us that

> every community has something of the character of an organic unit. It has a more or less definite structure and it has "a life history in which juvenile, adult and senile phases can be observed." If it is an organism, it is one of the organs which are other organisms.[3]

In other words, each community is an organism, even though it may be an organ of the larger community of which it is a part. It is perhaps sufficient to point out here that this statement is a contradiction in terms. In effect, the ecologists extend at will the concept of environment, so that more often than not it includes the geographical, physical, economic, and social environments; and the result is that or-

[2] See Clements, *Research Methods in Ecology* and *Plant Succession: an Analysis of the Development of Vegetation;* also J. W. Bews, *Human Ecology* (1935), chap. i.

[3] Park, "Human Ecology," *American Journal of Sociology,* XLII, 4. Although Park speaks here specifically of plant and animal "societies," since it comes under his discussion of "symbiotic community," and since he tells us that "to such a habitat and its inhabitants—whether plant, animal, or human—the ecologists have applied the term 'community'" (*ibid.,* p. 4), the statement equally applies to human communities.

ganism and environment merge into one another, so that the ecological organism is sometimes treated as though it were its own environment.

The extension of the concept of environment to other than the geographical one has another consequence. Plant and animal ecologies study sustenance and place relations between the organism and the environment, where the process of competition, or struggle for existence, is the basic process underlying these relations. Human ecologists claim a similar point of view.[4] However, in extending the idea of the environment beyond the geographical limits, they also extend the basis of the relations of the organism to the environment, and, in fact, these relations necessarily undergo a qualitative change. Consequently, if the environment includes such aspects as the social and the technological, the process of competition loses its ecological significance. Therefore, there is no justification for stressing competition and sustenance relations, as is done by plant and animal ecologies, any more than any other processes and relations. That is to say, if other processes, social or technological, are neither considered nor stressed by human ecologists, it is not because the scope of the subject matter precludes this, but rather because the school holds a monistic point of view with a peculiar emphasis upon competition. The validity of such a one-sided approach is inevitably a matter of controversy. It may have its adherents, but it has also been extensively criticized in scientific and philosophical literature, for reasons such as those suggested by Cohen and Nagel:

> Hasty monism, the uncritical attempt to bring everything under one principle and category, is one of the most frequent perversions of scientific method. This is certainly true of popular forms

[4] McKenzie, "The Scope of Human Ecology," in *The Urban Community,* edited by Burgess, p. 167, and Anderson and Lindeman *Urban Sociology,* p. 41.

of materialism, economic and other forms of determinism, subjective idealism, panlogism, and all other monistic doctrines according to which the absolute totality of all things is exhausted by some one category.[5]

In their use of the ecological conceptions, human ecologists have come up against the difficulties which invariably arise from a sweeping application of the natural sciences to phenomena of human group life. Consequently, in the attempt to reconcile the method with the requirements of the subject matter, they have been obliged to make gradual as well as sporadic changes in both their methodology and their approach. This has been done in several ways, such as by modifying the ecological concepts and by supplementing them with concepts from other natural sciences; by incorporating results of applied technological studies, such as city planning; and, finally, by trying to merge ecological with economic and sociological concepts.

The analogical treatment of human activities along the lines of those of animals and plants has brought many difficulties into the path of human ecologists, resulting in continual accretions to their system. In this way, they have avoided the restriction to the more organic and less evolved level of behavior which is implicit in their general formulations and in their definition of "community."

Whatever possibility there might have been of abstracting the ecological elements in human group life was curbed by the fact that the starting point of the ecologists was sociology. Trained in the tradition of this discipline, they were already imbued with the concepts which belonged to it and utilized these concepts explicitly and implicitly in the development of the conceptual scheme which they had borrowed from organic ecology. In using biological concepts they did not limit them to their original specific context.

[5] Morris R. Cohen and Ernest Nagel, *An Introduction to Logic and Scientific Method* (New York, 1934), p. 384.

They either gave them a new social and economic connotation, or, if these were concepts which had been in use both in biological and sociological references as, for example, competition, they included the latter usage in their treatment. In this way they have given the biological concept "dominance" an economic, technological, cultural, and social significance, while the concept "position" has been extended to economic and social status as well. "Succession," which refers in biology to the displacement of one species of animals or of one life-form of plants by another has been applied to the displacement of racial, age, economic, or cultural groups, institutions, utilities, structures, cultural factors, architectural styles; to sequences of technological inventions and cultural trends; and in short to anything and everything.

Translating biological concepts to cover social aspects and identifying the biological with sociological principles of cycles, human ecologists have comprehended the social group as an organismic unity within which social processes occur, and have applied such concepts to describe social factors as "gradients" and "natural history." They have included as objects of ecological study economic, political, and social institutions, and applied to them the same ecological laws as are assumed to pertain to human beings. At the same time they have put forth a claim that, with these "ecological" data as causes and indices of social phenomena, they are able to measure and put upon a quantitative basis the realm of the social.

The causal nexus found in biological sciences between these different categories has been held to by human ecologists more or less rigidly, for instance, in the relation of competition to distribution and mobility, or of symbiosis to dominance and succession, or again in the relation of different ecological processes to one another. The contrast between the chameleonic character of the concepts and the rigidity of the relation between them has inevitably resulted in a peculiar discrepancy between the descriptive and the interpretative phases of the theory of human ecology.

To cite one example, from the point of view of ecology the basic and universal process is competition as a determinant of distribution. In the application of this hypothesis, human ecologists have found that the element of choice, which is absent in plant and, to a great extent, in animal life, is a persistent factor among human beings. To account for this factor they have introduced the concept of selection, which is applied in a twofold way. The selective agent can be either the environment or else the human beings and their "institutions." The former is in accordance with the ecological principle of environmental determinism, while the latter vitiates this principle in stressing the element of conscious willing. Thus, inadvertently, human ecologists invite a more complex theory of causation which, however, they have not developed, failing to grasp the full significance of their postulates. Instead, they have emphasized the environmental selection, so that it is commonly the area which does the selecting, the sifting, the sorting, the allocating: "From the mobile competing stream of the city's population each natural area of the city tends to collect the particular individuals predestined to it."[6]

This lack of regard for the volitional factors is emphasized still more by the rigidity both of spatial structure and of processes which is imputed to the "community," where natural areas "seem to find, in some natural and inevitable manner, their predetermined places,"[7] and where "regions

[6] Zorbaugh, "The Natural Areas of the City," in *The Urban Community*, edited by Burgess, p. 223.

[7] Park, "The Urban Community as a Spacial Pattern and a Moral Order," in *The Urban Community*, edited by Burgess, p. 10.

within a city pass through different stages of use and occupancy in a regularity of manner which may eventually be predictable and expressible in mathematical terms."[8] In this way human beings become the objects of selection, while the areas assume an animistic rôle. It is thus that "the cities sift and sort and redistribute their ill-assorted populations into new groups and classes, according to new and unexpected patterns."[9] And again, it is thus that

> the city may be likened to a great sieve which sifts and sorts its human elements and arranges them in space in accordance with their economic efficiency and their rôle in the life of the community. The physical structure of the city—its buildings, streets, and transportation systems—constitute the mesh of the sieve, and competition among the human elements the dynamo which drives the machine.[10]

Human ecologists occasionally make references to such volitional factors as purpose, but even then usually to tell us how hopelessly the iron laws of nature determine it:

> The human community differs from the plant community in the two dominant characteristics of mobility and purpose, that is, in the power to select a habitat and in the ability to control or modify the conditions of the habitat. On first consideration this might seem to indicate that human ecology could have nothing in common with plant ecology where the processes of association and adjustment result from natural unmodifiable reactions; but closer examination and investigation make it obvious that human communities are not so much the products of artifact or design as many hero-worshipers suppose.[11]

[8] McKenzie, "The Scope of Human Ecology," in *The Urban Community,* edited by Burgess, p. 181.

[9] Park, "Sociology," in *Research in the Social Sciences,* edited by Gee, p. 12. It may be noted that Park's reference to "new and *unexpected* patterns" contradicts the idea of McKenzie, or, for that matter, of Park himself, that the configuration of areas and the distribution of the population is predetermined and inevitable and susceptible to mathematical prediction.

[10] McKenzie, *The Metropolitan Community,* p. 245.

[11] McKenzie, "The Ecological Approach," in Park, Burgess, *et al., The City,* pp. 64–65.

Even when ecologists speak of human selection they do not distinguish it from the factors of environmental selection, enumerating these as if they belonged to the same universe of discourse and not conceding to human volition its appropriate significance in relation to the theory as a whole. As a result it plays no part in their theory of causation, which consequently remains consistent with the general ecological principle of environmental emphasis.

The application of ecological analogy, the concomitant accretions of alien concepts from several other disciplines, and the modification of these have resulted not only in the deviation of the school from the ecological subject matter, but also in the change of the entire character and scope of the system. Human ecology is not alone in this, for most concepts and systems of concepts translated from one science into another, more specifically from the natural into social sciences, suffer similar consequences. The pitfalls would be less hazardous if the borrowed concepts readily responded to the subject matter to which they are applied, but generally the analogy is labored and, if anything, distorts rather than describes or explains reality. The extensive criticisms of the biological analogies of Spencer, Lilienfeld, Worms, Schäffle, Novicow, and others have brought in their wake a general distrust of this approach among later sociological schools, so that the reversion to such inclusive analogical treatment by human ecologists is quite unique and is significant in relation to the general trend of sociology.

Of great significance to the trend of sociology, however, are the methods and techniques instituted or adopted by this school and the focussing of attention upon localized and territorially delimited investigations. In the face of the theory, which reveals so many conflicting and inconsistent elements, the ecologists have succeeded in opening fields and stimulating concentration on specific areas of study. Numerous investigations of various urban areas have contributed illuminating sociological data and have put to a test new techniques in localized research. At first relying mainly upon case studies, they have come more and more to lean, in addition, upon statistical methods, recently employing the latter for the purpose of determining gradients of various phenomena. Of significance, too, is the development and application of the social research base map, an efficient way of presenting graphically a complex of numerous factors and of depicting their spatial changes over a period of time.

The ecologists' intensive investigation of small territorial units has served to elucidate and illustrate the specific processes manifested in urban and other areas and has given insight into the varied elements which go to make up our modern communities. Their exploration of the short-run processes of change, such as, for example, the assimilation of immigrant groups in the urban environment, has added valuable data to sociological literature. Likewise, some of the monographs on "problem" phenomena and studies of various social types and cultural groups are both of interest and of value. Moreover, the attention given to the study of various physical, technological, and economic factors has thrown into relief certain conditions of the social organization, for an analysis of which the sociologist has hitherto depended upon other disciplines.

A promising method, which has not as yet been given extensive application, but which ecologists advocate, is the delimitation of communities in terms of spatial concentration of the group's participation in various social, political, and economic activities. This revealing method was first employed by Galpin in the delimitation of rural communities and presented in his article, "The Social Anatomy of an Agricultural Community."[12] While its application to lo-

[12] *Agricultural Extension Station Bulletin 34,* Wisconsin, 1915.

cal areas within the city may be questioned on the grounds that participation in most of these areas is city wide, its use in rural sections and in relation to larger areas, such as the city or the metropolitan region, seems of great value as a means of sociological discovery.

Human ecologists have also contributed some studies which are of more ecological than sociological significance, if by "ecology" is meant the human aspect of sustenance relationships analogous to that prevailing among plant and animal communities. A good example of these is McKenzie's "Ecological Succession in the Puget Sound Region."[13] One of the least explored of the ecological fields, the regional survey would seem to lend itself to ecological methods and techniques and to promise to yield productive results.

While the generalizations on which ecology itself is assumed to rest are very broad and sweeping, yet, in their actual approach to their particular situations and problems and in their methods of investigation of them, most of the ecologists take a very modest and cautious stand. In fact, if anything, they may be criticized for too much caution in the interpretation of their data, often to the exclusion of significant generalizations for which their materials provide.

While this study has been essentially concerned with the coherence and significance of the theory of human ecology rather than the factual research carried out by the school, a question may be raised here as to the relation of theory and fact. We saw the inconsistencies revealed in the theory. Some of these have undoubtedly crept into the factual studies and weighted their interpretative aspects, since the theoretical conceptions serve as the starting point as well as the guiding principle of factual investigations. However, these studies do not reveal either the monistic approach nor

[13] *Publications of the American Sociological Society*, XXIII (Chicago, 1928), 60–80.

the a priori assumptions to anything like the same extent as does the theory. This would imply their contentment to relinquish the business of theory, for the most part, to a few leaders such as Park, Burgess, Wirth, and McKenzie. Such a division of labor may be claimed to make for efficiency, but it may also make for lack of unity between theory and facts, between doctrine and methods, and between approach and conclusions derived from factual analysis.

Yet only in so far as theory serves to classify and explain or describe facts is it of scientific value; only inasmuch as methods are tools of discovery or verification are they of relevance; only to the extent that researches are a means to scientific generalization or to the reorientation of the existent body of theory do they contribute to knowledge. For, as Goethe said, "*Theorie steckt bereits in den Tatsachen,*" and where consonance between theory and fact is foregone there is no science.

BIBLIOGRAPHY

Adams, G. C., "The Relation of General Ecology to Human Ecology," Ecology, Vol. XVI, No. 3, July, 1935.

Allee, W. C., Animal Aggregations, a Study in General Sociology, Chicago, The University of Chicago Press, 1931.

Anderson, Nels, The Hobo: the Sociology of the Homeless Man, Chicago, The University of Chicago Press, 1923.

——— and Eduard C. Lindeman, Urban Sociology: an Introduction to the Study of Urban Communities, New York, Alfred A. Knopf, 1928.

Bernard, L. L., editor, Fields and Methods of Sociology, New York, Farrar & Rinehart, Inc., 1934.

Bews, J. W., Human Ecology, London, Oxford University Press, 1935.

Booth, Charles, Life and Labor of the People of London, London and New York, Macmillan & Co., Ltd., 1889–1903.

Burgess, E. W., "The Determination of Gradients in the Growth of the City," Publications of the American Sociological Society, Vol. XXI, 1927.

——— "The Natural Area as the Unit for Social Work in the Large City," Proceedings of the National Conference of Social Work, 1929.

——— "Residential Segregation in American Cities," The Annals of the American Academy of Political and Social Science, No. 2180, November, 1928.

——— "What Social Case Records Should Contain to Be Useful for Sociological Interpretation," Social Forces, Vol. VI, 1927–28.

——— editor, The Urban Community, Chicago, The University of Chicago Press, 1925.

——— and R. E. Park, Introduction to the Science of Sociology, Chicago, The University of Chicago Press, revised edition, 1924.

Cavan, Ruth S., Suicide, Chicago, The University of Chicago Press, 1928.

Child, Charles M., "Biological Foundations of Social Integration," Proceedings and Papers of the American Sociological Society, Vol. XXII, June 21, 1928.

Child, Charles M., The Physiological Foundations of Behavior, New York, Henry Holt & Co., 1924.

Clements, F. E., Plant Succession: an Analysis of the Development of Vegetation, Washington, Carnegie Institution of Washington, 1916.

——— Research Methods in Ecology, Lincoln, Nebraska, The University of Nebraska Press, 1905.

Cohen, Morris R., and Ernest Nagel, An Introduction to Logic and Scientific Method, New York, Harcourt, 1934.

Columbia Encyclopedia, "Symbiosis," New York, Columbia University Press, 1935.

Cooley, Charles H., Human Nature and the Social Order, New York, Chas. Scribner's Sons, 1922.

Cressey, Paul G., The Taxi Dance-Hall, Chicago, The University of Chicago Press, 1932.

Durkheim, Emile, Le Suicide: étude de sociologie, Paris, F. Alcan, 1897.

Eubank, Earle E., The Concepts of Sociology, New York, D. C. Heath & Co., 1932.

Galpin, C. J., The Social Anatomy of an Agricultural Community, Agricultural Extension Station Bulletin 34, Wisconsin, 1915.

Gee, Wilson, editor, Research in the Social Sciences, New York, The Macmillan Co., 1929.

Goldenweiser, A., "Social Evolution," Encyclopaedia of the Social Sciences, edited by Edwin R. A. Seligman, and Alvin Johnson, New York, The Macmillan Co., 1931.

House, Floyd N., The Range of Social Theory, New York, Henry Holt & Co., 1929.

Hunter, Robert, Tenement Conditions in Chicago, Report by the Investigating Committee of the City Homes Association, Chicago, City Homes Association, 1901.

Hurd, Richard M., Principles of City Land Values, New York, The Record and Guide, 1911.

Kellogg, Paul U., editor, The Pittsburgh Survey, New York, The Charity Organization of the City of New York, 1909.

Longmoor, Elsa Schneider, *see* Young, Erle Fiske.

Lundberg, George A., Read Bain, and Nels Anderson, editors, Trends in American Sociology, New York and London, Harper & Brothers, 1929.

MacIver, Robert M., "The Historical Pattern of Social Change," Journal of Social Philosophy, Vol. II, No. 1, 1936.

——— Society, Its Structure and Changes, New York, Farrar & Rinehart, Inc., 1931.

McKenzie, R. D., "The Concept of Dominance and World Organization," The American Journal of Sociology, Vol. XXXIII, No. 1, July, 1927.

——— "Ecological Succession in the Puget Sound Region," Publications of the American Sociological Society, Vol. XXIII, 1928.

——— The Metropolitan Community, New York, McGraw-Hill Book Co., 1933.

——— The Neighborhood, a Study of Columbus, Ohio, Chicago, The University of Chicago Press, 1923.

Mowrer, Ernest R., Family Disorganization, Chicago, The University of Chicago Press, 1927.

——— The Family, Its Organization and Disorganization, Chicago, The University of Chicago Press, 1932.

Palmer, Vivien Marie, Field Studies in Sociology, Chicago, The University of Chicago Press, 1928.

Park, Robert E., Ernest W. Burgess, Roderick D. McKenzie, The City, Chicago, The University of Chicago Press, 1925, contains a bibliography by Louis Wirth.

——— "Human Ecology," The American Journal of Sociology, Vol. XLII, No. 1, July, 1936.

——— "Succession, an Ecological Concept," American Sociological Review, Vol. I, No. 2, April, 1936.

——— "Urbanization as Measured by Newspaper Circulation," The American Journal of Sociology, Vol. XXXV, No. 1, July, 1927.

——— "William Graham Sumner's Conception of Society," Chinese Social and Political Science Review, Vol. XVII, No. 3, 1933.

——— and E. W. Burgess, Introduction to the Science of Sociology, Chicago, The University of Chicago Press, revised edition, 1924.

Riis, Jacob, The Battle with the Slum, New York, The Macmillan Co., 1902.

——— How the Other Half Lives; Studies among the Tenements of New York, New York, Chas. Scribner's Sons, 1890 and 1914.

Ross, Frank A., "Ecology and the Statistical Method," The American Journal of Sociology, Vol. XXXVIII, No. 4, January, 1933.

Rowntree, Benjamin S., Poverty, a Study of Town Life, London, New York, The Macmillan Co., 1901, 1902.

Salisbury, Edward J., "Plants," Encyclopaedia Britannica, 14th edition, 1929.

Shaw, Clifford R., with the collaboration of F. M. Zorbaugh, H. D. McKay, and L. S. Cottrell, Delinquency Areas: a Study of the Geographic Distribution of School Truants, Juvenile Delinquents, and Adult Offenders in Chicago, Chicago, The University of Chicago Press, 1929.

Smith, T. V., and Leonard D. White, editors, Chicago: an Experiment in Social Science Research, Chicago, The University of Chicago Press, 1929.

Thrasher, Frederick M., The Gang, Chicago, The University of Chicago Press, 1927.

Warming, Eugenius, Oecology of Plants, Oxford, Clarendon Press, 1909.

Weaver, W. Wallace, West Philadelphia: a Study of Natural Social Areas, Philadelphia, privately published, 1930.

White, R. Clyde, "The Relation of Felonies to Environmental Factors in Indianapolis," Social Forces, Vol. X, May, 1932.

Wirth, Louis, "The Ghetto," The American Journal of Sociology, Vol. XXXIII, No. 1, July, 1927.

——— The Ghetto, Chicago, The University of Chicago Press, 1928.

——— "The Scope and Problems of the Community," Publications of the American Sociological Society, Vol. XXVII, No. 2, May, 1933.

——— "The Sociology of Ferdinand Tönnies," The American Journal of Sociology, Vol. XXXII, No. 3, 1926.

Woods, Robert A., The City Wilderness; a Settlement Study, Boston and New York, Houghton, Mifflin & Co., 1898.

Young, Erle Fiske, and Elsa Schneider Longmoor, "Ecological Interrelationships of Juvenile Delinquency, Dependency, and Population Mobility: a Cartographic Analysis of Data from Long Beach, California," The American Journal of Sociology, Vol. XLI, No. 5, March, 1936.

Zorbaugh, Harvey W., The Gold Coast and the Slum, Chicago, The University of Chicago Press, 1929.

INDEX